Tejidos

Teacher Edition
Libro del profesor

Megan Cory
Janet Parker
Catherine Schwenkler

www.waysidepublishing.com

Copyright © 2013 Wayside Publishing

All rights reserved. No part of this publication may be reproduced, stored in a retrieval system, or transmitted in any form or by any means, electronic, mechanical, photocopying, recording, or otherwise, without the prior written permission of the publisher.

Printed in USA

8 9 10 KP 19

Print date: **1150**

Softcover ISBN 978-1-938026-38-6

FlexText® ISBN 978-1-942400-13-4

Table of Contents

Welcome to *Tejidos* **2**
Organization and Features of Student Edition **3**
Tejidos Explorer Features **4**
Using the Teacher Edition **5–6**
Principles of Effective Teaching and Learning **7**
Overview of Common Core State Standards and
World-Readiness Standards for Learning Languages **8–9**
Scope and Sequence **10–22**

Teacher Notes, Student Learning Objectives, Pacing Guides and Answers

Manta 1 Familia y comunidades
Hilo 1 Estructura de la familia **23**
Hilo 2 Redes sociales **38**
Hilo 3 Ciudadanía global **53**

Manta 2 Vida contemporánea
Hilo 4 Viajes y ocio **66**
Hilo 5 Educación y carreras profesionales **80**
Hilo 6 Relaciones personales **95**

Manta 3 Belleza y estética
Hilo 7 Belleza y moda **110**
Hilo 8 Artes visuales y escénicas **123**

Manta 4 Identidades personales y públicas
Hilo 9 Héroes y personajes históricos **135**
Hilo 10 Identidad nacional e identidad étnica **149**

Manta 5 Desafíos mundiales
Hilo 11 Temas del medio ambiente **164**
Hilo digital Población y demografía **177**

Manta 6 Ciencia y tecnología
Hilo 12 Cuidado de la salud y medicina **193**

Appendices

A. Rubrics:
1. Analytic **210**
2. Holistic **216**
3. Student "I can do" statements **221**
4. Summative Assessments **226**

B. Grammar Guide **250**

Dear colleagues,

Welcome to the Teacher Edition for *Tejidos, comunicación auténtica en un contexto cultural.*

Tejidos is a thematic standards-based Spanish program that aims to engage intermediate level learners with authentic materials that align with the AP® global themes and sub-theme contexts in addition to the IB core and optional topics. This innovative program prepares students for courses in the year or semester prior to the AP® Language & Culture and IB Exams such as Advanced Level III, Level IV, Conversation, Pre-AP®, or Pre-IB courses.

Tejidos was created and organized with the high school student in mind. The sub themes were sequenced to be accessible to the intermediate-mid to intermediate-high level student, according to the American Council on the Teaching of Foreign Languages (ACTFL) scale, at the beginning of the course with the expectation that the student will reach the pre to low-advanced level by the end of the course. Reference the 2012 ACTFL Performance Descriptors for Language Learners in *Tejidos* Explorer in Teacher Resources or on the ACTFL website, www.actfl.org.

The *Tejidos* program provides students:

- Authentic and motivating content to learn and use Spanish for purposeful communication
- Spanish-only instruction with scaffolding, glossing, and strategies for support
- Additional support, resources, and extension activities in *Tejidos* Explorer
- Integration of language and culture in real-world contexts
- A diverse range of authentic materials from Latin America and Spain
- Opportunities for communication in all modes with pair work and group work interwoven throughout each activity
- Individual and collaborative performance-based tasks and assessments
- A deeper understanding of the interconnection of the cultural products, practices, and perspectives that form the worldview of Hispanic cultures
- Opportunities to make cultural comparisons
- Grammar and use of language in context
- A variety of rubrics to measure their performance

The **Tejidos Teacher Edition** includes a scope and sequence, detailed instructions for each activity, answers to specific exercises within each activity, and suggestions to tailor activities and assessments to the students' level.

Student Learning Objectives at the beginning of each *hilo* align with the *World Readiness Standards for Learning Languages* in addition to the *English Language Arts and Literacy Common Core State Standards*. These objectives are also found in **Explorer**.

We hope that you and your students enjoy *Tejidos, comunicación auténtica en un contexto cultural*. Please contact us with comments and suggestions at waysidepublishing.com/contact-us/.

Tejidos authors,

Megan Cory
Janet Parker
Catherine Schwenkler

Organization and Features of the Student Edition of *Tejidos*

Tejidos is a Spanish-only standards-based program that was developed using Backward Design. There are six units *(mantas)* representing the six AP® global themes and the three IB core topics that are subdivided into one, two, or three chapters *(hilos)* per *manta* that provide in-depth study into the recommended contexts and subthemes. Overarching **essential questions** frame each thematic *hilo* with motivating learning activities that engage students with authentic texts – video, audio, articles, blogs, interviews, and literature written for native Spanish-speakers.

Chapter (hilo) *organization:*

- Each *hilo* begins with a magazine style spread that includes the essential questions, an overview of the *hilo,* and its table of contents.
- An introductory activity or provocation, *Introducción,* introduces the theme.
- A pre-assessment, *Antes de empezar,* activates background knowledge and vocabulary in addition to immersing students into the content of the theme.
- Two or three essential questions align with four to seven activities per *hilo*.
- Each activity includes at least one *formative assessment* that can be scored using a rubric found in the appendices of the Teacher Edition and in *Tejidos* Explorer. Additional formative assessments in Explorer can be scored and entered into the online grade book.
- The *hilo* culminates in a *summative performance-based assessment* or *Evaluación final*.

Additional features in each hilo:

Icons: Colorful icons symbolize all the communication modes, culture, comparisons, connections, student journal, and Explorer materials.

Strategies for speaking, reading, listening, and writing, including sentence starters and transition phrases are interwoven throughout the student edition in blue text boxes.

Use of language (grammar) in context is featured in each *hilo* in green text boxes. There is not a specific sequence to the grammar as it is driven by the language use in the context of the authentic sources. Refer to the grammar guide to find specific grammar points.

Culture: cultural products, practices, and perspectives are integrated throughout each thematic *hilo*. A detailed explanation is provided to the teachers and students in the student edition and Teacher Edition. Students have numerous opportunities to make cultural comparisons. **Additional cultural information** connected to each activity is included in separate purple shaded text boxes.

Real world performance tasks and assessments are embedded throughout *Tejidos* such as emails, tweets, texting, Facebook status comments, podcasts, blog entries, interactive journals, website contests, etc.

- **Formative assessments:** Every activity has one or several of the following evaluative components that can be assessed at the teacher's discretion: *¡Te toca a ti!, ¡Tu opinión cuenta!, Reflexión, ¿Qué aprendiste?* and *¡A tejer!* Formative assessments also appear in *Tejidos* **Explorer**. Rubrics for all communication modes are in **Explorer** and in the appendix of the Teacher Edition.
- **Summative performance-based assessments** *(Evaluación final)* framed in authentic contexts appear at the end of each hilo with specific criteria, checklists, and additional scaffolding in **Explorer.**

Vocabulary is highlighted in dark orange vocabulary text boxes throughout the *hilo* but not in every activity. Vocabulary is glossed in the authentic texts with a Spanish synonym or definition; each *hilo* ends with a comprehensive list of synonyms or definitions in Spanish of the key words organized by activity. A section of *Expresiones* *útiles* appears in the vocabulary list at the end of each *hilo*.

Diario: The authors highly recommend that students keep a journal to record class notes, answers to activities, reflections, and questions they may have. The *diario personal* icon appears frequently throughout the student text. The teacher has many options that may include an interactive journal, to provide feedback and comment on students' progress, or an online journal that the teacher and student can access. The journal also serves as a portfolio in the sense that it shows student progress over time.

Organization and features of *Tejidos* Explorer *(Guía digital)*

The Wayside Publishing *Tejidos* Explorer (*Guía digital*) is an integral component of the *Tejidos* program providing access to a variety of support materials such as interactive quizzes and further scaffolding for activities. **Explorer** also includes forums where students can participate in interpersonal writing and speaking activities, as well as links to authentic materials, extension activities, online resources, and rubrics.

There is an additional **Hilo Digital** (*Población y demografía, Manta: Desafíos mundiales*) not present in the student text.

RECURSOS: Students and teachers will be able to take full advantage of the endless Web 2.0 resources available in *Tejidos* **Explorer**. Each hilo of **Explorer** contains the following items accessible to both students and teachers:

- Audiovisual materials
- Scaffolding for some activities in each hilo
- Vocabulary practice, which includes quizzes, flash cards, and matching
- Contextualized grammar activities
- Additional activities such as discussion forums and open-ended questionnaires
- Final evaluation/summative assessment support such as specific criteria and checklists
- Additional useful links
- Rubrics: "I can do" rubrics, holistic & analytic in all communication modes
- Maps of the Spanish-speaking world
- Generic graphic organizers such as the Y-chart and Facebook Message/Comment
- Blank black and white and color maps of Spain, Latin America, and the Caribbean
- PDFs of Spanish-Spanish, Spanish-English, and English-Spanish glossaries

SÓLO PARA LOS PROFESORES: Teachers will be able to access additional resources within the **RECURSOS** folder.

- Automatized, editable, and exportable Grade book and roster
- A place to store files and share them with your students.
- For multiple-choice quizzes in **Explorer,** the correct answer may appear differently in the Student Edition than in **Explorer.** The reason is that the answers are digitalized and randomized in **Explorer.** See formative assessment on **Using the Teacher Edition** for more details.
- Objectives by hilo
- A lengthy additional activity for Hilos 1 and 6
- Additional language teaching and hilo specific links
- Complete access to the student **Explorer** course. That is, teachers see just what students do with the exception of the resources mentioned here, which are available to teachers only.

Using the *Tejidos* Teacher Edition

The *Tejidos* Teacher Edition aims to guide you as you plan and prepare to teach with the student edition, written exclusively in Spanish, for the purpose of keeping classroom communication in Spanish. *Tejidos* is designed to be a flexible program to meet the needs of a variety of courses and intermediate level students. The Table of Contents outlines the contents of the Teacher Edition for your reference.

The **scope and sequence** for all the *hilos* is at the beginning of the Teacher Edition in a table format that includes the essential question aligned with the respective activities, the authentic sources *(fuentes)*, the vocabulary categories, grammar in context, and types of formative assessments.

Forty-five states, the District of Columbia, four territories, and the Department of Defense Education have adopted the **Common Core State Standards.** The *American Council on the Teaching of Foreign Languages* (ACTFL) aligned the *World-Readiness Standards for Learning Languages* with the *CCSS English Language Arts and Literacy Standards*. The complete document appears in the Teacher Professional Resources link in **Tejidos** Explorer. The **Student Learning Objectives** for each hilo align with these official documents focusing on the function, context, communication, and cultural awareness domains in which the student needs to demonstrate performance.

The Teacher Edition **Teacher Notes** pages align with the Student Edition, referencing the page numbers, icons, and outline of the *Tejidos* textbook. The **Student Learning Objectives** for each *hilo* appear at the beginning of the Teacher Notes pages, which are tabbed in the upper right hand corner for easier access. A Pacing Guide for each *hilo* includes suggestions for what students can complete outside of class. Each activity includes instructions in English, when appropriate and helpful for teacher use, however not every part of each activity requires additional instructions. **Answers** to exercises are provided in shaded text boxes as well as samples of student answers where appropriate.

Formative assessments and homework suggestions have been noted throughout each *hilo* and address all modes of communication integrating culture and cultural comparisons. The Teacher Notes pages suggest which parts of the activities can be used as formative assessments in addition to the following sections: *Reflexión, ¿Qué aprendiste?, ¡A tejer!* and to a lesser degree *¡Te toca a ti!* and *¡Tu opinión cuenta!*. **Tejidos** Explorer includes exercises from the *hilo* activities that also lend themselves to use as formative assessments; these can be submitted, scored online, and entered into the online grade book. For multiple-choice quizzes, the correct answer may appear differently in the Student Edition than in **Explorer**. The reason is that the answers are digitalized and randomized in **Explorer**. The correct answers given in the Teacher Edition correspond to the questions and answers as they appear in the Student Edition. If your student is taking a quiz in **Explorer** and you would like to help them identify the right answer, refer to the answer as given in the Teacher Edition and its corresponding answer in the Student Edition. For example, if the answer given in the Teacher Edition is "B" the correct answer is that which appears next to "B" in the Student Edition.

Analytic, holistic, student "I can do" rubrics, and summative assessment rubrics, specific to each hilo, are in the Teacher Edition Appendix A. The rubrics align with the 2012 ACTFL Performance Descriptors for Language Learners for the Intermediate mid to high range, with some features of Low Advanced range in the "Exceeds expectations" category. It is suggested that you use the generic rubrics to score student performances in the respective communication modes. The rubrics are posted in the Recursos, Rúbricas section of **Explorer** for student and teacher access. There is an explanation of how to convert rubric scores to percentages in a footnote of each analytic rubric.

The **Explorer icons** in the Student Edition and in the Teacher Edition indicate that there is significant *"apoyo adicional,"* additional support, in **Explorer** that includes: printable and editable graphic organizers, tables, charts, checklists for final evaluations, and optional activities that align with the essential questions of the *hilo*.

STARTALK-Endorsed Principles for Effective Teaching & Learning and Characteristics of Effective Language Lessons

See examples online: https://startalk.umd.edu/principles/

- Implementing a standards-based and thematically organized curriculum
    - Every lesson derives from a standards-based unit that culminates in students developing the ability to engage in spontaneous, unrehearsed communication for real-world purposes.
    - Each lesson has clearly stated cultural objectives that indicate what students will be able to do and what they need to know by lesson's end.
    - Research and theory determine the instructional experiences and the order in which they take place to ensure that students can meet the lesson's cultural and language performance objectives.
- Grammar is not the focus of the course, unit, or lesson. The teacher teaches grammar as a tool for communication, avoiding meaningless rote drills and ensuring that all practice requires attention to meaning.
- Facilitating a learner-centered classroom
    - Students learn vocabulary from input (hearing or reading) and from using vocabulary in language-rich contexts such as stories, hands-on experiences, picture descriptions, or subject-matter content.
    - The teacher provides frequent, varied classroom opportunities for students to interpret and express meaning for real-world purposes.
    - In every class session, the teacher provides paired or small group activities that engage students in using the language for meaningful communication.
- Using the target language and providing comprehensible input for instruction
    - The teacher uses the target language at least 90 percent of the time.
    - The teacher uses a variety of strategies to make language comprehensible, monitors student comprehension, and makes adjustments as necessary.
    - The teacher avoids the use of translation by using verbal and non-verbal strategies and also avoids eliciting translation from students.
- Integrating culture, content, and language in a world language classroom
    - Cultural instruction focuses on perspectives—not just products and practices.
- Adapting and using age-appropriate authentic materials
    - The teacher uses authentic materials and designs tasks appropriate to the language proficiency and age level of the learners.
    - The teacher uses a range of authentic print and non-print materials in a variety of technological formats.
- Conducting performance-based assessment
    - The teacher uses formative assessment of student performance during the course of the lesson to adjust instruction as needed.
    - The teacher and students use feedback about the quality of student performance relative to the lesson's and unit's instructional targets.

The bulleted lists of characteristics provide guidance for reflecting on observed lessons. They focus exclusively on world language-specific behaviors, and do not include critical but more generic characteristics of effective instruction (e.g., time management and engaging all learners).

Reproduced with permission from: STARTALK Endorsed Principles for Effective Teaching & Learning and Characteristics of Effective Language Lessons, STARTALK Project, National Foreign Language Center, University of Maryland College Park, 2008.

Alignment of the World-Readiness Standards for Learning Languages with the Common Core State Standards

Performance Expectations

The *Common Core State Standards for English Language Arts (ELA) and Literacy in History/Social Studies, Science, and Technical Subjects* contain four strands: Reading, Writing, Speaking and Listening, and Language. These four strands are represented in the *World-Readiness Standards for Learning Languages, Revised 2014* by the three Communication standards (Interpersonal, Interpretive, and Presentational) and the level of proficiency demonstrated. In addition, the standards of the other four goals areas for learning languages – Cultures, Connections, Comparisons, and Communities – support and align with the *Common Core*. These standards describe the expectations to ensure all students are college-, career-, and world-ready.

The *Common Core* strands of **Reading, Writing, Speaking and Listening** are captured in the *World-Readiness Standards for Learning Languages'* goal area of **Communication**, by emphasizing the purpose behind the communication:

- Interpersonal (speaking, writing)
- Interpretive (reading, listening, viewing)
- Presentational (writing, speaking, visually representing)

In the description of reading in the *Common Core* document, the use of both literary and informational texts is suggested. This same balance is identified in the *World-Readiness Standards for Learning Languages*.

In the description of writing in the Common Core document, a balance of writing to explain, to persuade, and to convey experience is suggested. These same purposes for writing are identified in the *World-Readiness Standards for Learning Languages*.

The *Common Core* strand of **Language** is described for language learners through proficiency levels that outline three key benchmarks achieved in world language programs given sufficient instruction over time:

- Novice (the beginning level, regardless of age or grade)
- Intermediate
- Advanced

Many factors influence the rate of progress through these three proficiency levels and the level learners acquire by the end of high school. Chief among those factors are time and the degree of immersion in the second language. Students who begin study of a language in middle school or high school generally acquire an intermediate level of proficiency.

Aligning the National Standards for Learning Languages with the Common Core Standards

Common Core State Standards for
English Language Arts and
Literacy in History/Social Studies, Science,
and Technical Subjects
- Reading
- Writing
- Speaking and Listening
- Language

National Standards for Learning Languages
Three Modes of Communication
- Interpersonal
- Interpretive
- Presentational

ACTFL Proficiency Guidelines
- Novice
- Intermediate
- Advanced

Speaking and Listening → Interpersonal

Listening / Reading → Interpretive

Language → Proficiency Levels

Speaking / Writing → Presentational

Reproduced with permission from ACTFL

Tejidos Scope & Sequence

Tejidos offers six thematic units *(mantas)* based on the 2014 AP® Spanish Language and Cultures themes and the 2013 IB core and optional topics that are subdivided into 13 thematic chapters *(hilos)*. Each *hilo* weaves a variety of authentic texts, such as videos, audios, blogs, interviews, articles, and literature that align with two or three essential questions, providing the overarching goals of the *hilo* for the student. *Hilo* activities integrate the *World-Readiness Standards for Learning Languages* focusing on the five Goal Areas: Communication, Cultures, Connections, Comparisons, and Communities standards. Student Learning Objectives for each chapter align with the *World-Readiness Standards for Learning Languages* and the *Common Core State Standards* for English Language Arts and Literacy.

Manta 1: Familia y comunidades
Hilo 1: Estructura de la familia
IB: Relaciones personales

Activity	Authentic source(s)	Vocabulary topics	Grammar in context/ Strategies	Formative Assessments
Introducción: ¿Qué sabes de la familia hispana de hoy en día?	**Entrevista con jóvenes latinos Parte 1**	Family, origin, daily life	Strategies: Conversing with a friend	Interpretive (T/F) Interpersonal speaking
Antes de empezar: ¿Cómo describes a los miembros de una familia?	**Fotografías**	Family members, descriptions: physical and personality	Strategies: Writing an informal email	Interpersonal writing
Pregunta esencial 1: ¿Cómo es la familia hispana de hoy en día?				
1. ¿Cuáles son las diferencias entre las familias modernas y tradicionales?	**Arte:** Silva, Lomas Garza Imágenes de familias	Traditions, values	Comparatives and superlatives	Presentational writing, Cultural comparisons
2. ¿Cómo es la estructura de la familia hispana en la actualidad?	**Edublog:** Tipos de familia	Types of families, changes, statistics	Strategies: Writing in a journal	Interpretive (M/C) Cultural comparison: application & analysis
Pregunta esencial 2: ¿Cuáles son los papeles que asumen los miembros de una familia hispana?				
3. ¿Qué esperan mis padres de mí?	**Tiras cómicas:** Baldo	Roles of family members		Interpersonal speaking & writing, Presentational writing
4. ¿Estás de acuerdo con estos consejos prácticos para tus padres?	**Blog:** Consejos de un profesor de educación y psicología	Professional advice to parents of teens	Familiar imperative/ commands	Interpersonal speaking & writing, interpretive reading, presentational speaking
Pregunta esencial 3: ¿Qué piensan los jóvenes de la familia hispana en la actualidad?				
5. ¿Cómo es la familia latina de hoy en día?	**Entrevista con jóvenes latinos Parte 2**	Cultural perspectives: Hispanic family life in the U.S.	Strategies: Use of present subjunctive: giving advice	Cultural comparison: Interpersonal writing or presentational speaking
6. ¿Cuáles son las tradiciones familiares que debemos conservar?	**Literatura:** "La última piñata" *(Canícula)* por Norma Cantú	Cultural perspectives: Family traditions and celebrations	Strategies: Text comprehension and meaning	Presentational writing options
Evaluación final/ Summative Assessment: *Participa en un concurso*	Reference to all sources	Reference to all vocabulary	Comparatives, superlatives, present subjunctive Strategies: Making references, transition phrases	Creating a podcast: Interpretive, Presentational writing & speaking

Manta 1: Familia y comunidades
Hilo 2: Redes sociales
IB: Comunicación y medios

Activity	Authentic source(s)	Vocabulary topics	Grammar in context/ Strategies	Formative Assessments
Introducción: ¿Qué harías tú?	**Video:** "De aquí no pasas"	Useful expressions, social networking	Strategies: Conversational expressions	Interpersonal writing
Antes de empezar: ¿Con qué frecuencia usas las redes sociales?	**Tuit Tuit:** "Los adolescentes y las redes sociales" Ministerio Ed, Argentina	Social networking		Interpersonal speaking & writing (Tuit), Interpretive (T/F), Cultural comparison, Presentational Writing
Pregunta esencial 1: ¿Por qué usamos redes sociales y por qué nos importan?				
1 ¿Por qué usan los jóvenes las redes sociales?	**Informe educacional y artículo periodístico:** El referente, Argentina	Internet, social networking, technology		Cultural comparison, Interpretive (T/F)
2 ¿Cómo evolucionan las redes sociales con los cambios en la vida social y con los avances de la tecnología?	**Audio digital en línea:** "Spanish Newsbites"	Internet, privacy, social networking		Interpretive (fill-ins), Presentational writing, Interpretive (T/F), Interpersonal writing
3 ¿Qué semejanzas y diferencias existen entre los adolescentes de España, América Latina y los Estados Unidos con su uso de las redes sociales?	**Estudio de investigación:** Statistics from Burón and Martín, University of Camilo José Cela	Internet, social networking, technology, statistics,	Strategies: Informal letter/e-mail, Similarities & differences	Interpersonal speaking & writing, Cultural comparisons, Interpretive (fill-ins), Presentational writing
Pregunta esencial 2: ¿Cuáles son las ventajas y desventajas de las redes sociales?				
4 ¿Cuáles son los riesgos de Internet y las redes sociales?	**Encuesta:** "Los riesgos en Internet y en las redes sociales" Ministerio de Ed, Argentina	Internet safety, Internet advice, social networking		Interpersonal speaking & writing, Presentational speaking & writing, Cultural comparisons
5 ¿Cuáles son los papeles de jóvenes y padres en el uso responsable de las redes sociales?	**Blog:** Educafamilia	Technology, family roles in internet safety	Formal imperative, Present subjunctive	Interpersonal speaking & writing Interpretive: vocabulary matching, Presentational speaking & writing
Pregunta esencial 3: ¿Cómo cambia la manera de interactuar entre nosotros cuando usamos las redes sociales?				
6 ¿Cómo cambia la comunicación familiar con el uso de la tecnología?	**Video:** "La familia digital from Generaciones Interactivas	Technology, social networking, family roles through technology		Interpersonal speaking & writing, Culture: products, practices, perspectives, Presentational speaking,
7 ¿Cómo escribimos en un español abreviado en las redes sociales?	**Textear con amix**	Technology shorthand (texting)		Interpersonal speaking, Presentational writing,
Evaluación final/ Summative Assessment: Voces de jóvenes en un blog	Reference to all sources	Reference to all vocabulary	Reference to all grammar	Writing a blog: Interpretive, Presentational writing, interpersonal speaking

Manta 1: Familia y comunidades
Hilo 3: Ciudadanía global
IB: Cuestiones globales

Activity	Authentic source(s)	Vocabulary topics	Grammar in context/ Strategies	Formative Assessments
Introducción: ¿Qué pueden hacer los jóvenes para mejorar el mundo?	**Documental:** Liga Española de la Educación	Global citizenship, awareness		Interpersonal speaking
Antes de empezar: ¿Qué necesita el mundo actual?	**Documental:** Liga española de educación	Global citizenship: needs and challenges		Interpersonal speaking, Cultural comparison, Presentational speaking
Pregunta esencial 1: ¿Por qué necesitamos los ciudadanos globales?				
1 ¿Qué es un/a ciudadano/a global?	**Blog:** Educadores y educadoras para una ciudadanía global	Citizenship, human rights		Presentational writing, Interpersonal speaking
2 ¿Por qué necesitamos los ciudadanos globales?	**Folleto de publicidad:** Liga Española de la Educación	Global needs, poverty, hunger, policies, volunteering	Subordinate "si" clauses with the conditional and imperfect subjunctive	Interpersonal speaking, Presentational speaking & writing
Pregunta esencial 2: ¿Qué características debe tener un/a ciudadano/a global?				
3 ¿Cómo se define un/a ciudadano/a global?	**Blog y documental:** Liga española de la educación	Implications of global citizenship, Defining a global citizen		Presentational speaking & writing, Interpersonal speaking
4 ¿Qué es el voluntariado?	**Radio emisión:** Fundación pies descalzos	Non-profit organizations, volunteering		Interpersonal speaking, Presentational writing
Pregunta esencial 3: ¿Cómo contribuyen los jóvenes al bienestar de las comunidades?				
5 ¿Cómo pueden cambiar el mundo los jóvenes voluntarios?	**Texto impreso y video:** ArmandoPazOEA	Volunteering	Strategies: Reflecting about learning	Interpersonal speaking & writing Presentational writing
6 ¿Qué puedes hacer tú para hacer una diferencia en tu comunidad?	**Anuncio de servicio público:** Plataforma del voluntariado de España (PVE)	Volunteering, refugees	Use of the subjunctive with "para que"	Presentational speaking & writing, Interpersonal speaking, Interpretive: fill-ins
Evaluación final/ Summative Assessment: Plan de acción	Ashoka Jóvenes Changemakers	References all vocabulary	Reference to all grammar Strategies: Comparing and contrasting, giving an opinion	Collaborative Action Plan interpersonal, presentational writing & speaking Cultural comparisons

Manta 2: Vida Contemporánea
Hilo 4: Viajes y ocio
IB: Ocio

Activity	Authentic source(s)	Vocabulary topics	Grammar in context/ Strategies	Formative Assessments
Introducción: ¿Por qué te gustaría conocer un nuevo país?	**Video:** Descubre Chile	Travel, Maps, Chile		Interpersonal speaking, Presentational writing
Antes de empezar: ¿Qué sabes de Chile y su cultura?	**Video Turístico:** Fundación Imagen de Chile	Chile, Culture of Chile		Interpersonal speaking, Presentational writing, Cultural Products, Practices, Perspectives
Pregunta esencial 1: ¿Cómo se planifica un viaje a un país donde se habla español?				
1 ¡Volemos a Chile!	**Búsqueda de Internet-** Viajes	Traveling, Travel planning, Activities, Money exchange		Interpersonal speaking, Presentational speaking & writing, Cultural comparison, Interpretive fill-ins
2 ¿Quieres explorar Chile?	**Horario de Turbus**	Regions of Chile, Bus schedule, Activities, Packing	Conditional	Interpersonal speaking & writing Cultural comparison, Presentational speaking
Pregunta esencial 2: Como viajero, ¿cómo se puede experimentar la vida cotidiana de otro país?				
3 ¿Cuáles son tus costumbres cuando viajas?	**Narración:** "Viajes" by Cortázar *(Historias de cronopios y de famas)*	Travel customs, Preparing to travel		Interpersonal speaking, presentational speaking & writing
4 ¿Qué puedes aprender y conocer al viajar?	**Radioemisión, Documental, y artículo periodístico:** Expedición Tahina-Can	Reconstruction of a country post-natural disaster, Socio-cultural realities	Preterit tense: irregulars, spelling changes & uses Strategies: Analyzing products, practices, and perspectives	Interpersonal speaking, Presentational speaking & writing, Culture: products, practices, perspectives
Pregunta esencial 3: ¿Cómo se entiende el ocio desde la perspectiva local?				
5 ¿Cómo puedes pasar un día tranquilo en familia?	**Folleto turístico:** Parque metropolitano de Santiago	Parks, Schedules, Services, Food		Interpersonal speaking & writing Cultural comparisons
6 ¿Qué piensan los chilenos sobre el ocio?	**Entrevista auditiva**	Free-time in Chile, Family past-times, Sports, Typical food		Interpersonal speaking, Presentational speaking & writing, Cultural comparisons
Evaluación final/ Summative Assessment: *Viaje virtual*	Reference to all sources	Reference to all vocabulary	Reference to all grammar Strategies: Useful expressions for a presentation	Plan a class trip to a Spanish-speaking country, Interpersonal Interpretive: research Presentational speaking & writing

Manta 2: Vida contemporánea
Hilo 5: Educación y carreras profesionales
IB: Relaciones sociales

Activity	Authentic source(s)	Vocabulary topics	Grammar in context/ Strategies	Formative Assessments
Introducción: ¿Qué significa aprender?	**Tira cómica:** Fabian Landa	School, learning		Presentational writing, Interpersonal speaking
Antes de empezar: *Tuiteando sobre #educación:*	**Tuits:** Various Twitter users	Education, school, learning		Interpersonal speaking & writing, Presentational writing
Pregunta esencial 1: ¿Cómo son los sistemas educativos en varias partes del mundo hispanohablante?				
1 ¿Educación pública o privada en Argentina?	**Audio:** Viviana Allegri, Principal of a public school in Argentina	Public vs. private education	Three uses of the passive voice with "ser" and "se" Strategies: comparisons, expressing opinions	Interpersonal speaking, Presentational writing, Cultural comparisons
2 ¿Qué causa la deserción escolar?	**Estadísticas y gráficas:** Gobierno del Estado de Baja California en México	Levels of schooling, Drop-out rates, Statistics		Interpersonal speaking, Presentational writing
Pregunta esencial 2: ¿Cómo nos prepara la educación para nuestra vida futura?				
3 ¿Cómo sirve la educación secundaria en la preparación para la universidad?	**Artículos y documental:** Alejandro de la Parra; Ministerio de Educación, Cultura y Deporte, Gobierno de España	Educational systems, Preparing for college	Present subjunctive	Interpersonal speaking & writing, Culture: products, practices, perspectives Presentational speaking & writing, Interpretive (T/F)
4 ¿Cómo se elige una institución universitaria o educación superior?	**Informes y consejos:** editorcarlos; Alejandro de la Parra, InfoFácil	Choosing a college, Giving advice	Direct and indirect object pronouns	Interpersonal speaking, Presentational speaking & writing
Pregunta esencial 3: ¿Cómo se elige una carrera profesional?				
5 ¿Cómo puedes elegir una carrera apropiada y atractiva para ti?	**Encuesta:** Elegir Carrera	Choosing a career, Professional dispositions/growth	Preterit and imperfect	Interpersonal speaking & writing, Culture: products, practices, perspectives Presentational writing
6 ¿Qué factores influyen al elegir una carrera?	**Artículo informativo:** Coyuntura Económica	Considering a career, Personal strengths/ preferences, Careers		Interpersonal speaking, Cultural comparisons, Presentational speaking & writing,
Evaluación final/ Summative Assessment: *Futuras carreras*	Reference to all sources	Reference to all vocabulary	Reference to all grammar Strategies: Connectors, use of imperfect and preterit	Career Fair: Interpretive research Presentational speaking & writing, Interpersonal speaking

Manta 2: Vida contemporánea
Hilo 6: Relaciones interpersonales
IB: Relaciones sociales

Activity	Authentic source(s)	Vocabulary topics	Grammar in context/ Strategies	Formative Assessments
Introducción: ¿A quién amas tú?	**Álbum de fotografías**	Interpersonal relationships, Emotions,		Interpersonal speaking & writing, Presentational writing,
Antes de empezar: *Amor adolescente*	**Tira cómica:** Baldo	Friendship, Romantic relationship		Interpersonal speaking, Presentational writing
Pregunta esencial 1: ¿Cómo la comunicación afecta nuestras relaciones familiares?				
1 *¿Son normales los conflictos entre hermanos?*	**Radioemisión:** La rivalidad	Sibling/Family relationships	Verbs ending in –ar, -er, -ir, with changes in spelling; "Cuanto más"+ Present subjunctive; Use of verb "deber" Strategies: Formal correspondence	Interpersonal speaking & writing Presentational writing Interpretive audio: (MC)
2 *¿Cómo afectan a los padres las decisiones de sus hijos?*	**Cuento:** "No oyes ladrar los perros" by Juan Rulfo	Parent – child relationships	Verbs with haber: Present perfect, (Preterit perfect), present perfect subjunctive, pluperfect, Pluperfect subjunctive, conditional perfect	Interpersonal speaking, Presentational speaking & writing, Interpretive (T/F)
Pregunta esencial 2: ¿Cómo nos definen nuestras amistades?				
3 *¿Por qué son valiosos los amigos en nuestra vida?*	**Poema y refranes:** Zaid; "Mi amigo"; Proverbios y refranes	Friendship	Uses of subjunctive	Interpersonal speaking, Presentational speaking
4 *¿Sabes que hay un Día Mundial de la Amistad?*	**Artículo periodístico:** Infoluque	Day of friendship		Interpersonal speaking, Presentational writing, Cultural comparisons
5 *¿Cómo nos influyen los amigos?*	**Refranes y testimonio:** Educar el carácter	Influence of friends		Presentational speaking, Interpersonal speaking
Pregunta esencial 3: ¿Cómo formamos nuestras ideas y expectativas del amor?				
6 *¿Cómo formamos nuestras ideas y expectativas del amor?*	**Arte:** "Serenade" by Francisco Cerón	Romantic relationships		Presentational speaking & writing, Interpersonal speaking & writing
7 *¿Cómo influyen las expectativas en una relación romántica?*	**Poesía:** "Me gustas cuando callas" by Neruda *(Veinte poemas de amor y una canción desesperada.)*	Expectations of romantic relationships	Verb "gustar" in an interpersonal context Strategies: Literary techniques and terms	Interpersonal speaking, Cultural comparisons, Presentational writing
Evaluación final/ Summative Assessment: *Cortometraje*	Reference to all sources	Reference to all vocabulary	Reference to all grammar	Create a short film, Presentational speaking & writing, Interpersonal speaking & writing

Manta 3: Belleza y estética
Hilo 7: Definiciones de la belleza
IB: Diversidad cultural

Activity	Authentic source(s)	Vocabulary topics	Grammar in context/ Strategies	Formative Assessments
Introducción: ¿Puedes tú definir la belleza?		Beauty		Interpersonal speaking & writing, Cultural comparisons
Antes de empezar: ¿Por qué es difícil definir la belleza?	**Las aceras de Madrid**	Beauty, Defining beauty		Interpersonal speaking, Presentational writing
Pregunta esencial 1: ¿Cómo varían las definiciones de la belleza en otras culturas?				
1 ¿En qué se ha basado la belleza a través de la historia?	**Artículo informativo:** Suite 101	Beauty in history	Ordinal and cardinal numbers Strategies: Writing an informative text	Presentational writing, Cultural comparisons
2 ¿Qué otros conceptos de belleza hay en otras culturas?	**Textos informativos:** Ruiz; Cimacnoticias	Cultural concepts of beauty	Using relative pronouns to connect one or more phrases	Presentational writing, Culture: products, practices, perspectivas Interpersonal speaking, Cultural comparisons
Pregunta esencial 2: ¿Quién tiene el poder de definir la belleza y la moda?				
3 ¿Quién decide lo que está de moda?	**Artículo periodístico:** El Economista	Fashion		Presentational writing, Interpersonal speaking & writing
4 ¿Cómo influyen los famosos en nuestra moda?	**Fotografías**	Famous people, fashion		Interpersonal speaking & writing
Pregunta esencial 3: ¿Cómo se puede concientizar a la gente de una definición más amplia de belleza?				
5 ¿Pueden los productos culturales cambiar nuestras perspectivas sobre la belleza?	**Fotografías, artículo y video:** Telemundo47, Dove	Cultural products, beauty, fashion, advertising	Nosotros commands	Interpersonal speaking & writing, Presentational speaking & writing, Cultural comparisons
6 ¿Eres más que una imagen?	**Artículo de opinión:** stop-obsesion	Beauty, Youth, Consumerism		Interpersonal speaking, Presentational speaking & writing
Evaluación final/ Summative Assessment: Diseñar un conjunto	Reference to all sources	Reference to all vocabulary	Reference to all grammar Strategies: Describing, persuading, making connections	Designing a new look: Presentational writing & speaking, Interpretive: research, Interpersonal speaking

Manta 3: Belleza y estética
Hilo 8: Artes visuales y escénicas
IB: Diversidad cultural

Activity	Authentic source(s)	Vocabulary topics	Grammar in context/ Strategies	Formative Assessments
Introducción: *¿Qué tipo de arte te gusta más?*	**Imágenes de arte** Artes plásticas: definiciones	Various artforms: visual art, scenic art, Graffiti, Applied art, Music		Interpersonal speaking, Presentational writing, Culture: products, practices, perspectives
Antes de empezar: *¿Cómo se describe el arte?*	**Murales** by Aurelio Grisanty	Music, Murals, Describing art	Strategies: Describing art	Presentational speaking & writing, Interpersonal writing
Pregunta esencial 1: ¿Cómo interpretan los artistas la realidad y la fantasía en sus obras?				
1 *¿Cómo inspiran las obras surrealistas de Salvador Dalí a Lady Gaga?*	**Arte surrealista y fotografía:** El Fan Terrible Blog	Surreal art, fantasy		Presentational speaking & writing, Interpersonal speaking, Cultural comparisons
2 *¿Quiénes serán los amantes?*	**Cuento** "Continuidad de los parques" by Cortázar	Fantasy literature	Gerunds with pronouns Strategies: Text comprehension	Interpersonal speaking, Presentational speaking & writing
Pregunta esencial 2: ¿Cómo refleja el arte la perspectiva cultural?				
3 *¿Qué se puede ver "detrás de" un mural?*	**Murales:** Herrón; Estrada	Murals, interpreting murals, farm workers,	Impersonal "se"	Interpersonal speaking & writing, Presentational speaking & writing, Cultural comparisons
4 *¿Qué tienen en común los bailes del Caribe?*	**Bailes del Caribe**	Caribbean dances, Bachata music, Salsa dancing		Interpersonal speaking, Culture: products, practices, perspectivas Presentational speaking & writing, Cultural comparisons
Evaluación final/ Summative Assessment: *Visita al museo*	Reference to all sources	Reference to all vocabulary	Reference to all grammar Strategies: Questions to ask the artist	Presenting art in a museum: Interpretive research Interpersonal speaking Presentational writing

Manta 4: Identidades personales y públicas
Hilo 9: Héroes y personajes históricos
IB: Diversidad cultural

Activity	Authentic source(s)	Vocabulary topics	Grammar in context/ Strategies	Formative Assessments
Introducción: *¿Reconoces a estos íconos del mundo hispanohablante?*	**Imágenes**	Famous people		Interpersonal speaking, Presentational writing, Culture: products, practices, perspectives
Antes de empezar: *¿Cómo han influido en la historia los héroes y personajes públicos?*	**Más imágenes**	Famous people		Culture: products, practices, perspectives, Interpersonal speaking, Presentational speaking
Pregunta esencial 1: ¿Cómo expresan los seres humanos su identidad en diversas situaciones?				
1 *¿Cómo cambiamos nuestro comportamiento para cumplir con las expectativas de los demás?*	**Poema:** "A Julia de Burgos" by de Burgos	Identity, Forming identity		Interpersonal speaking & writing Presentational writing
2 *¿Cuál es el legado que nos dejó Lorca?*	**Biografía y poema:** Maurer; "La guitarra" by Lorca	Legacy, Spanish Civil War,	Adverbs	Interpersonal speaking, Presentational speaking & writing
Pregunta esencial 2: ¿Cómo puede un individuo contribuir a definir la identidad de una nación?				
3 *¿Cómo se convirtió Eva Perón en una leyenda?*	**Biografía y documental:** Biografías y Vidas	Social justice, human rights	Irregular preterit	Presentational speaking & writing, Interpersonal speaking
4 *¿Cómo puede el testimonio de una persona transformar la situación política de una nación?*	**Biografía y documental:** Rigoberta Menchú, Fundación Rigoberta Menchú	Peace, Indigenous rights		Interpersonal speaking, Presentational speaking & writing
Evaluación final/ Summative Assessment: *Una cena inolvidable*	Reference to all sources	Reference to all vocabulary	Reference to all grammar	Dinner with a famous Hispanic person: Presentational speaking & writing, Interpretive research, interpersonal speaking

Manta 4: Identidades personales y públicas
Hilo 10: Identidad nacional e identidad étnica
IB: Diversidad cultural

Activity	Authentic source(s)	Vocabulary topics	Grammar in context/ Strategies	Formative Assessments
Introducción: ¿Cuáles son las partes de mi identidad?	**Tu identidad**	Personal identity		Presentational speaking & writing
Antes de empezar: ¿De dónde eres?	**Nacionalidades**	Nationalities, cities, countries		Interpersonal speaking, Presentational speaking & writing, Culture: products, practices, perspectives
Pregunta esencial 1: ¿Cómo se expresan los distintos aspectos de la identidad?				
1 ¿Cómo se puede expresar la identidad a través de la literatura?	**Narración:** "Mi nombre" by Cisneros *(La casa en Mango Street)*	Identity, names	Perfect conditional, "Como si"	Interpersonal speaking, Presentational speaking & writing
2 ¿Qué conexión hay entre los distintos aspectos de Frida Kahlo al ver sus retratos?	**Autorretrato:** Frida Kahlo	Identity, self-portrait		Interpersonal speaking, Presentational writing
Pregunta esencial 2: ¿Cómo se unen distintas culturas para formar una identidad étnica?				
3 ¿Cómo ha influido el mestizaje en la cultura latinoamericana?	**Poesía:** "Balada de los dos abuelos" by Guillén	Biracialism, Mestizo	Strategies: Reading, Literary devices: metaphors	Interpersonal speaking, Cultural comparisons, Presentational speaking & writing
4 ¿Cuáles son los diversos aspectos de la identidad étnica de Latinoamérica?	**Letra de canción:** "Latinoamérica" by Calle 13	Latin American ethnicity	Possessive pronouns	Interpersonal speaking, Presentational speaking & writing, Culture: products, practices, perspectives
Pregunta esencial 3: ¿Cómo influye el idioma en la identidad de una persona?				
5 ¿Cómo se une un idioma a gente de diferentes identidades?	**Videos y correo electrónico:** El díaE (Instituto Cervantes)	Language and identity, Native languages in Latin America		Presentational speaking & writing, Interpersonal speaking & writing
6 ¿Cuál es la situación lingüística actual en España?	**Artículo informativo y documental:** Just Landed; Rincón del vago	Languages and dialects in Spain		Interpersonal speaking, Presentational speaking & writing, Cultural comparisons
Evaluación final/ Summative Assessment: ¡Los idiomas sí cuentan!	**UNESCO,** Reference to all sources	Reference to all vocabulary	Reference to all grammar Strategies: Research	Presentation on the preservation of native languages in Spanish-speaking countries: Interpersonal speaking, interpretive research, Cultural comparisons, Presentational speaking & writing

Manta 5: Desafíos mundiales
Hilo 11: Temas del medio ambiente
IB: Asuntos globales

Activity	Authentic source(s)	Vocabulary topics	Grammar in context/Strategies	Formative Assessments
Introducción: ¿Qué sabes del calentamiento global?	**Video:** Calentamiento global, Israel Rojas, Ecuador	Global warming, Environmental concerns		Presentational speaking & writing, Interpersonal speaking
Antes de empezar: ¿Quiénes son las víctimas del calentamiento global?	**Artículo:** Pingüinopedia	Effects of global warming on animals, Penguins		Presentational writing, Interpersonal speaking, Linguistic comparisons,
Pregunta esencial 1: ¿Cuáles son las causas del calentamiento global?				
1 ¿Cuáles son las cinco causas principales del calentamiento global?	**Blog:** Un blog verde	Causes of global warming, emissions, deforestation		Linguistic comparisons, Presentational writing, Interpersonal speaking & writing
2 ¿Cuál es tu huella de carbono personal?	**Calculadora:** Huella de carbono	Carbon footprints, Carbon dioxide emissions		Presentational writing, Cultural comparisons, Interpersonal speaking
Pregunta esencial 2: ¿Cuáles son los efectos del calentamiento global?				
3 ¿Cuáles son los efectos del cambio climático en España?	**Revista digital:** Greenpeace España	Climate change: health & environmental effects		Interpersonal speaking & writing, Presentational speaking & writing, Cultural comparisons
4 ¿Te puedes enfermar debido al calentamiento global?	**Anuncio publicitario y noticias:** El Mundo; La Onda Verde de NRDC	Illnesses, global warming	Prepositions: "por" and "para" Strategies: Cultural comparisons	Interpersonal speaking, Presentational speaking & writing, Cultural comparisons
Pregunta esencial 3: ¿Cómo se puede combatir el calentamiento global?				
5 ¿Qué pueden hacer los jóvenes para combatir el calentamiento global?	**Artículo periodístico y consejos:** La Nación	Protecting the environment: Recycling, environmentally friendly lifestyle changes	Familiar imperative with pronouns	Interpersonal speaking & writing, Cultural comparisons, Presentational speaking,
6 Juntos, ¿cómo podemos mejorar el medio ambiente?	**Documental y Facebook:** UNESCO; Jóvenes Frente al Cambio Climático	Environmentally friendly lifestyle changes	Present subjunctive Strategies: Listening and note-taking, Participating in a Socratic debate	Interpersonal speaking, Cultural comparisons
Evaluación final/Summative Assessment: Folletos y anuncios publicitarios	**Cuidemos nuestro planeta** Reference to all sources	Reference to all vocabulary	Reference to all grammar	Brochure and public service announcement about a global challenge: Interpersonal speaking, Interpretive research, Presentational speaking & writing

Manta 5: Desafíos mundiales
Hilo Digital: Población y demografía
IB: Asuntos globales

Activity	Authentic source(s)	Vocabulary topics	Grammar in context/ Strategies	Formative Assessments
Introducción: ¿Qué sabes de la emigración?	**Gráficas e imágenes:** World Bank	Immigration, Emigration, Migration		Interpersonal speaking
Antes de empezar: ¿Qué sabes de las experiencias de los inmigrantes hispanos?	**Video**	Immigrant experiences		Presentational writing, Interpersonal speaking
Pregunta esencial 1: ¿Cuáles son las razones por que la gente elige migrar a otro país?				
1 ¿Qué les motiva a la gente tomar la decisión de emigrar de su país de origen?	**Documental y foro:** Witness for peace; Me Quiero Ir	Motives for emigrating,	Progressive tenses	Interpersonal speaking, Interpretive (T/F), Presentational writing, Cultural comparisons
2 ¿Cuáles son algunos países que atraen a los emigrantes y por qué?	**Podcasts y artículos:** Me Quiero Ir; UNICEF	Choosing a country to which to emigrate,	Prepositions "por" and "para"	Interpersonal speaking, Presentational writing, Interpretive: (T/F)
Pregunta esencial 2: ¿Cuáles son los desafíos a los que se enfrentan en el proceso de emigrar a otro país?				
3 ¿Cómo es el proceso de inmigrar legalmente y conseguir ciudadanía en los EE.UU?	**Documental oficial del gobierno de EE.UU.**	Naturalization, Citizenship, Visas	Passive voice	Presentational speaking & writing, Interpersonal speaking
4 ¿Cómo es la experiencia al cruzar la frontera?	**Video y artículo académico:** Moreschi	Borders, Crossing borders,		Interpersonal speaking, Presentational writing
Pregunta esencial 3: ¿Cuáles son los desafíos a los que se enfrentan los emigrantes en un nuevo país?				
5 ¿Cómo se adapta un emigrante a un nuevo país?	**Consejos de emigrantes**	Adapting to a new country, Advice, Stages of emigration	Use of the past participle as an adjective	Interpersonal speaking, Presentational speaking
Evaluación final / Summative Assessment: *Foro digital*	Reference to all sources	Reference to all vocabulary	Reference to all grammar Strategies: Persuasive argument	Analyze personal histories of emigrants based on Essential questions Interpersonal speaking, Interpretive: research, Presentational speaking & writing

Manta 6: Ciencia y tecnología
Hilo 12: Cuidado de la salud y medicina
IB: Salud

Activity	Authentic source(s)	Vocabulary topics	Grammar in context/ Strategies	Formative Assessments
Introducción: ¿En qué consiste vivir sano?	**Video My fitbook:** online source	Healthy living, exercise, proper diet		Presentational speaking & writing, Interpersonal speaking
Antes de empezar: ¿Qué necesita una comunidad para que la gente tenga una vida saludable?	**Guía de comunidad:** Caja de Herramientas Comunitarias; Comunidad Saludable	Healthy communities, Contributing to community health	Negation and "pero"/"sino"	Interpersonal speaking, Presentational speaking & writing, Cultural comparisons
Pregunta esencial 1: ¿Cómo coexisten las prácticas de la medicina tradicional y la moderna?				
1 ¿Medicina Tradicional o Medicina Científica? ¿En verdad somos tan diferentes en lo esencial?	**Revista científica:** Scientific Electronic Library Online Peru	Modern/scientific medicine, traditional/natural medicine		Interpersonal speaking, Presentational speaking & writing
2 ¿En qué se basa la medicina mapuche?	**Entrevistas:** Tahina-Can; Monografías.com; Carolina Andrea Neculhueque Rivera	Mapuche medicine, Traditional medicine, Natural medicine		Interpersonal speaking, Presentational speaking & writing, Culture: products, practices, perspectives
Pregunta esencial 2: ¿Cómo varía el cuidado de la salud en distintas regiones del mundo hispano?				
3 ¿Cómo está liderando España en el campo médico?	**Audio:** Spanish Newsbites	Modern medicine, Organ donation		Presentational speaking & writing, Interpersonal speaking
4 ¿Cómo varía el cuidado de la salud en areas rurales vs. urbanas?	**Artículo informativo:** Programas de las Naciones Unidas para el Desarrollo de Peru	Health in rural areas/Urban areas		Interpersonal speaking & writing, Presentational writing
Pregunta esencial 3: ¿Cómo influye la comunidad en la salud del individuo?				
5 ¿Cómo se puede concientizar a una comunidad sobre su salud?	**Fotonovela:** National Diabetes Education Program	Diabetes, Health awareness		Interpersonal speaking & writing, Presentational speaking & writing
6 ¿Qué hacen las promotoras para influir en la salud de su comunidad?	**Documental**	Promoting healthy habits		Presentational writing, Interpersonal speaking, Culture: products, practices, perspectives, Cultural comparisons
Evaluación final/ Summative Assessment: Feria de la Salud	Reference to all sources	Reference to all vocabulary	Reference to all grammar Strategies: Writing	Health Fair: Interpersonal speaking, Interpretive research, Presentational speaking & writing

MANTA 1 Familias y comunidades

Hilo 1 Estructura de la familia

Essential questions:
- ¿Cómo es la familia de hoy en día?
- ¿Cuáles son los papeles que asumen los miembros de una familia?
- ¿Qué piensan los jóvenes de la familia de hoy en día?

Student Learning Objectives

Interpersonal Communication: Spoken and/or Written Conversations

- Exchange information about modern and traditional families, roles of family members, traditions, and daily life.
- Express opinions about the social and cultural changes in family life and roles of family members, including parents' expectations of teens.
- Compose interpersonal messages such as emails or social media comments about roles of family members, traditions, and daily life.
- Compare, contrast, and express perspectives on changes in traditional and modern Hispanic families, including the family structure and roles of family members.
- Give advice to friends and family members regarding what parents can do to educate and guide their teens.

Interpretive Communication: Print, Audio, Audiovisual, and/or Visual Sources

- Demonstrate comprehension of content from authentic texts and audiovisual sources about the family, including blogs, interviews, and short narratives.
- Describe significant details from audiovisual interviews about the social and cultural changes in the lives of Hispanic families in the U.S.
- Interpret a message from an author in order to agree or disagree about advice to parents of teens.
- Determine the author's point of view regarding the changes in family structure in a Spanish-speaking country.

Presentational Communication: Spoken and/or Written Presentations to a Variety of Audiences

- Plan, produce, and present a written and oral digital product to a Spanish-speaking audience related to changes in the family structure, roles of family members, and modern-day family life.
- Apply, analyze, and compare census bureau statistics from Chile and the U.S. to determine the changes in families over a period of time.
- Express opinions on the changes in traditional and modern families, including Hispanic families in the U.S.
- Produce reflections and journal entries to demonstrate understanding of changes in family structure, roles of family members, and modern-day family life.

Relating Cultural Practices to Perspectives:

- Investigate, explain, and reflect on the relationship between the practices of traditional and modern-day families and the perspectives (beliefs/values/attitudes) of teens from Hispanic cultures.

Relating Cultural Products to Perspectives:

- Investigate, explain, and reflect on the relationship between the products (art and literature reflecting modern-day and traditional families) and perspectives (beliefs/values/attitudes) of Hispanic cultures.

Making Connections:

- Make connections to content knowledge about art and literature as it relates to traditions of Hispanic cultures.

Acquiring Information and Diverse Perspectives:

- Interpret and analyze statistics about families from Chile over a period of time.

Language Comparisons

- Make linguistic comparisons of familiar commands, cognates, comparisons, and superlatives to parallel structures in English.

Cultural Comparisons:

- Compare changes in family life and roles of family members, including parents' expectations of teens in the U.S. and Spanish-speaking countries.
- Evaluate similarities and differences of birthday celebrations in the U.S. with those in a Hispanic culture.

School and Global Communities:

- Interact with Spanish speakers about changes in family life and roles of family members, including parents' expectations of teens from Hispanic cultures.

Lifelong Learning:

- Set goals and reflect on progress in using Spanish for enjoyment, enrichment, and advancement.

Suggested Lesson Plan Sequence/Pacing Guide
Manta 1 Familias y comunidades
Hilo 1 Estructura de la familia

Focus according to Essential Question Pages in SE	Day (based on 60 min class)	Classroom Activities	Homework/ Formative assessment/ Exit pass
La familia de hoy en día pp. 6–13	1	* Introduce unit with overview hook for summative assessment * *Antes de empezar* activity: video interviews * Group work: *Antes de empezar* activities with thematic vocabulary	* ¡Te toca a ti! assignment: Write an email to one of the teenagers from the video
	2	* Group work: Artwork activity to discuss the traditional vs. modern Hispanic family	* ¿Qué aprendiste? Comprehension check
	3–4	* Interpretive reading of blog post "Tipos de familia" * Group work: Statistical analysis and presentation	* ¿Qué aprendiste?/¡Tu opinión cuenta! responses
Los papeles y expectativas de la familia pp. 13–18	4	* Interpretive reading "Baldo" comic strip activity to discuss parent expectations and rules	* ¿Qué aprendiste? Comprehension check
	5	* Interpretive listening to audio program on "La rivalidad" * Write an email asking for advice on a family problem	* Possible extension: Respond to a classmate's email
	6	* Interpretive reading of online parenting advice column * Prepare comments to post to the blog with your response	* (As needed by your students) Prepare answers to "interview" questions for next day
Los puntos de vista sobre la familia pp. 18–25	7	* Interview with a classmate * Interpretive listening to student interviews about their perspective on family * Comparison between your family and theirs	* Facebook message and/or leave a voicemail for one of the interviewees
	8	* Analysis of cultural products, practices and perspectives in artwork * Vocabulary inference activity while reading short story * Visualization and summary activities	* ¿Qué aprendiste? Connection between artwork and literature
	9–10	* Present Evaluación final summative assessment * Workshop time for student planning and pre-writing	* Summative assessment graphic organizer and outline
	11–12	* Workshop time for planning and practicing summative assessment	* Record and submit podcast for summative assessment

Hilo 1 Estructura de la familia

Introducción ¿Qué sabes de la familia hispana de hoy en día?

Student book page 6
Time estimate: 35–45 minutes

 A Organize students into pairs and have them describe their families according to the prompting themes in the student text.

« | » | Video script

Entrevista con dos jóvenes latinos de la Ciudad de Nueva York (Parte I)

Anfitriona con Erik

Estimados televidentes, bienvenidos a la transmisión de MundoLatino donde el programa de hoy, Enfoque en la familia, trata de la estructura de la familia hispana.

Para ver lo que está pasando en la familia hispana de hoy en día, vamos a entrevistar a dos jóvenes latinos de la ciudad de Nueva York. Primero quisiera presentarles a Erik de Puerto Rico.

Gracias por venir a nuestra emisora hoy para hablar un rato sobre tu familia con los televidentes. Ahora, vamos a hacerte unas preguntas sobre la estructura de tu familia

En primer lugar, ¿me podrías decir de dónde es tu familia?

Erik: Mi familia y yo somos puertorriqueños.

¿Cuándo llegaron ustedes aquí?

Erik: Mis papás tienen casi diecisiete años aquí en este país, yo tengo como dos años. Tengo un hermano de doce años que nació aquí.

¿Con quién vivías antes si solamente llegaste hace dos años?

Erik: Antes yo vivía en Puerto Rico con mi abuelita, una tía mía y una prima.

¿Con quiénes vives ahora?

Erik: Ahora vivo con mis papás y mi hermano que acabo de conocer hace unos años.

¿Dónde vive tu familia extendida?

Erik: Tengo familia extendida aquí en este país y también tengo más familia en Puerto Rico pero no nos vemos mucho porque no viajamos tanto.

Gracias Erik por describir a tu familia. Un poco más tarde esperamos platicar más contigo para conocer tus opiniones más a fondo.

Anfitriona con Michelle

Ahora seguimos con el segundo punto de vista estudiantil. Gracias Michelle por estar con nosotros, y aportar tu voz a nuestros televidentes. Me gustaría hacerte algunas preguntas de tu familia.

En primer lugar, ¿podrías describir a tu familia, sus orígenes y cuándo vinieron aquí?

Michelle: Pues, mi mamá llegó aquí a los Estados Unidos hace veinticuatro años. Vino cuando tenía dieciséis años en busca de un trabajo en una fábrica pero era un poco difícil encontrar un trabajo aquí.

En Colombia, ella vendía flores en el mercado. Siguió trabajando hasta que tuvo a mi hermano mayor de soltera, y de allí comenzó trabajando en limpieza.

Después conoció a mi papá de Ecuador. Son de diferentes culturas pero se llevan bien y para mí es muy divertido conocer las dos culturas.

Entonces ¿con quiénes vives ahora?

Michelle: Vivo con mis dos padres y mis dos hermanos. Mi hermano mayor está en la universidad y el otro es menor que yo.

En cuanto a tu familia extendida, ¿cómo es, dónde viven y se ven mucho?

Michelle: Pues, la familia de mi mamá es muy pequeña y tiene dos hermanos, uno que vive en Colombia y el otro está acá en Nueva York.

No ve mucho al hermano en Colombia porque se preocupa por mi hermano menor si lo deja para viajar a Colombia. De todos modos lo ve dos veces al año, lo llama y le manda dinero a la familia. Desde que era niña, vemos a mi tío que vive en NY cada viernes.

La familia de mi papá es bien grande porque tiene cinco hermanas y dos hermanos.

Mi papá aún tiene muchos tíos allá en Ecuador que todavía no ha conocido.

Aunque su familia es muy grande no se ven tanto porque viven en diferentes distritos de la ciudad de Nueva York. A veces los vemos en los días festivos.

Muchas gracias, Michelle, y de nuevo a ti, Erik, por estar aquí con nosotros. Después de una pausa y unas noticias, volveremos a preguntarles más sobre sus opiniones sobre la familia de hoy en día. Me despido de nuestros televidentes por ahora.

  B Students will watch an introduction to a video interview of two Latin American teenagers in the U.S. who speak about their families. Students will complete the organizer that is in *Tejidos* **Explorer**.

  D Check students' comprehension with the true/false statements. Have them compare answers including the justification for correct answers and the correction for false statements.

Answers to Part D:
1. Cierta
2. Falsa- su hermano nació en los EE.UU.
3. Cierta
4. Falsa- la mayoría vive en PR menos los papás y su hermano que viven en NYC.
5. Cierta
6. Falsa- dos hermanos
7. Cierta
8. Cierta
9. Cierta

Antes de empezar: ¿Cómo describes a los miembros de una familia?

Student book page 7
Time estimate: 30–40 minutes plus assign e mail as homework

Have students refer to the pictures to activate previous vocabulary related to the family. You may opt to use additional photographs in class and request that students bring in a picture of a family (theirs or any another family.) Complete the chart that is also found in **Explorer**. They can use vocabulary from part A of the Introduction and access the last page of the hilo for additional vocabulary.

Secondly, each group of 3 or 4 students will choose two photos (one large family and one small one) to describe in detail: physical and personality characteristics and relationships to each other. You may want them to share out a description of one of the photos.

¡Te toca a ti!

The e-mail may be assigned as homework. The template is in **Explorer** (Recursos, Organizadores gráficos). You may use one of the interpersonal writing rubrics to score it. The following is a model for the e-mail:

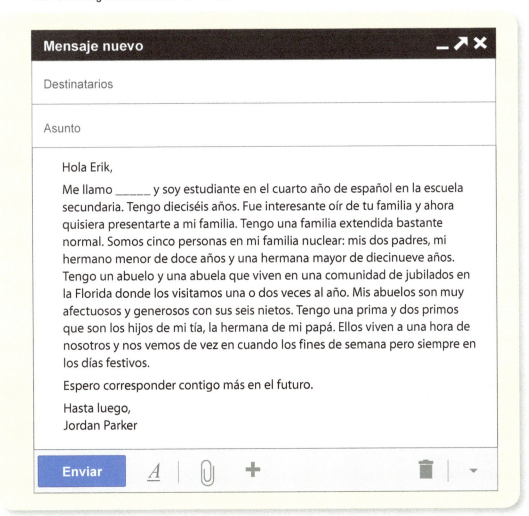

¿Cómo es la familia hispana de hoy en día?

Actividad 1 ¿Cuáles son las diferencias entre las familias hispanas modernas y tradicionales?

Student book page 8
Time estimate: 60 minutes. HW: Assign ¿Qué aprendiste?, an individual reflection for HW.
Grammar in context: comparatives and superlatives to compare family members in artwork and images

A Students will pair up to complete two Y chart organizers (in **Explorer**, Recursos, Organizadores gráficos). One student will choose a painting and the other student will select one of the photos. You may want to give half of the pairs in the class a blue sticky note and the other half a yellow sticky note to assign which visuals they will analyze. Give them a time limit (5 minutes). The questions that they will answer are on p. 9 in text.

B Each pair will now join up with another pair so that each group of four students represents the four different visuals in the text. They will answer the questions in part B after sharing out the information in their Y chart. Then students need to come to a consensus on any differences they see in the images between modern and traditional families. Lastly they will talk about similarities and differences of the Hispanic families and other families that they know.

Another option for A and B is to place four Y charts in the four corners of the classroom. Give each photo a number and write the number in the center of the Y chart. Divide the students into four groups, give each group a number and a different color marker. Have them move to a corner of the room with their books. At their station, they will have a limited amount of time to complete the 3 sections of the Y chart.

1. Write exactly what they see in "veo"
2. Write what they think is happening in "pienso"
3. Write what they wonder or would like to know in "quisiera saber"

After two or three minutes, use a signal or alarm to indicate a rotation to the next station in numerical sequence. Tell them to move in numerical sequence to the next photo with the same color marker. Read what the former group has written and then add more information. Repeat this process until they have completed working on all four visuals. Reduce the time limit each time. Begin with three minutes, then two minutes 30 seconds, then to two minutes, then one minute. Have students select the best comments to share out.

 ¿Qué aprendiste?

This is a formative assessment. For differentiation purposes, have students answer one of the questions or both. To grade it, use the presentational writing rubric (holistic or analytic) in **Explorer** and in the Teacher Edition appendices. .

¿Cómo es la familia hispana de hoy en día?

Actividad 2 ¿Cómo es la estructura de la familia hispana en la actualidad?

Student book page 10
Time estimate: 1st day: 60 minutes, 2nd day: 30–40 minutes.
HW: Assign Part C for HW after reading in class.

 A Before reading the monograph from an educational website in Chile, *Tipos de familias*, have students form small groups to discuss the two bullet points about the types of families they know and if they think the same types of families exist in Spanish-speaking countries.

 B The text is divided into five sections in order to reference information when discussing and answering the questions. There is a space in **Explorer** for students to submit answers to the questions about sections 1 and 3 of the reading. Read the first section of the text together as a class in order to determine the purpose of the article. Then have students read section 2 individually and complete the organizer in **Explorer**, then pair up to compare the information they noted about each type of family.

 C Before doing this part, tell students to read sections 3, 4 y 5 individually and to think about the social effects on the Hispanic family due to changes in types of families. Have them form an opinion as to whether they agree with the blog or not.

Answers to Part C:
1b. Explicar la complejidad de la familia.
2c. La familia es imprescindible para que los hijos sobrevivan y crezcan lo mejor posible.
3b. Hay veces que los padres no son capaces de cumplir con su deber y esperan que las escuelas hagan este trabajo.
4a. sección 1, líneas 11–12.
4b. sección 5 líneas 61–65.
4c. sección 2 líneas 20–25.
4d. sección 2 líneas 39–43.

¿Qué aprendiste?

 In pairs, students will compare and analyze the two graphs comparing types of families in Chile and the U.S. at about the same time in history.

1. Students have to mention three changes that have occurred in each country.
2., 3. Students will create two bar graphs: 1) Chile in 1992 and 1998 and 2) the U.S. in 1990 and 2000.
4. What are the similarities and differences between the two countries? Have them share out one similarity and one difference.

If students have access to a computer they can create bar graphs using the Charts menu in Microsoft Word.

Here is a sample of what a graph would look like for Qué aprendiste question 2:

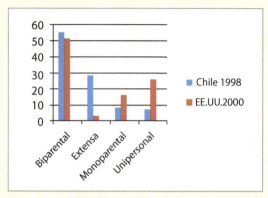

¡Tu opinión cuenta!

Have students record their opinions in their journals about changes in the structure of the family over the last two or three decades. This can be a homework assignment or a 10–15 minute reflection at the end of class. If you prefer, they can write it on a separate page to submit.

¿Cuáles son los papeles que asumen los miembros de una familia hispana?

Actividad 3 ¿Qué esperan mis padres de mí?

Student book page 13
Time estimate: 30 minutes–45 minutes

 A As students read through the cartoons, have them focus on the guiding questions in the student text on page 13. Ask them to rank the cartoons A – D based on how often they have the similar discussions with their own parents (1 being the least and 4 being the most).

 B You can utilize a variety of technology resources for this activity.

1. www.polleverywhere.com: Create four polls for each theme portrayed in the cartoons and invite students to post their "Twitter" messages using the links and poll codes. They can respond using iPods, iPads, computers or cellphones.

2. This activity also asks students to respond using Twitter format as if they are Baldo tweeting after each conversation. They can use Twitter accounts and hashtag (#) the theme. They can also connect with a class twitter page by tagging with the @ symbol. Cel.ly is another website (no need to type in .com, just cel.ly) that functions much like Twitter but is better suited for education.

3. www.todaysmeet.com is a website that allows you to create "virtual rooms." Send the link to your students via email and they can respond to the polls or questions using computers, iPads or mobile devices.

If you do not have easy access to technology, pass out sticky notes in four different colors, one for each cartoon theme. Have your students write their 140 character messages on the sticky-notes. Once they have finished have four large posters up in the front of the room and have students organize their messages by theme.

If you are using one of the digital tools mentioned above, have students respond and comment on what others have written, or 'retweet' comments they like by adding on to the Tweet. For the sticky notes, have students read what others have written to spark a class discussion about how parents and children communicate.

¡Tu opinión cuenta!

Students will role-play person A and person B interviewing each other about their roles in the family and opinions about parental roles. They will record each other's answers in writing or on a digital device. They will then share their classmates' answers with the class. They can compare similarities and differences among their answers.

¿Qué aprendiste?

Questions 1 and 2 will be a paraphrase/summary of the class discussion and question 3 will be a personal opinion. Students may write this reflection as a homework assignment or in class as a closing task for this activity.

¿Cuáles son los papeles que asumen los miembros de una familia hispana?

Actividad 4 ¿Estás de acuerdo con estos consejos prácticos para tus padres?

Student book page 16
Time estimate: 45–60 minutes, the blog may be assigned as homework
Grammar in context: familiar commands in the context of giving advice to your parents.

A Vocabulary in the text is italicized to highlight words whose meanings can be inferred from context of the advice that the professor gives to parents on page 17. Students can search for the italicized word in context to help with matching it to the definition. The chart is provided in **Explorer** for students to complete.

Answers to Part A:
1. D
2. K
3. G
4. H
5. I
6. B
7. C
8. E
9. J
10. A
11. F

B Have students read the introduction to the advice to parents on page 16 and then comment on the bulleted sentence starters.

C While reading the ten pieces of advice that the professor gives to parents so that they can get along better with their teens, have students individually decide if they agree or disagree with the advice.

¡Te toca a ti!
Have students form groups of 3 or 4 to discuss their answers to the advice column.

¿Qué piensan los jóvenes de la familia hispana en la actualidad?

Actividad 5 ¿Cómo es la familia latina de hoy en día?

Student book page 18
Time estimate: 45 min with HW (assign Part D. Option 1 or 2 for HW)
Grammar in context: Present subjunctive (as noted in strategy box on pg. 18)

« » Video script

Entrevista con dos jóvenes latinos de la Ciudad de Nueva York (Parte II)

Anfitriona con Erik

Bienvenidos de nuevo a mundo latino donde seguimos con las entrevistas en nuestro programa, Enfoque en la familia.

Volvemos a hablar con Erik. Hola Erik. Gracias por describirnos a tu familia anteriormente. Quisiera hacerte unas cuantas preguntas más sobre tu familia.

Por favor cuéntanos desde tu punto de vista, sobre todo porque has vivido en Puerto Rico y ahora vives en Estado Unidos, ¿cómo ha cambiado tu familia desde que llegó a los Estados Unidos?

Erik: Pienso que la familia aquí es un poquito más unida que la familia que tenía en Puerto Rico, porque allí todos vivíamos separados. No había mucha comunicación y la mayoría de la familia vivía en diferentes ciudades. Tampoco vivía con mis papás. Entonces cuando llegué aquí, vi que la mayor parte de mi familia vive aquí en New York y es más unida. Ahora tengo mejor comunicación con mis papás por vivir aquí con ellos.

Entonces dentro de la casa, ¿cuáles son los papeles que asumen los diferentes miembros de la familia? Por ejemplo, ¿quién hace los quehaceres y los trabajos de casa?

Erik: Mis dos papás trabajan. Mi papá trabaja de chef en un restaurán durante el día. A veces mi mamá trabaja durante el día, pero también por la noche.

En cuestión del trabajo de la casa, todos contribuimos, por ejemplo mi padre contribuye la comida y yo también contribuyo porque lavo, friego, trapeo, barro- hago de todo un poco.

Sin embargo, puedo decir que mi mamá hace la mayor parte del trabajo. Mi papá no hace mucho en la casa pero nos ayuda cuando puede.

Si pudieras darles unos consejos para ser buenos padres, ¿qué les aconsejarías?

Erik: Para ser buenos padres les aconsejaría que brindaran y apoyaran a sus hijos en cualquier momento. También para ser buenos padres, necesitan respetar la opinión de cada miembro de la familia.

Les aconsejaría que los dos ayudaran en las situaciones económicas en vez de dejar todo para la mamá. Por ejemplo, el papá no debe ser machista como decimos en Latino América. El papá no debe pensar solo en sí mismo sino también ayudar con todo lo que pueda.

Les diría a mis padres que siempre trataran de salir adelante y estar juntos a su familia de manera que sean un buen ejemplo para que los hijos tengan éxito y los padres puedan darles un buen modelo.

¿Qué expectativas tienen tus padres para ti?

Erik: Mis padres tienen muchas expectativas. Quieren que me gradúe de la secundaria y después de la universidad. Después tal vez esperan que siga con un doctorado. Quieren que llegue a lo alto, lo máximo que pueda. Quieren lo mejor para mí, para mi vida y más que nada, que yo tenga éxito.

Muchas gracias, Erik. Agradecemos tu participación y aporte.

Anfitriona con Michelle

Ahora nos toca oír algo más de Michelle. Gracias, Michelle, por estar con nosotros de nuevo y para aportar tu opinión y experiencia para que te escuchen otros jóvenes. Ya describiste un poco a tu familia. Me gustaría hacerte unas cuantas preguntas más sobre la estructura de tu familia.

¿Cuáles son los papeles que asumen los diferentes miembros de tu familia?

Michelle: Mis padres trabajan, mi papá de cocinero en un restaurante y mi mamá limpia casas. Los dos tienen sus maneras de pagar los gastos de familia, por ejemplo mi papá paga por la renta, la luz y el gas; mi mamá paga por los teléfonos, cosas para nosotros como la ropa y la comida. Si necesitan pagar por alguna otra cosa, hablan y lo arreglan entre ellos.

¿Quién hace el trabajo de la casa?

Michelle: Como mi papá está en casa por las mañanas, limpia la casa y hace la comida. Cuando mi mamá llega por la tarde, ella recoge a mi hermano y nos cuida a nosotros. Ellos se turnan para estar con nosotros dependiendo de su horario de trabajo. Durante las vacaciones nosotros, los hijos, limpiamos la casa.

Me parece que tu familia es muy unida. ¿Me puedes comentar sobre las expectativas que tienen tus padres respecto a ti?

Michelle: Francamente entre mis hermanos, yo soy la más floja, y por eso mis padres esperan más de mí, porque quieren una vida mejor para mí.

Ellos no quieren que limpie casas ni que encuentre un trabajo en tiendas; quieren que trabaje en algo que me guste, que haga muy buen dinero, que ayude a otras personas y que tenga mi propia familia.

No quieren que tengamos la vida que ellos tuvieron la cual era muy dura.

Antes de terminar, ¿algún consejo, que querrías darles a tus papás, sobre su papel de papás?

Michelle: Yo les diría que sigan haciendo lo que están haciendo, empujándome a mí y a mis dos hermanos, porque hemos logrado a niveles que nosotros nunca pensamos que podíamos.

Pues mi hermano ya está en la universidad y es el primero de nuestra familia para graduarse. Es muy importante para mi familia porque tienen orgullo de él y es un honor de ser el primero. Además ahora, nosotros, vemos lo que podemos lograr.

¿Y tú piensas que vas a poder lograr esas expectativas?

Michelle: Yo creo que sí. Sí, porque mis padres siempre me han apoyado, y pues mi hermano también me ha apoyado. Yo he visto que él sí puede, y yo creo que yo también puedo tener éxito.

Anfitriona con Erik

Vuelvo a hacerle la misma pregunta a Erik. ¿Tú piensas que podrás lograr las altas expectativas que tus papás tienen de ti?

Erik: Yo pienso que sí. Yo voy a lograr todas las expectativas que ellos tienen para mí. Soy una persona que nunca se rinde. He tenido muchas malas experiencias en mi niñez pero siempre he tratado de salir adelante. Yo sé que voy a cumplir todas las metas que me propongo. Ellos van a sentirse orgullosos de mí.

Estupendo Erik y Michelle, los felicito a los dos y de parte de nuestro programa, Enfoque en la familia, les agradecemos mucho su participación y las aportaciones hechas a nuestra audiencia.

Este programa ha sido transmitido en MundoLatino *en Nueva York.*

B You may need to explain and/or model to students how to take notes here, as they may not have had much practice taking notes while listening. Remind students that they cannot write full sentences or expect to transcribe everything they hear; rather, they should be noting key words and information. You can model this on the board for them during the first few lines of dialogue.

C As on the AP exam, students can hear auditory sources twice. Here they need to mark each statement as *Cierta* or *Falsa* and correct the false statements.

Answers to C:
1. Cierta
2. Falsa – Toda la familia de Erik contribuye algo.
3. Falsa – Los padres de Erik esperan que se gradúe de la universidad y después que siga con un doctorado.
4. Cierta
5. Falsa – Los padres de Michelle comparten responsabilidad para el presupuesto de la casa.
6. Cierta
7. Falsa – Quieren que tenga una mejor vida y que trabaje en algo que le guste.
8. Falsa – Su hermano fue el primero de la familia en graduarse de la universidad.
9. Cierta

 ¿Qué aprendiste?

 Students may need assistance with connectors used to make comparisons (discuss similarities and differences in Spanish). They can refer to hilo 2, pg 42.

 D For Option 1, students can access the Facebook message template in **Explorer,** and for Option 2 can record themselves speaking in **Explorer.**

¿Qué piensan los jóvenes de la familia hispana en la actualidad?

Actividad 6 ¿Cuáles son las tradiciones familiares que debemos conservar?

Student book page 20
Time estimate: 60 minutes plus writing assignment

 A Before starting this part of the activity, you will want to explain the 3 P's (products, practices, and perspectives) of culture from the *World-Readiness Standards for Learning Languages*. This is in **Explorer** as Apoyo adicional for student access: **Lengua y cultura: los productos, prácticas y perspectivas**. An English summary appears at the end of this activity.

 B Have two pairs of students form a group of four to begin to analyze the Barbacoa painting. Project the Barbacoa painting onto the screen for all to see (or reference in their books). In their small groups, have them record the products or practices that they see in the painting. Then ask them what meaning or value the practice or product has in the Hispanic culture. In some cases regarding the piñata, it may be the history that will explain the meaning of how the practice was started. See the culture box in this activity to view a video on the origin of the piñata (see **Explorer** *Fuentes audiovisuales* for Act 6) or ask students to do the research.

 C Create a class organizer on chart paper to share the information to display to the class. Ask students to make a list of some products and practices that define our current day culture in order to get them to fully understand the concept of what those products or practices say about a culture.

Examples of U.S. Products
1. Carros/autopistas
2. Comida rápida (McDonald's/Burger King)
3. Diet foods/Slim Fast/Meal replacement bars

Examples of corresponding U.S. Practices:
1. Speed on Highways/Interstates
2. Eating in cars due to being in a hurry
3. "Thin is in"

 D The vocabulary box titled "Al leer" previews vocabulary in context from the narrative "La última piñata." Have students infer the meaning from context as they read. There is a vocabulary activity in **Explorer**.

 E Have students draw the scene that they visualized after reading the narrative followed by writing a summary of their drawing. You may have them do this as homework individually or work in pairs in class. The answer to the fill-in regarding the age of Nena's sister: Espy was three years old "Esperanza tiene apenas tres años."

Note: Norma Cantú lived on the border between Mexico (Nuevo Laredo) and the U.S. (Laredo) in the late 40s and early 50's. Have students research the laws of that time to determine life on the border and the impact on crossing the border between Mexico and the U.S.

¿Qué aprendiste?

Students have three differentiated options to demonstrate what they learned in this activity. The main question asks them to explain what literature or art communicates about the Hispanic culture, in this case, Mexico.

 Teacher Note: See teacher professional resources link in **Explorer** relating to culture standards. This is the Spanish version for students that appears in the Apoyo Adicional Act 6:

 Lengua y cultura: productos, prácticas y perspectivas
La lengua y la cultura se relacionan íntimamente. Cuanto más se sabe de la cultura de una región, mejor se puede usar su lengua para comunicarse con las personas que la hablan. Por eso, es muy importante estudiar la cultura de los países hispanohablantes a través de los siguientes tres elementos:

- **productos: lo que produce una cultura**
  ejemplos: objetos cotidianos, pinturas, tecnologías, literatura, viviendas, bailes, música, tradición oral e instituciones (gobiernos, sistemas de educación.)
- **prácticas: el comportamiento aceptado por los miembros de una cultura**
  ejemplos: conducta social, saludos, tradiciones, celebraciones, comportamiento diario como el ir de compras, y uso formal o informal del trato entre personas.
- **perspectivas: las creencias que guían a los miembros de una cultura**
  ejemplos: actitudes ante hechos sociales, valores, importancia de la familia, interdependencia, libertad y respeto a la privacidad.

 English summary: *Language and culture: products, practices, and perspectives:* Culture and language are intimately interrelated. The more one knows about the culture of a region, the more you can use their language to communicate with the people. In order to communicate in culturally appropriate ways, students need to have knowledge about "what to say and do when and where." The activities in *Tejidos* are designed so that students are learning about different levels of culture while they are learning and practicing Spanish.

The three interrelated components of a culture are products, practices, and perspectives, referred to as the "3 Ps":

- **Products** (what a culture produces, tangible or intangible) such as paintings, technologies, literature, homes, dance, music, and institutions (government, education.)
- **Practices** (how a culture behaves or acceptable social behaviors) such as greetings, gestures, traditions, celebrations, shopping practices, table manners, use of formal or informal forms of address, and dating behaviors.
- **Perspectives** (the world view of the culture, the why or justification of the products and practices) such as attitudes, beliefs, importance of family, ownership, freedom, and respect for privacy.

 Additional activity: "**Tres generaciones**" by Rosaura Sánchez is a story about three generations of Mexican-American women living in the United States that is in **Explorer** in the **Teachers Only** site. It is a complete activity with exercises and scaffolding available to those who may want to use it with their classes. It connects with all the essential questions of this hilo.

Essential questions:
- ¿Cómo es la familia hispana de hoy en día?
- ¿Cuáles son los papeles que asumen los miembros de una familia hispana?
- ¿Qué piensan los jóvenes de la familia hispana en la actualidad?

Hilo 1 Evaluación final — ¿Qué piensan los jóvenes de la familia hispana de hoy en día?

Student book page 24
Time Estimate: 2 class periods (this will depend on if time is given to work on this at home, or if students will need to do recordings in class).
Grammar in context: present tense, comparisons, superlatives, present subjunctive

As you prepare your students for this summative assessment, be sure to spend some time working on paraphrasing the question when they compose their response. The question being asked should be clear in the responses that students give. For example, in this final evaluation I the student can rephrase the question to say "En la familia hay una variedad de papeles que los miembros pueden asumir" or "En nuestra sociedad de hoy en día, la familia moderna es diferente de la familia tradicional." From there, the student can continue their presentation with examples and evidence from the resources in the chapter.

You can also provide additional help to students who might be struggling to get started. You can give them the "main idea" as a starting point, knowing that very soon, with examples like the one that follow, they will be able to do this on their own. At the beginning of the year students might need additional support in starting a presentation like this.

As students begin this summative assessment, you can use the graphic organizer and an outline for students in **Explorer (Evaluación final)** to help show them the thought process used to start and develop a cohesive oral presentation. There is a sample summative assessment with answers in **Explorer** (Recursos, Sólo para los profesores).

MANTA 1 Familias y comunidades

Hilo 2 Redes sociales

Essential questions:
- ¿Por qué usamos las redes sociales y por qué nos importan?
- ¿Cuáles son las ventajas y desventajas de las redes sociales?
- ¿Cómo cambia la manera de interactuar entre nosotros cuando usamos las redes sociales?

Student Learning Objectives

Interpersonal Communication: Speaking and Writing
- Exchange information about advantages and disadvantages of social networking.
- Express opinions about social and cultural changes in families and communities due to social networking.
- Exchange messages such as emails, blogs, or social media posts about appropriate use of social networks.
- Compare, contrast, and express perspectives about social networking preferences and opinions of teens in Spanish-speaking countries and the U.S.
- Compare and contrast forms of communication in social relationships and family life before and after social networking.
- Give advice to educate others on responsible use of social networks.
- Explain how consumers' usage of social networks influence advances in technology.

Interpretive Communication: Print, Audio, Audiovisual, and/or Visual Sources
- Demonstrate comprehension of content about social networking from authentic texts, blogs, surveys, audio, and audiovisual resources.
- Describe and analyze significant details from audio and audiovisual sources about changes in forms of communication in families and communities.
- Interpret a message from an author in order to agree or disagree about advice to parents of teens.
- Evaluate the author's purpose from authentic texts, surveys, and blogs regarding social networking among teens.
- Interpret and analyze statistics about usage of social networking in Spanish-speaking countries.

Presentational Communication: Spoken and/or Written Presentations to a Variety of Audiences
- Participate in a social media forum to express and defend opinions about the role of social media in social and cultural changes of families and communities.
- Create an oral or written publication on the responsible use of social networks.
- Produce reflections and journal entries to demonstrate understanding of the influence social networking has on relationships, both friends and family.
- Record telephone messages to express personal opinions about advantages and disadvantages of social networking.

Relating Cultural Practices to Perspectives:
- Investigate, explain, and reflect on social networking practices and the perspectives (beliefs/values/attitudes) of Hispanic cultures.

Relating Cultural Products to Perspectives:
- Investigate, explain, and reflect on the use of products (devices) and the perspectives (beliefs/values/attitudes) of Hispanic cultures.

Connections: Connect with Other Disciplines
- Make connections to content knowledge about technology as it relates to social networking.

Connections: Acquire New Information
- Use new information about technology to expand content knowledge.

Comparisons: Language
- Make linguistic comparisons of cognates and familiar and plural imperative verb forms.

Comparisons: Culture
- Compare similarities and differences among teens' use of social networks in the U.S. and Spanish-speaking countries.
- Analyze, compare and contrast survey results about use of social networks in Spanish-speaking countries and the U.S.

School and Global Communities:
- Interact with Spanish speakers about changes in relationships and family life due to social networking.

Lifelong Learning:
- Set goals and reflect on progress in using Spanish for enjoyment, enrichment, and advancement.

Suggested Lesson Plan Sequence/Pacing Guide
Manta 1: Familias y comunidades
Hilo 2: Redes sociales

Note: Workshop days (working on projects in class) are flexible and should be inserted in the sequence per your class' specific needs and abilities. Students may be able to complete work more or less quickly outside of class.

Focus according to Essential Question Pages in SE	Day (based on 60 min class)	Classroom Activities	Homework/ Formative assessment/ Exit pass
El uso e importancia de las redes sociales pp. 30–42	1	* Introduce unit with video hook "Qué harías tú" and poll * *Antes de empezar* poll, reading and response	* True/False and Tuit cultural comparison activities can be assigned as homework
	2	* Reading, then mapping information and opinions * Post reading activities: Summarize and evaluate texts	* ¿Qué aprendiste? summaries and ¡Tu opinión cuenta! oral presentation
	3	* Finish review of yesterday's texts on social networks * Listening to audio source (twice) with vocabulary and comprehension activities	* ¿Qué aprendiste? responses
	4 + workshop(s)	* Interactive reading and analysis of graphs with comprehension checks * Creation of survey to administer to others + Workshop day (insert in sequence as you deem best) for analyzing student survey data and drafting letter to professors with this information. *Additional writing workshop day can be included as per the needs of your students.*	* Fill in the blanks during reading activity * Students administer survey and complete final draft of letter outside of class
Ventajas y desventajas de las redes sociales pp. 43–50	5	* Categorize vocabulary while reading and comprehension check following text * Think – pair – share on cultural differences	* ¿Qué aprendiste? Informal letter using informal commands
	6–7 + workshops	* Grammar focus and pre-reading conversation * Two close readings of texts for vocabulary and content * Group conversations * Workshop days (insert in sequence as you deem best) for work on formative assessment project and presenting to class	* Students will develop and polish their formative assessment projects outside of class
Las redes sociales y nuestra manera de interactuar pp. 51–59	8–9	* Video (all the way through and in fragments) and discussion * Cultural analysis * Group role plays and presenting to class * Practice with abbreviations for texting in Spanish	* ¿Qué aprendiste? cultural analysis and ¡Tu opinión cuenta! Evaluation * Tweeting practice
	10	* Finish review of "amix" and watch/respond to video on texting while driving * Present *Evaluación final* summative assessment * Workshop time for student planning and pre-writing	* Summative assessment: students prepare interview and their own experiences
	11–12	* Workshop time for planning and writing summative assessment	* Draft, edit and submit final blog entry for summative assessment

Hilo 2 Redes sociales

Introducción: ¿Qué harías tú?

Student book page 30
Time estimate: 30 minutes

To start this unit it is important to think about the technology that you can integrate in the activities that we include in the Student Edition and in **Explorer**. We know that every school is different and that the rules and policies associated with technology use are varied. Before teaching this unit, read the activities and suggestions we offer about how to incorporate technology. Find out what technology your school allows and that you have at your disposal. Even though we offer many options it is important that you use the best option for your situation.

Show the video to your class. After viewing, take a poll to find out if your students think the girl should go to the party or not. There are a wide variety of websites that allow for class polling like www.polleverywhere.com, www.edmodo.com, www.todaysmeet.com, www.wallwisher.com and www.cel.ly.com. Based on the technology you have available, decide which is the best tool to ask your students "¿Qué harías tú?" **Explorer** has a Facebook status template for students to fill out.

If there is no way for you to incorporate technology in this lesson, pass out one color sticky note to students who think she should go to the party and another color to those who think she should not go to the party. Have them write their reasoning on the paper and then place them up in front of the room. If you are doing the class poll, project it onto a screen or TV so that students can read their classmates' responses. Invite your students into a discussion in which they explain their answers. Focus the discussion on reasons they give to defend their opinions, i.e. the dangers of social media, the responsibility of parents, and how teenagers can make good decisions about how they use the Internet.

Antes de empezar: ¿Con qué frecuencia usas las redes sociales?

Student book page 31
Time estimate: 45 minutes

 A Give your students the opportunity to ask ten classmates the question presented in the text. You can structure this using an activity like *inside-outside circles* or you may choose to give them a certain period of time to get responses from ten people. You can also do a quick poll of the entire class using www.edmodo.com or www.polleverywhere.com. These sites make it very easy to create polls, for students to respond, and to collect the data from their answers. Depending on how you would like to structure this activity you may choose either option.

  B Have your students read the short excerpt and the statistics that accompany it in the graphic that is reproduced here. The graphic in the First printing of the Student Edition misprint; the correct graphic is below and is also accessible to students in **Explorer**, Antes de empezar Apoyo adicional.

 C Ask your students to read through the questions and answer true or false. If the statement is false, have them rewrite it so that it correctly reflects the information in the reading.

> **Answers for Part C**
> **a.** Falsa - El 80 porciento de usuarios de redes sociales tienen entre doce y treinta años.
> **b.** Cierta
> **c.** Cierta

   D Now that students have seen this additional table, have them make this comparison. Students compare the results of the survey that they completed in part A with the responses shown in the correct table from Part B. Ask them to write a Tweet, which they can submit electronically using Edmodo or polleverywhere.com, in which they communicate in 140 characters or less, the similarities or differences between the statistics they collected and those provided in the table.

¿Por qué usamos redes sociales y por qué nos importan?

Actividad 1 ¿Por qué usan los jóvenes las redes sociales?

Student book page 32
Time estimate: 2 45-min class periods with homework

A. There is a vocabulary exercise in **Explorer** that students can take as a pre-assessment in class or do as a homework assignment if they all have access to Internet.

Answers for A:
1. rodeado
2. La espontaneidad
3. El anonimato
4. La pantalla
5. los riesgos
6. inmerso
7. ceder
8. suelen

B. You can use the information on the Injuve site linked in **Explorer** to help students understand what *Injuve* is (and it could be a good way to solicit their opinions about this kind of governmental agency, and their goals and programs!) There is a graphic organizer for this section in **Explorer**.

C. There is a graphic organizer for this section in **Explorer**. The first two columns are based on the texts; the last two columns provide students with an opportunity to express their opinion and prepare to share it with classmates. It is important that they justify their opinions!

¿Qué aprendiste?

You can choose to have students present their summaries to the class, via phone message to you, or by recording themselves digitally in **Explorer**. Alternatively, you can ask them to prepare their written summary for display in the classroom.

¡Tu opinión cuenta!

There is a space in **Explorer** for students to record their answers here. Alternatively, you can set up a voicemail system like Google Voice to have students leave you messages. (This is free on a Gmail account and sends you an email notification that you have received a voicemail. You can listen to students' responses online and send the audio file back to them with your written comments via email, so that they can listen to themselves – great feedback!)

Note to teachers: "No te metas en mi Facebook" de Esteman
This song by Esteman has a link to a karaoke version in **Explorer** Enlaces for Actividad 1. Students can sing along!

¿Por qué usamos redes sociales y por qué nos importan?

Actividad 2 ¿Cómo evolucionan las redes sociales con cambios en la vida social y con avances de la tecnología?

Student book page 36
Time estimate: 30 minutes

 A Before listening to the audio in this activity, have your students complete the matching activity in this section to help them define these eight words that will help them with their comprehension of the text. This is available to take as a vocabulary quiz in **Explorer**.

Answers for A:
1. G   4. A   7. D
2. F   5. B   8. E
3. H   6. C

 B Play the audio for your class so that they can hear the brief radio announcement. The first time ask students to focus on the main idea.

 C The second time you play the audio, have them complete the sentences in Part C. This is also an online quiz in **Explorer**. Go over the answers in part C before moving on to part D.

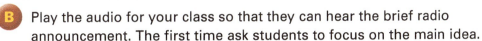

« | » | **Audio script**

2008 termina. ¿El fenómeno español del año en Internet? No hay duda: Tuenti. Con sólo dos años de vida, esta red social es el tercer sitio en tráfico de visitas en España, después de Google y MSN. Tuenti tiene casi el mismo número de usuarios que Facebook en su versión española, unos dos millones y medio, pero más del doble de visitas y de más tiempo. ¿Están menos ocupados los jóvenes y adolescentes? Puede ser. Tuenti está hecho por y para ellos. Cuatro amigos con poco más de 20 años lo crearon en 2006. Hoy son un equipo de 35.

El éxito de Tuenti se resume en tres ideas: la especialización, la privacidad, y la localización. A diferencia de Facebook, de carácter más internacional, o MySpace, cada vez más destinado al entretenimiento y la música, Tuenti es para jóvenes, la mayoría de ellos estudiantes universitarios y de secundaria. No es una empresa con versión española, nació en español. A Tuenti sólo se accede por invitación de amigos. Una vez dentro, la privacidad funciona como en el mundo real. Si el contacto es profesional, se puede ver sólo este perfil (fotos, vídeos). Si es de amistad, se pueden ver más cosas.

Pero el futuro de Tuenti y de las otras redes sociales está en la localización: el móvil. Funciona como un gran sistema colectivo de correo electrónico. Puedes saber dónde están y qué hacen tus amigos en cada momento y unirte a ellos. En este caso, la tecnología va por detrás. Tuenti y Facebook ya existen en el teléfono móvil. Puedes ver las fotografías, pero aún no es posible subirlas desde el propio teléfono. Tampoco los vídeos. Es sólo cuestión de tiempo.

Answers for Part C:
1. red social
2. usuarios
3. 20, 2006, 35
4. nació
5. fotografías, teléfono

 1. After your students have listened to the audio, answered the questions in part C and gone over the questions as a class, give them a few moments to answer the questions in the table on page 37 with the correct answers, true or false. If the answer is false, ask them to rewrite the statement in a complete sentence.

Answers for Part D:
1. Cierta
2. Cierta
3. Falsa - La mayoría de los usuarios de Tuenti son estudiantes universitarios y de secundaria.
4. Cierta
5. Falsa - Los usuarios de Tuenti pueden controlar la privacidad de su perfil y lo que sus amigos pueden ver de su página.
6. Falsa - En el futuro, Tuenti se va a centrar en los móviles y el acceso móvil.
7. Falsa - Los usuarios de Tuenti pueden ver las fotos desde su móviles, pero solo pueden subirlas de una computadora.

 2. Give your students an opportunity to ask a partner the three questions provided in the text and record their answers. As a class, discuss their answers to the questions.

 Ask your students to read the brief announcement and view the image from the Tuenti website. You can discuss as a class how the site responded to the perceived need of its users that was discussed in the audio.

 ¿Qué aprendiste?

Have students respond in a short blog-style essay to the question provided at the bottom of page 37.

¿Por qué usamos redes sociales y por qué nos importan?

Actividad 3 ¿Qué semejanzas y diferencias existen entre los adolescentes de España, América Latina y los Estados Unidos con su uso de las redes sociales?

Student book page 38
Time estimate: 1st day reading and discussions 45–60 minutes
2nd day (may be several days later)- collecting responses, analyzing data and presenting findings to class- 60 minutes

Activity activator: quotes from *Hoy Tecnología*: Have students read the quotes and ask them what they find or don't find surprising using these sentence starters that require the use of the present subjunctive tense: (no) me sorprende de que…. + present subjunctive. You may want to review irregular present subjunctive if needed. (An acronym for irregular verbs is DISHES = D- dar, I –ir, S-ser, H- haber, E-estar, S-saber.)

C Have students work with a partner while reading through the information and the graphics to complete the missing information. Have them share out the missing information with the class or you may want to collect their answers. Go to your **Explorer** course for a PDF of this activity.

> **Answers to Part C:**
> 1. Ecuador, España
> 2. Tuenti, FB, Hi5
> 3. Compartir o subir fotos, comentar las fotos de mis amigos
> 4. Muy a menudo

D **Después de leer:** Have the class create a short survey asking classmates or students in other classes the same four questions in this activity. There is Apoyo adicional available in **Explorer**. Some ideas include:

- Ask students to predict where students in the U.S. would fall in this survey.
- Survey options: 1) Survey several other Spanish classes in your school (or to another school), 2) create a survey monkey online and post the link on a public site so other Spanish students can access the link and take the survey. Post a link to the survey in a class wiki or blog.
- The U.S. student survey will ask the same questions and answers as used in the survey by Professors Burón and Martín. The answer choices will be for the United States only.
- One student will type in the questions and possible answer choices for the survey.
- After the link is posted, you may have to give the students a day or two to complete the survey before collecting the responses. When collecting the responses, use the analysis feature in survey monkey to tally the answers. This will allow them to compare the U.S. students' responses to the responses of Latin American and Spanish students

in the graphics. It is important to print a copy of the responses and the analysis of the responses.

- Students will then analyze and explain the results and compare the United States to the other Spanish-speaking countries.

Students will write a formal letter to the professors Burón and Martín in Madrid with the results of the survey of the U.S. students so they can include the U.S. in their next research study. Apoyo adicional for creating a formal letter, a printable email template and a digital forum for submitting the formal letter are available in **Explorer**.

a. After the surveys have been administered and answers collected, have students work individually, in pairs or in small groups to analyze two, three or four of the questions.

b. They will compare the results of the U.S. students with the six Latin American countries and Spain for each question summarizing the similarities and differences among the Spanish-speaking countries and the U.S.

c. Have them use an organizer (bar or pie graph) comparing similarities and differences. It does not have to be a "finished product" organizer; a sketch will serve the same purpose.

d. Write a formal letter to analyze the results for one of the questions. The analysis will compare similarities and differences of adolescents in Spain, Latin America and the U.S. A sample analysis follows. The analysis will include an original conclusion summarizing the perceived reasons for the differences. The strategy boxes on page 42 of the Student Edition provides important guidance on how to structure this letter.

e. The letter can be scored using the analytic interpersonal writing rubric.

Sample analysis of a different survey question to be included in a letter to Professors Burón and Martín

Mensaje nuevo

Destinatarios

Asunto ¿Cuántas veces al día usas redes sociales?

La opción más seleccionada en todos los países es "varias veces al día". El país con más de 50% es los Estados Unidos con más de 65% de los adolescentes usando las redes varias veces al día. El país que sigue es México con 50% usando las redes varias veces al día. Después en orden son Venezuela (45%), España (42%), Argentina (40%), Ecuador (38%) y el último país con solamente 36% de los adolescentes usando las redes varias veces al día es Colombia.

Los resultados nos informan que los adolescentes que tienen acceso a las redes están usándolas con mucha regularidad durante el día. Es probable que haya más uso en los Estados Unidos porque el estudio tuvo lugar en 2011 y ahora en ____ (año) es normal que los números de adolescentes en las redes aumentan. ¡Las redes evolucionan con los cambios en la vida social y los avances tecnológicos que entonces causan un mayor número de usuarios por ser la fuente no solamente de la vida social sino también escolar y académica!

Enviar

¿Cuáles son las ventajas y las desventajas de las redes sociales modernas?

Actividad 4 ¿Cuáles son los riesgos del Internet y las redes sociales?

Student book page 43
Time estimate: 60 min with HW (write email for ¿Qué aprendiste?)
Grammar in context: familiar commands

A Have students interview each other (interview 2 or 3 other students) and take notes that they will use later to make comparisons in part C.

B Here students categorize vocabulary according to what they already know, can understand as a cognate, or do not know (for these, encourage them to infer the meaning from context). This graphic organizer is also available in **Explorer** as Apoyo adicional for this activity.

C Answers to Part C for los argentinos:
1. Sí 2. Sí 3. a veces 4. a veces 5. Sí

D Have students compare similarities and differences of practices and perspectives of Argentine adolescents and the students in your class using notes from part A. Discuss: What could lead to some of these similarities and differences? There is a Venn Diagram graphic organizer available in **Explorer** or students can make their own.

¿Qué aprendiste?

Remind students how to use familiar commands when writing e-mails and text messages (grammar box on page 17 of the Student Edition: hilo 1 – activity 4). The email can be done for homework, submitted in **Explorer** or by using the email template and can be graded using the interpersonal writing rubric.

¿Cuáles son las ventajas y desventajas de las redes sociales modernas?

Actividad 5 ¿Cuáles son los papeles de jóvenes y padres en el uso responsable de las redes sociales?

Student book page 46
Time estimate: (Activity) 45 mins–90 mins/(Evaluation) 1 day to 1 week
Grammar in context: present subjunctive, formal Usted and Ustedes commands

B This vocabulary activity is available in **Explorer**.

Vocabulary answers for Part B: (continued on next page)
Consejos para el uso responsable de Internet
1. D 2. A 3. B 4. E 5. C

El papel de la familia ante las redes sociales en Internet

6. C	**9.** C
7. A	**10.** B
8. E	

 C There is a handout in **Explorer** to guide students with the reading. Depending on the time you have available for this activity, there are several options. You can choose the option that works best with your curriculum and pacing.

- You can have students read one article for homework and do the associated activities. The following day in class they can complete the second reading and activities.

- Another option would be to have half of the class read one article while the other half reads the second article. If you have a 90-minute block to complete this lesson students can read both articles.

- **Jigsaw option:** Another way to divide up the two articles would be to jigsaw parts of the articles. Part B is set up as a jigsaw so that students will be working on one section of the article, defining the vocabulary and extracting the suggested information for the table. Divide the class into approximately 5 groups of 5 (depending on the size of your class, the articles are divided into 5 sections). Each group is responsible for identifying the vocabulary in bold, defining it in context of the article (word reference.com) and extracting the factual information requested on the chart. It is essential that every student be prepared to share the information with another group.

Based on your decision above about how to break up the reading, this part of the activity may also look different. If all students have read both articles the first step here will be more of a comprehension check. Did both students find the main points of the article? What did anyone miss? This will give them a chance to work together to fill in any gaps.

If the students are working in pairs where each has read a different article, there will be more to discuss because students will need to summarize the key points of the article to help their partner complete the table and understand the article they did not read and vice versa.

  D As the expert student shares out the vocabulary and corresponding advantages, disadvantages, and suggestions, the others will add it to their handouts (notebooks), and complete the organizer.

  ¡A tejer!

 For this formative assessment you can choose what works best for your particular students and the available technology. Depending on the time available you can either assign it for homework outside of class, you can give one class period to complete the posters or pamphlets in class, or you can allow students both time in class and at home. **Explorer** provides a space where students can submit their letters or links to their digital products. Also, be sure to direct students to the appropriate rubrics for presentational speaking and writing to help guide their work.

¿Cómo cambia la manera de interactuar entre nosotros cuando usamos las redes sociales?

Actividad 6 ¿Cómo cambia la comunicación familiar con el uso de la tecnología?

Student book page 51
Time estimate: 60 minutes for video and discussion, 30–45 for interpersonal role plays: 20 minutes planning and 15–20 minutes sharing out presentations
Grammar in context: subjunctive for opinions

A As a pre-assessment to find out what students know before watching the video, have students predict what might happen in the video by referring to the screen shots of each segment of the video (in **Explorer** for Hilo 2, Activity 6, Part D.)

B We suggest that the conversation groups for the interpersonal discussions consist of a mix of male and female students, if possible.

C Have students watch the video one time through to get the gist of what is happening, their first impressions, and if they would recommend it to their friends.

D At this time, the video can be broken down into segments (see start and stop times below). You can watch more than one segment at a time, but it is broken down here so you can pause and debrief about what happened and what was said after each capítulo (chapter) and what was said. There is a graphic organizer in **Explorer** under Apoyo adicional that can be used as a handout to guide students in discussing the video, with the same the bulleted comments as on pages 52–53.

« »

"La familia digital":
Start and stop times for different sections

Después de ver Capítulo 1 del video: (.01– .56)
Después de ver Capítulo 2 del video: (.56 –1:38)
Después de ver Capítulo 3 del video: (1:38 – 2:30)
Después de ver Capítulo 4 del video: (2:30–3:12)
Después de ver Capítulo 5 del video: (3:12–4:07)
Después de ver Capítulo 6 del video: (4:08–5:31)
Después de ver Capítulo 7 del video: (5:31–6:27)
Después de ver Capítulo 8 del video: (6:27–fin)

¿Qué aprendiste?

The video gives students an overview of family life in a modern day family in Spain. Students will identify products and practices in the video and then determine the perspective of each product and practice. Students can work in pairs, recording their ideas in their journals, and then share with the class. As an extension have them make a cultural comparison to the same products and practices in the U.S. In **Explorer** refer to the **Recursos, Sólo para los profesores** section for a link to an explanation of products, practices and perspectives.

Here are some possible answers:

Los productos: las tecnologías: el móvil, el ordenador y las redes sociales

Las prácticas: los usos de las tecnologías: el móvil (fotos), el ordenador- el Internet para hacer compras y usar las redes sociales para socializar y comunicar

Las perspectivas:
- usa el móvil: para guardar información de los amigos, comunicar con los amigos y sacar fotos
- usa el ordenador: para entrar al Internet, hacer las compras
- usa las redes sociales para crear una imagen y ser parte de algo

E This is an impromptu conversation between two students who role-play a parent and daughter or son. Give them a limited time (10–15 minutes) to prepare what they want to say, then they should film or record with a flip cam or on the space provided in **Explorer**. Upload to a computer to show in class. This can be scored with a holistic interpersonal speaking rubric.

Note to teacher: Check out the link provided in **Explorer** to the web channel for Generaciones Interactivas to see their other videos.

¡Tu opinión cuenta!

Go to your **Explorer** course to download or print the Facebook message template in organizadores gráficos.

¿Cómo cambia la manera de interactuar entre nosotros cuando usamos las redes sociales?

Actividad 7 ¿Cómo escribimos en un español abreviado en las redes sociales?

Student book page 55
Time estimate: 30 min with homework

B This chart shows abbreviations commonly used in chat and text in Spanish. The third one down has a ? so that students infer what it could be from the information already given. (The answer is por qué). On the following page #2 on the list of rules also asks students to guess; the answers are "escribo" and "salgo".

The links provided in **Explorer** for this activity bring you to many other amix examples. Students could peruse for homework and practice writing SMS-style.

¡Te toca a ti!

This is good for in-class practice before students practice on their own at home. A copy of the graphic organizer is available in **Explorer**.

> **Answers for ¡Te toca a ti!**
> **Forma completa en español:**
> Estoy en casa
> Nos vemos mañana
> ¿Tienes tiempo para salir?
>
> **Forma abreviada en amix (there is more than one possible answer here!)**
> Ven xa aca x favor
> Abla bn, no t scucho
> Amix no salg xq no tngo tiemp

¿Qué aprendiste?

For part E you can use cel.ly which is very similar to Twitter, but has been created for use in education to allow students a place to post their #GraciasRedesSociales tweets using their cellphones. You can make the settings so that students can "retweet" their classmates' tweets and comment back making the activity interpersonal. You can also use one of the polling websites we have mentioned in this chapter for students to post and read what others are writing. Depending on the technology policy and availability at your school this can be done for homework or in class.

Culture box: After watching the video from the link in **Explorer**, have students discuss the different points. You may want to open this up to a whole-class discussion afterward.

Essential questions:
- ¿Por qué usamos redes sociales y por qué nos importan?
- ¿Cuáles son las ventajas y desventajas de las redes sociales?
- ¿Cómo cambia la manera de interactuar entre nosotros cuando usamos las redes sociales?

Hilo 2 Evaluación Final - *Redes sociales*

Student book pages 58 - 59
Time estimate: 1 day to present, plan Part I and pre-write Part II; workshop days to compile, draft and edit final blog entries
Grammar in context: present, imperfect, present subjunctive and past subjunctive

This is a combination of descriptive, informative, and persuasive writing. Some students will need additional support with one or more parts of the task. To structure all parts of the task with sufficient scaffolding and examples for students, go to your **Explorer** course for more support.

Options for who students can interview in Part I:

1. Someone older in their family (the interview would be in whatever language is spoken at home);

2. Solicit opinions and experiences from various people through social media (for example, publish the question ¿Cómo era la vida antes de las redes sociales? and wait for answers)

3. Interview faculty and staff at the school!

In any of those cases, the student would present a written report in Spanish to you with a summary of the content of that interview and his/her conclusions.

Options for publishing student blog entries:

1. The forum provided in **Explorer** is a ready-to-use option!

2. Create a class blog or individual blogs using one of these sites:
- Blogspot.com
- Wiki sites
- Wordpress.com
- Edublogs.com

3. Write their blog entry on paper/on the computer and hand it in; you could potentially "publish" them on a wall or in another public place.

4. Look for a public site that could welcome these kinds of blog entries – perhaps your school site, or a local newspaper.

An additional – and recommended – piece of the project not mentioned in the book is to ask students to comment on each others' blog entries. As time allows this is preferable, since this is how blogs work in real life, and it adds an interpersonal writing activity. Be clear about your expectations for what and how much they would write, and consider the best way to administer this part of the project for appropriate participation and your record-keeping.

MANTA 1 Familias y comunidades

Hilo 3 Ciudadanía global

Essential questions:
- ¿Por qué necesitamos los ciudadanos globales?
- ¿Qué características debe tener un/a ciudadano/a global?
- ¿Cómo contribuyen los jóvenes al bienestar de las comunidades?

Student Learning Objectives

Interpersonal Communication: Speaking and Writing
- Exchange information about the role and contributions of young global citizens in local and global communities.
- Express opinions about challenges and needs of local and global communities.
- Exchange messages such as e-mails, blogs, or social media posts about local and global community challenges and needs.
- Describe the characteristics and actions of a global citizen.
- Describe and provide examples of volunteerism.
- Explain the influence of technology and social media on responding to global community needs.
- Collaborate with peers on local or regional community challenges and needs.

Interpretive Communication: Print, Audio, Audiovisual, and/or Visual Sources
- Demonstrate comprehension about contributions of global citizens from authentic texts, websites, brochures, blogs, audio, and audiovisual resources.
- Describe and analyze significant details from audio and audiovisual sources about the importance and benefits of volunteerism.
- Evaluate the author's purpose from authentic texts, promotional materials, websites, and blogs regarding volunteerism among teens.
- Interpret and evaluate volunteer organizations and groups in Spanish-speaking countries.

Presentational Communication: Spoken and/or Written Presentations to a Variety of Audiences
- Convince others to volunteer as global citizens.
- Describe the benefits of volunteerism to a community in need.
- Present a persuasive proposal on the challenges and needs of a local or regional Hispanic community.
- Reflect on the role an individual plays in collaborating to improve the world.
- Produce reflections and journal entries to demonstrate understanding that contributions of global citizens can improve the world.

Relating Cultural Practices to Perspectives:
- Investigate, explain, and reflect on the relationship between the practice of volunteerism and the perspectives (beliefs/values/attitudes) of Hispanic cultures.

Relating Cultural Products to Perspectives:
- Investigate, explain, and reflect on the relationship between the products produced by global citizens (food and educational programs) and the perspectives (beliefs/values/attitudes) of Hispanic cultures.

Connections: Connect with Other Disciplines
- Make connections to content knowledge about local and global community needs and challenges.

Connections: Acquire New Information
- Use new information about global citizens to expand content knowledge.

Comparisons: Language
- Make linguistic comparisons of cognates, *si* clauses with imperfect subjunctive and conditional and subjunctive with *para que*.

Comparisons: Culture
- Compare similarities and differences on volunteerism among teens in the U.S. and Spanish-speaking countries.

School and Global Communities:
- Interact with Spanish speakers about the needs of local and global communities and the contributions of global citizens.

Lifelong Learning:
- Set goals and reflect on progress in using Spanish for enjoyment, enrichment, and advancement.

Suggested Lesson Plan Sequence/Pacing Guide

Manta 1: Familias y comunidades
Hilo 3: Ciudadanía global

Note: Workshop days are flexible and should be inserted in the sequence per your class' specific needs and abilities. Students may be able to complete work more or less quickly outside of class.

Focus according to Essential Question Pages in SE	Day (based on 60 min class)	Classroom Activities	Homework/ Formative assessment/ Exit pass
La importancia de ciudadanos globales pp. 64–70	1	* Introduce unit with video hook and vocabulary practice * Activate previous knowledge, brainstorm global issues * Watch and respond to video; prioritize issues, presentations	* Oral presentation after group work
	2	* Pre-reading vocabulary exercise * Active reading and categorizing vocabulary from text * Deductive process to create definition of global citizen	* Vocabulary categorization
	3	* Finish review of yesterday's text; Think-Pair-Share reflection * Pre-reading vocabulary and prediction activities * Jigsaw group work activity	* Reflexión
	4 + workshop(s)	* Group presentations with audience participation sheet + Workshop day (insert in sequence as you deem best) for work on ¡Te toca a ti! task and possible presentation to class or to a small group	* Group presentation * ¡Te toca a ti! individual research
Carácterísticas de un/a ciudadano/a global pp. 71–75	5	* Class brainstorm about global citizens * Two close readings of the text * Two viewings of the video * Synthesis activities represent a global citizen	* Graphic organizers for text and video * Poem can be assigned as homework
	6	* Finish synthesis work from yesterday; present to class * Vocabulary preview for next text * Active reading and follow-up conversation * Summarizing ¿Qué aprendiste? task	* Post-reading interpersonal task as exit slip * ¿Qué aprendiste? task for homework
Las contribuciones de los jóvenes pp. 75–81	7	* Think-Pair-Share about Amando Paz foundation * Y-chart activity with video * Make connections and expand notes with song and text * Response through interpersonal writing and reflection	* ¡Tu opinión cuenta! Interpersonal writing task * Reflexión journal prompt
	8	* Pre-viewing graphic organizer * Two directed video viewings: vocabulary, grammar * Respond with spoken opinion and journaling	* ¡Tu opinión cuenta! presentational speaking task * Reflexión journal prompt
	9	* Review expectations for summative assessment: collaborative action plan and individual assessment * Workshop time for planning and writing summative assessment	* Group work and presentations * Draft, edit and submit individual reflection for summative assessment
	10	* Present group plans to class	

Hilo 3 Ciudadanía global

Introducción ¿Qué pueden hacer los jóvenes para mejorar al mundo?

Student book page 64
Time estimate: 20 minutes
Grammar in context: Reflexive verbs

    A   You will watch the video two times for this "hook" and it is important that the first time, it is without sound. It helps students to form their impressions and start thinking of the necessary vocabulary before adding the language. After watching the trailer without sound, have students predict what they think the documentary will be about, recording the vocabulary, that they needed, on a chart.

    B   The shaded vocabulary box contains key terms that students may find useful in discussing this topic; introduce the language into the discussion at some point if students are searching for these words or if they have not yet used them.

Antes de empezar ¿Qué necesita el mundo actual?

Student book page 65
Time estimate: 40 min

    A   **1.** This brainstorming session will indicate what students are interested in, what they already know, and what language they have to talk about global and local issues in Spanish. During or after the whole-class brainstorm, you might make a poster with the final list of ideas (or ask a student to do so) that can remain visible in the classroom for the rest of the hilo. Students will have to continue building awareness and vocabulary of the issues throughout the hilo, and choose one issue to focus on for their final project.

   3. Be sure to ADD or SUGGEST the following items to the list, if not offered by students, to build vocabulary that will appear later in the hilo:
- Los desafíos/Los retos/Las injusticias
- La pobreza
- El género
- El medio ambiente
- La educación
- La discriminación

B Students will watch the video clip of the "objetivos del milenio" as identified by La Liga española de la educación. Pause the video after each objective so they have time to write each objective on the same list as they brainstormed in part A; have them create a separate column or section of their journal. After they finish the list, they will compare the objetivos del milenio to the class list in a Venn diagram (found in **Explorer**, Recursos, Organizadores gráficos). At this time, have each group present their top three concerns, justifying their choices, for global citizens in the 21st century.

1. Erradicar la pobreza extrema y el hambre
2. Educación básica para todos
3. Igualdad de oportunidad para el hombre y la mujer
4. Reducir la mortalidad infantil
5. Mejorar la salud en la maternidad
6. Avanzar la lucha contra el VIH y otras enfermedades
7. Asegurar un medio ambiente sano y seguro
8. Lograr una sociedad global para el desarrollo.

¿Por qué necesitamos los ciudadanos globales?

Actividad 1 ¿Qué es un ciudadano global?

Student book page 65
Time estimate: 1 60-minute class plus 30 minutes; for homework assign the reading on page 67 (also in **Explorer** so students can mark it up with highlighting colors)
Possible resource: Universal declaration of human rights

A 3. This is important practice for students to work with vocabulary in context, and such hard-to-define terms as "citizenship"!

> **Answers for Part A 3 (in order):**
> pertenecemos; comprometernos; reclamar; plantear; logramos; cumplido; indignado/a; erradicar; difundir

B This is a great activity to help students identify what they do know, and find cognates, instead of only seeing (and getting stressed about) the words that they do not know. This text, available in **Explorer** for students to annotate, contains a lot of key vocabulary for the hilo, so take your time with the activities in "A" and encourage students to look for what they do know, first, and then work together on what they don't. The initial reading with highlighting colors can be a homework assignment, but definitely give students time to work together and with dictionaries to find what they don't know, and discuss together as a class to check for comprehension.

C Ideally students are finding specific words and examples here from the text. The text offers a lot of information so this breaks it up into descriptors – values – actions. You might suggest that students look for the adjectives and verbs first. When going over this graphic organizer as a class, require that students justify their answers by referring back to the text.

 D Again, this is an opportunity for students to ground their answers in the text, not just speculate. Circulate and check that groups are speaking in Spanish and referring back to the text. You might ask each group to comment on one of the examples to the rest of the class.

  Reflexión

 This could be a good opportunity to do a whole-class brainstorm after students reflect individually and discuss in pairs. You might put the categories on the board and list examples under each. Wait for students to be able to justify their examples.

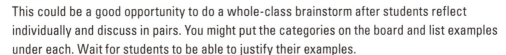
¿Por qué necesitamos los ciudadanos globales?

Actividad 2 ¿Por qué necesitamos los ciudadanos globales?

Student book page 68
Time estimate: 2 60-minute classes with homework (individual reflection and research)
Grammar in context: Si clauses in past subjunctive/conditional tenses

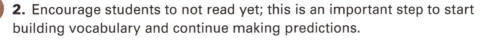 **A** **2.** Encourage students to not read yet; this is an important step to start building vocabulary and continue making predictions.

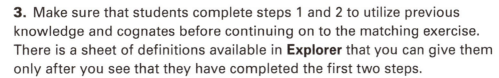 **3.** Make sure that students complete steps 1 and 2 to utilize previous knowledge and cognates before continuing on to the matching exercise. There is a sheet of definitions available in **Explorer** that you can give them only after you see that they have completed the first two steps.

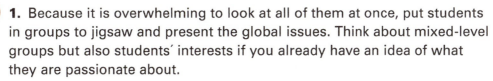 **B** **1.** Because it is overwhelming to look at all of them at once, put students in groups to jigsaw and present the global issues. Think about mixed-level groups but also students´ interests if you already have an idea of what they are passionate about.

 2. As noted in the document in **Explorer** with instructions for students, feel free to expand/adjust the expectations for the group poster and presentation. Depending on the size of your class and time available, you could expand this activity. Also, you can ask students to present the key vocabulary to the class in a variety of ways. You may want to give them options, or ask them to follow a model that you often use for presenting new vocabulary. It is important that the student presenters use the vocabulary in context, in discussing the global problem in their presentation.

3. This is a simple graphic organizer (available in **Explorer**) to help students be attentive audience members. It is a good chance to remind them that another group's issue might be the one that they want to explore in more detail in this hilo's final project, so listen up!

C For this grammar practice, students may need further scaffolding for the construction of verbs in the past subjunctive and conditional. Expand the grammar review and practice as necessary.

 ¡Te toca a ti!

This formative assessment is important in helping students reflect on the information given in group presentations, and discern an issue they'd like to explore further here and in their final project. Encourage students to think of other issues that are important to them – it is not limited to the global challenges presented in this text. For the research part of this assignment, you may want to model appropriate use of Internet-based resources. For example you could do a search in front of the class for articles on AIDS (SIDA) in Spanish-speaking countries. Show students how to identify authentic sources and summarize information without plagiarism.

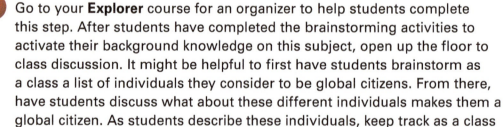

¿Qué características debe tener un/a ciudadano/a global?

Actividad 3 ¿Cómo se define un/a ciudadano/a global?

Student book page 71
Time estimate: 1 60-minute class with homework, plus 15 minutes
(to finish final synthesis activities)
Grammar in context: "Si" clauses in present/future tenses

A Go to your **Explorer** course for an organizer to help students complete this step. After students have completed the brainstorming activities to activate their background knowledge on this subject, open up the floor to class discussion. It might be helpful to first have students brainstorm as a class a list of individuals they consider to be global citizens. From there, have students discuss what about these different individuals makes them a global citizen. As students describe these individuals, keep track as a class of the characteristics or traits they share. As a class choose the 10 most important characteristics of a global citizen.

B As students read the first time (this text also available in **Explorer** for students to annotate) have them look for those action words in the definitions of the characteristics. Later students will use these to write *si* clauses. The second portion can be assigned for homework individually or completed by pairs as the activity suggests. You can also divide students into groups of 3 and give each group a characteristic. As a group they can come up with a definition and post them around the room for the duration of the unit.

  Show the video twice to your class. The first time, allow students to simply listen for vocabulary they are familiar with and give them time to process what they are seeing and hearing. The second time, have students fill out a chart with a list of characteristics and actions they hear the young people say describe a global citizen.

> **Sample answers:**
> En el video los jóvenes describen a un ciudadano global en estas palabras:
> Tolerancia, igualdad, cariño, libertad de expresión, comprensión, confianza, respeto, compañerismo,
> Empatía, responsabilidad, universalidad, sin discriminación, libertad, solidarios, Sensibilidad,
> Cooperación, generosidad, perteneciendo a una sola tierra

   1. As a synthesis activity, have students put it all together from what they already knew (from reading and observing) about global citizens. Below are a list of options for how you can do this activity in class:

a) If your students have easy access to technology have them create a Wordle (www.wordle.net) using the characteristics and actions they believe define a global citizen. Remind them that the more often they type in a word or phrase the larger it appears in the wordle.

b) In groups of 3 or 4, have students draw a silhouette of a human (they can do this by having one student lie down on a big sheet of white paper and together they can trace the outline). Then they can fill it in with words and images that depict the characteristics and actions of a global citizen.

c) Purchase a set of human cut outs (these are often made of blank white cardboard paper) and have students fill it with words, phrases and images that describe a global citizen.

 2. The poem can either be done in addition to the human silhouettes/word clouds or can be used instead of the option described above.

¿Qué características debe tener un/a ciudadano/a global?

Actividad 4 ¿Qué es el voluntariado?

Student book page 73
Time estimate: 45 minutes
Grammar in context: Si clauses with present and future tenses

Culture box: Before your students do the short reading about "voluntariado," have them listen to the brief Spanish news audio clip about Shakira's NGO (Non-governmental organization), La Fundación Pies Descalzos. This audio was recorded shortly after the earthquake in Haiti (2010), when Shakira, along with many other celebrities, was working to provide aid. We have included a link to Shakira's Foundation in **Explorer** if you would like students to dig into the vocabulary or extend this into something more meaningful in class. Depending on the time you have, you can also have them listen to the audio then have them respond to a few questions before moving on to the activity.

« | » Audio transcript

Todos con Haiti

No hay tiempo que perder. Shakira lo sabe. Pocos días después del terrible **terremoto** de Haití, la reconstrucción del país es urgente. Los **miles** de niños víctimas de la tragedia **necesitan comida**, agua, casas, pero también necesitan **escuelas**. La *Fundación Pies Descalzos* que la cantante **creó** en Colombia en el año 2003 sabe de eso. Más de 6.000 niños que estaban en una situación **desfavorecida asisten** hoy a los colegios de la *Fundación* **en todo el país**. Allí reciben educación, comida, **atención sanitaria** y, **según la propia cantante,** mucho afecto **para construir** un futuro mejor.

Toda esta experiencia, **fondos** e infraestructuras **ha querido aprovechar la estrella colombiana** para construir una escuela en Haití. El proyecto **es conjunto con** otras organizaciones humanitarias. **Arquitectura para la Humanidad** construirá el edificio. **Otras ONG darán** otros servicios: agua, asistencia sanitaria o alimentación. Shakira ha sido una de las artistas que ha participado en el **teletón mundial "Esperanza por Haití", celebrado** en Los Ángeles **el pasado viernes 22, junto con** estrellas como Madonna, Bono, de U2, Christina Aguilera, Alicia Keys y Sting. En **otro medio con menos difusión,** en la británica Universidad de Oxford, *Shakira explicaba* **hace pocos días** a los europeos el trabajo de Pies Descalzos en Colombia y sus **proyectos** para el futuro.

B This activity is available in the Vocabulario section of your **Explorer** course.

Vocabulary answers for Part B:
1. gratuito = regalado
2. beneficiar = mejorar
3. desinteresada = altruista
4. ejercer = practicar
5. calidad de vida = bienestar
6. un aporte = contribución
7. brindar = ofrecer voluntariamente
8. vincularse = unirse
9. sin fines de lucro = sin ganancias
10. hacer frente = enfrentarse
11. reciprocidad = intercambio
12. gratificante = satisfactorio
13. enfrentarse = confrontar
14. remuneración = salario
15. esfuerzo = aporte

 C Here you can have students type the central ideas of the text and post them to a class blog or they can create marketing flyers with images that can be put up around the room.

 ¿Qué aprendiste?

Assign students to task options where they will be successful, for differentiation, and judge their performance on whatever option they complete. Consider posting student work in the hallway or in another way that is visible to the school community, since Shakira is a recognizable celebrity!

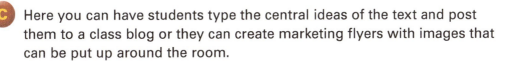

¿Cómo contribuyen los jóvenes al bienestar de las comunidades?

Actividad 5 ¿Cómo pueden cambiar el mundo los jóvenes voluntarios?

Student book page 75
Time estimate: 60 min
Grammar in context: Have students use the present subjunctive for recommendations in "Tu opinión cuenta"

 B Have students watch the video the first time without sound so students concentrate on the visuals in order to record their impressions on the Y organizer (available in **Explorer**, Recursos, Organizadores gráficos). Have them work in pairs and then share out 1) ONLY what they saw, 2) what they think is happening, 3) what they would like to know.

 C Continue adding information to the organizer and as an option, discuss the words to the song and the music video that are in the enlaces in **Explorer**. The song is easy to understand especially if you have the words for reference. The hondureños are very patriotic and are proud of their country.

¡Tu opinión cuenta!

This Facebook comment is an individual interpersonal writing and is written as a recommendation: Recomiendo que ... (present subjunctive). Students need to include rationale for their recommendation based on the criteria outlined in the bullet points. This can be collected for a quick comprehension check (formative assessment).

Sample answer:

¡Amanda! Me encantan las aportaciones que ustedes hacen a su comunidad. Te recomiendo que invites a los niños de la escuela primaria a participar ¡Ellos son el futuro! Es gratificante ayudar al entorno.

Optional: Have students research information about the OEA (Organización de Estados Americanos) y el USAID (United States Agency for International Development) who sponsored the "Héroes Cotidianos" for the Amando Paz contest. There is a link in **Explorer** for this website that includes links to the facts and ideas "que te servirán para construir un cambio en tu comunidad país o región".

¿Cómo contribuyen los jóvenes al bienestar de las comunidades?

Actividad 6 ¿Qué puedes hacer tú para hacer una diferencia en tu comunidad?

Student book page 78
Time estimate: 50 minutes
Grammar in context: si clauses with imperfect subjunctive and conditional; present subjunctive with para que...

A As an option, this can be assigned as homework and presented orally to the class the following day.

B As students watch the brief video have them jot down a few words that capture some of the problems that global citizens attempt to solve.

Video script

No es lo que hago, es por qué lo hago.

(Note: After they finish part D, you can turn on the Spanish subtitles that are accurate in this video)

1. **Sonia:** Si vieras como las personas refugiadas reconstruyen su vida en nuestro país, entenderías porque dedico horas de mi vida a asesorarles jurídicamente. No es lo que hago, es por qué lo hago.
2. **David:** Para que todos tomemos conciencia de las dificultades cotidianas que tienen las personas con discapacidad.
3. **Angelina:** Para que todas las personas mayores se sientan acompañadas.
4. **Rubén:** Para que todas las personas nos sintamos libres de definir nuestra orientación sexual o identidad de género.
5. **Bea:** Para que los bosques vuelvan a crecer en zonas desertificadas.

Hacer voluntariado es querer cambiar el mundo, y hacerlo.

C **Answers:**
1. D   2. C   3. A   4. B

D **Answers:**
Sonia: vieras, entenderías
David: tomemos
Angelina: se sientan
Ruben: nos sintamos
Bea: vuelvan
Grammar in common: Si clause with imperfect subjunctive and conditional and subjunctive after para que...

¡Tu opinión cuenta!

This is a formative assessment that can be scored with a presentational speaking rubric. Students need to use subjunctive tenses and *si* clauses to convince classmates to participate in a community project. Students can record themselves in **Explorer**.

Reflexión

This can be a formative assessment for presentational writing or a homework journal grade.

There is an additional video embedded in **Explorer** that may be accessed by students for more information on motivating teens to volunteer and what kind of traits you need to have: **Es tu momento. Hazte voluntario con Javier:**

HILO 3 Ciudadanía global

Essential questions:
- ¿Por qué necesitamos los ciudadanos globales?
- ¿Qué características debe tener un/a ciudadano/a global?
- ¿Cómo contribuyen los jóvenes al bienestar de las comunidades?

Hilo 3 Evaluación Final — *Suéñalo, Hazlo*

Student book page 80
Time estimate: Two 60 minute class periods
Grammar in context: Si clauses with present and future tenses; imperfect subjunctive & conditional in persuasive writing in the context of a proposal, action plan and reflection.

Note to teachers: Introduce students to the final project early in this *hilo* so they can be thinking about an idea for their global citizen project for the summative assessment.

There will be two parts to the summative assessment:

1. Collaborative proposal and action plan: two 60 minute class periods once they have their idea- we suggest two to three members depending on your class size and how seriously the students work together

2. Individual reflection (150-200 words):
- summarize the idea of the project
- reflect on how the student's traits, passions and interests of a global citizen will contribute to the project's success
- reflect on how he/she will take action if they can carry out this project. (may be assigned outside of class to submit for an individual grade)

The detailed instructions are in **Explorer** for the students to follow. Have students refer back to the first and second hilos for expressions to include in their writing.

Suggestions:
- If there is a local or regional Hispanic community agency, have a student call and request information about the needs of the local Hispanic community. This is an opportunity for students to put their Spanish language skills into action to improve the well-being of their local or regional Hispanic community such as raising awareness of needs within the Hispanic community, providing English classes for parents (and childcare for children) , tutoring students after school, helping w/HW, practicing reading, mentoring a little brother or little sister, coaching a soccer team, getting the elderly (tercera edad) motivated to help younger children, working together on a project, etc.

- The sponsoring organization is Ashoka Changemakers. You may want the students to watch a 5-minute video about the organization on their web site. www.joveneschangemakers.org

- You may want the students to present their proposal and action plan to the rest of the class who will serve as the selection panel. We suggest that you invite other Spanish teachers and their classes to "judge" the presentations. You may want to use a "ballot" using the criteria from the rubrics for them to complete. Choose the best three, four or five to send to the organization.

MANTA 2 Vida contemporánea

Hilo 4 Viajes y ocio

Essential questions:
- ¿Cómo se planifica un viaje a un país donde se habla español?
- Como viajero, ¿cómo se puede experimentar la vida cotidiana de otro país?
- ¿Cómo se entiende el ocio desde la perspectiva local?

Student Learning Objectives

Interpersonal Communication: Speaking and Writing
- Exchange information about traveling to and within a Spanish-speaking country.
- Express opinions about travel and leisure preferences and experiences.
- Exchange messages such as emails, blogs, or social media posts about travel plans to and within a Spanish-speaking country.
- Engage in discussions about travel plans to a Spanish-speaking country including where, when, how, and what to do and bring.
- Explain the influence of technology and social media on travel planning and accessing cultural information.
- Collaborate to create a detailed travel itinerary to a Spanish-speaking country.

Interpretive Communication: Print, Audio, Audiovisual, and/or Visual Sources
- Interpret, apply, and evaluate information from authentic texts, websites, brochures, blogs, audio, and audiovisual resources on travel and leisure in Spanish-speaking countries.
- Describe and analyze significant details from audio and audiovisual sources about travel and leisure in Spanish-speaking countries.
- Interpret, analyze, and compare family life, social life and leisure time activities among young people from Hispanic cultures from audio sources.
- Interpret vocabulary in a literary context by making inferences.

Presentational Communication: Spoken and/or Written Presentations to a Variety of Audiences
- Organize and present a detailed travel itinerary to a Spanish-speaking country.
- Analyze and evaluate travel itineraries.
- Plan and create a persuasive publication to convince others to travel to a Spanish-speaking country.
- Produce reflections and journal entries to demonstrate understanding of travel and leisure practices and perspectives in Hispanic cultures.
- Record messages about cultural similarities and differences regarding travel and leisure.

Relating Cultural Practices to Perspectives:
- Investigate, explain, and reflect on the the relationship between the practices of travel and leisure and the perspectives (beliefs/values/attitudes) of Hispanic cultures.

Relating Cultural Products to Perspectives:
- Investigate, explain, and reflect on the relationship between cuisine and the perspectives (traditions/values/attitudes) of the Hispanic cultures studied.

Connections: Connect with Other Disciplines
- Make connections to content knowledge about geography, forms of travel, places to visit, and leisure time activities.

Connections: Acquire New Information
- Apply new information from authentic sources about travel and leisure in Hispanic cultures to prepare a trip to a Spanish-speaking country.

Comparisons: Language
- Make linguistic comparisons of cognates, preterit, conditional, future, and subjunctive verb forms and uses.

Comparisons: Culture
- Compare similarities and differences about social lives among young people and/or families in the U.S. and in Spanish-speaking countries.

School and Global Communities:
- Interact with Spanish speakers about travel and leisure in Hispanic cultures.

Lifelong Learning:
- Set goals and reflect on progress in using Spanish for enjoyment, enrichment, and advancement.

Suggested Lesson Plan Sequence/Pacing Guide

Manta 2: Vida contemporánea
Hilo 4: Viajes y ocio

Note: Workshop days are flexible and should be inserted in the sequence per your class' specific needs and abilities. Students may be able to complete work more or less quickly outside of class.

Focus according to Essential Question Pages in SE	Day (based on 60 min class)	Classroom Activities	Homework/ Formative assessment/ Exit pass
Planificar un viaje pp. 88–95	1	* Introduce unit with video hook and reflection * *Antes de empezar* activities: Video, cultural analysis, reactions	* Journal reflections
	2–3	* Planning a trip: Group jigsaw activity and Internet research * Sharing out findings and opinions * Tell others about your trip	* Students will likely have to work on Internet research outside of class * Activity 2 Parte C can be assigned as HW (formative assessment)
Experimentar la vida cotidiana de un país extranjero pp. 95–104	4	* Infer vocabulary while reading "Viajes" for comprehension * Role-play and sharing out in class	* Pre-reading of "Viajes" can be assigned as HW with vocabulary activity * ¿Qué aprendiste? Role plays
	5–6	* Reading, listening and viewing activities from "Tahina-Can" * Respond to documentary clip * Discussion to connect back to hilo 3	* ¿Qué aprendiste? Formative assessment – to complete outside of class
El ocio desde la perspectiva local pp. 105–115	7	* Viewing, reading and responding to brochure from el Parque Metropolitano de Santiago	* Any or all of Parte C "Reflexiones sobre el ocio"
	8	* Vocabulary practice * Listening to audio in sections with comprehension checks * Responding to content in speaking and writing	* ¡A tejer!, ¡Tu opinión cuenta! presentational speaking and interpersonal writing tasks
	9 + Workshop day(s)	* Present summative assessment – **you may want to do this earlier in the unit so that students begin to work ahead of time** * Students begin working in pairs and organizing their ideas and research * Extra days to work in class as possible	* Students develop and polish their projects outside of class
	10–11	* Students present projects to class (this may take one or two days)	

Hilo 4 Los viajes y el ocio

Introducción ¿Por qué te gustaría conocer un nuevo país?

Student book page 88
Time estimate: 20 minutes (Part C 2 journal activity can be assigned as HW)

This is a short viewing activity to "hook" students for the unit ahead. The *Antes de empezar* activity that follows also includes a short video and the opportunity for students to discuss Chilean culture.

Reflexión

Have students respond to the prompt in their journals.

A 1. Knowledge of geography is lacking for far too many of our students! *Tejidos* **Explorer** includes many maps, in black and white and in color, under the *Resources* section that can help give students more practice.

2. Group students into pairs and have them discuss the questions in the text to find out their background knowledge of Chile.

B Feel free to watch the video 2 to 3 times and allow students to start their vocabulary brainstorm on the 2nd or 3rd time.

C After students view the video, have them converse with a partner to discuss what they learned about Chile using the notes they took during the video. Either as homework or a quick post viewing assignment have them write in their journals about 4 things they would like to experience in a trip to Chile.

Antes de empezar: ¿Qué sabes de Chile y su cultura?

Student book page 89
Time estimate: 30–40 min (final journal activity can be assigned as HW)

A In order to activate students' background knowledge of Chile, have them brainstorm in small groups using a T-chart. After 3–4 minutes, have them stop and write the items they brainstormed on the board, one representative from each group can write in graffiti format (writing words/ phrases randomly, i.e. diagonally, etc. on the board or chart paper). Review what everyone wrote and they should be able to explain what they wrote if it is not obvious. They can also dispute the products or practices if they think they are not correct.

- The first brainstorm will be products of Chile: (what people use and produce) many examples are on the video: wine, olive oil, fruits, copper, education, poets (Neruda, Mistral), weavings

- The second brainstorm will be practices of the Chilean people (what people do) Ex: soccer, trekking, fishing, asados/parrilladas (barbecue), parapentes (para-gliding)

  B Watch this video in **Explorer** "Secuencias de Chile." This promotional video gives an overview of Chile's products and some practices; it may be viewed twice to get all the information to add to their brainstorm sessions.

¿Cómo se planifica un viaje a un país donde se habla español?

Actividad 1 ¡Volemos a Chile!

Student book page 90
Time estimate: 90 minutes

This activity is a great way to get students interested in the topic of travel by getting them into the mindset of a traveler. Students will use the links we provide in **Explorer** to find out how to travel to Chile and where to stay once they get there.

There are many *Enlaces* for this activity in **Explorer**, the name of each link corresponds to a specific part of the activity. Be sure to check these one more time before students begin the assignment in case any of them are no longer functioning. You can also research any other websites you would like for them to use.

We recommend that you jigsaw this activity in the interest of time; split students into groups of 4 and then each of them will be responsible for one of the steps: pp 90-91 of the Student Edition includes 4 steps, each with a research component. Those responsible for the same step in the other groups can collaborate to find the information. After time to research in their "expert" groups, have them get back together in their original groups to share the information and take notes on what their group members found.

Another option is to classify the groups of students into different types of travelers: business, luxury travel, economy and eco-tourism. Each group would have different interests in mind as it relates to price, amenities and quality. This is a great way to have students understand how individuals or groups plan travel from different perspectives.

The culture box on page 92 has students convert money to see how far their USD (or whichever currency there is where students live) will take them in their journeys.

Answers for page 92

1. 32.59 USD
2. 3,116.88 CLP
3. 12,501.19 CLP
4. 350.22 USD

1. 35.80 EUR= 21,733.68 CLP = 45.18 USD
2. 263,000 CLP = 546.78 USD = 433.22 EUR
3. 80.00 USD = 63.38 EUR = 38,479.98 CLP

¿Cómo se planifica un viaje a un país donde se habla español?

Actividad 2 ¿Quieres explorar Chile?

Student book page 93
Time estimate: 90 min, Part C formative assessment can be assigned for HW
Grammar in context: Conditional to discuss potential plans (Part A 2), Future to discuss plans in Part C email or voice message

A 1. In the last activity your students read a brief overview of the different regions of Chile to decide when would be the best time of year to travel there. Now, provide them with the links (all in **Explorer**, but explained here) to dig a little deeper to decide where they want to go, what they will do there and what they will need to bring.

a. http://www.chileestuyo.cl/regiones.html *This website hosts a plethora of information about travel within Chile. Students can read information about each region and watch a video giving more information about what to do and see there. They can find out more about how to get there, where to stay when you do, specific cities, places to visit, activities to keep you busy, and tips to keep you safe.*

b. http://www.chileestuyo.cl/folleteria/folletos.html *We have included several of these in* **Explorer** *as PDFs, but have your students go to this site to view all of the brochures provided by Chile es TUYO.*

c. http://www.descubrechile.cl/region/index.html *A site with destinations categorized by region. Includes images and information about specific sites of interest to travelers.*

d. http://www.youtube.com/user/CHILE365/videos?sort=dd&flow=grid&view=0&page=1 *This YouTube channel hosts a variety of short videos (about 1 to 5 minutes in length) about a variety of tourist destinations that will help your students visualize the sites they plan to see on their visit.*

2. At this point students should have done enough research to be able to share their hopes for a trip with a classmate. This exercise makes them accountable of their research thus far. It will be helpful to tell them that they will need all of their information ready for the conversation. You can use the Venn Diagram as evidence of their conversation and a way to check their work thus far. This is a possible formative assessment.

B After students have discovered more about their destination, they will use the Turbus link (Enlaces for Activity 2 in **Explorer**) to book a bus ticket to travel from Santiago to their destination. If they are going to visit one of the islands, they will also need to explain how they will arrive at their final destination.

C You can assign either one or both of these formative assessments as time and your students' needs allow; also feel free to assign some students number 1 and others number 2 if you would like to assess either their writing or speaking skills.

1. There is a space to record this presentational oral assessment in **Explorer**.

2. Students can use the email template provided in **Explorer** or write an email from their own accounts and copy you!

Como viajero, ¿cómo se puede experimentar la vida cotidiana de otro país?

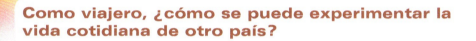

Actividad 3 ¿Cuáles son tus costumbres cuando viajas?

Student book page 95
Time estimate: 60 minutes (assign "Viajes" for HW the night before with the vocabulary exercise in the student text, part C)

A **Activator:** Students will converse about how their family makes travel plans: *planes en detalle con anticipación, planes con unas semanas de anticipación o espontáneamente.*

Culture box: Have students watch the short interview with Julio Cortázar on "Historia de cronopios y famas." The link is in the hilo 4 **Explorer** for activity 3. It is worth watching so students get a deeper understanding of Cortázar and his literary works.

B The three bulleted points provide background information on political symbolism of the cronopios, famas y esperanzas that students will need to know for the Reflexión at the end of the activity. Go through it carefully with students to make sure they understand.

C Students read for comprehension of content and interpret the meaning of the vocabulary from the context.

Vocabulary answers for Part C:
1. Labrar (un acta)
2. Inmuebles
3. Valijas
4. Llover a gritos
5. De guardia
6. Pernoctar
7. Cuatelosamente
8. Un acta
9. En ronda
10. Averigua
11. Diligencias

D Students categorize each of the "personajes" by their actions and then determine their characteristics. Have students personalize the characteristics to people they know. The organizer is available in **Explorer**.

> **Part D Answers:**
> If students can effectively justify their answer choices, there may be more than one answer for each characteristic.
>
> Buscan la sencillez (E)
> Defienden el orden establecido (F)
> Son generosos (E)
> Sienten las emociones profundamente (F)
> Son formales (F)
> Viven en el presente (C)
> No tienen ambición (E)
>
> No son perfectos (C)
> Tienen inclinaciones artísticas (C)
> Son soñadores (C)
> Son organizados (F)
> Son ignorantes y aburridos (E)
> Son rígidos (F)
> Son desordenados (C)
> Son idealistas (C)

¿Qué aprendiste?

1. Students will describe the characteristics of three travelers on the virtual trip to Chile in this chapter, describing the behaviors of a cronopio, fama and esperanza.

2. Role play: divide students into groups of three and each one will take on the characteristics of a fama, cronopio or esperanza on their trip to Chile (from Actividades 1 and 2). You may want them to plan it one day and share out the next day, this is meant to be spontaneous one short scene about getting ready in the hotel room, eating at a restaurant, waiting in lines at an amusement park, etc. Other students will interpret and decide which traveler is the cronopio, fama or esperanza.

Culture box: This references sites linked in **Explorer** relating to Neruda's life as a *viajero:* watch a brief video and read more about his life as a world traveler.

Como viajero, ¿cómo se puede experimentar la vida cotidiana de otro país?

Actividad 4 ¿Qué puedes aprender y conocer al viajar?

Student book page 99
Time estimate: 2 60-minute classes with a formative assessment to complete outside of class
Grammar in context: Future, preterit

A 2. Students should use strategies for making inferences in context and using prior vocabulary knowledge to determine the meanings of the words. Definitions are provided on the vocabulary page at end of hilo.

B As students read for comprehension, have them infer italicized vocabulary from context.

C. This comprehension check can be assigned for HW after reading the text. Note that is divided into two parts #1-#4 and #5-#8. It is also available to take digitally as a quiz in **Explorer**.

Answers for Part C:

1. D
2. C
3. A
4. B

5. H
6. E
7. F
8. G

D. This is where students can share what they know about the earthquake that took place in Chile in February, 2010. Then have students watch the documentary in **Explorer** (activity 4 fuente audiovisual), focusing on the perspectives of the people of Chile and how they reacted to the disaster. See if they can make a connection to any other disasters, natural or otherwise.

E. Students will have seen the documentary and will now read the details of the Spanish university student expedition. As they read, have them jot down details in their journals in order to write a blog entry to their classmates back in Spain, as if the students were members of the expedition. Review the past tense, *el pretérito indefinido,* with students at this time, found on page 102 of the textbook.

F. Students, as if they were an "expedicionario", write a blog addressing the bullet points. This blog entry can be assigned as a formative assessment or homework assignment.

G. Students will access the activity 4 audio recorded by a student on the expedition. Have them listen to the audio recording at least two or three times while taking some notes about the content. The recording is by a male college student who is talking about a relaxing day including a visit to a craft fair in the morning and a visit to the hot springs near Valdivia Chile in the afternoon. This can be done as a formative assessment (quiz) in **Explorer**.

« | » | Audio script

Narrador:
Cuaderno de viaje - Habla Jauma Muntada, expedicionario en Chile.

Jauma Muntada:
Hoy los expedicionarios nos hemos bañado en las termas "El pozo". Las termas están situadas al aire libre y están rodeadas de una naturaleza abrupta: el calor del agua contrastada con el clima frío, que incluso ha dejado caer algunas gotas. Así pues, nos hemos puesto el bañador y hemos estado disfrutando del agua durante parte de la tarde. La experiencia ha sido gratificante y ha ayudado a relajarnos y a descansar un poco. Antes de esto, por la mañana, hemos ido a una feria artesana, en Villarrica. Estaba llena de objetos hechos de madera: pendientes, llaveros, cubiertos, etc. Por eso, analizando todo el día, cabe destacar que ha sido una jornada tranquila e ideal para descansar.

H. Have students compare their notes from the audio recording and then answer the comprehension questions.

Answers for Part H

1. B
2. B

3. B
4. A

¿Qué aprendiste?

These are two formative assessment options for higher level thinking skills: analysis (presentational writing) and evaluation (presentational speaking).

1. **Analysis:** Students will need to analyze the products, practices, and perspectives of Chilean culture. Students imagine that their Spanish class meets with the students from Spain to hear about their expedition to Chile. Students will analyze one product and/or one practice, and the respective perspective, that they learned from the reading and audio in this activity.

2. **Evaluation:** Students need to convince their parents that they should participate in an expedition to Chile. They should prepare their oral presentation as if their parents do not want them to go. Include what they know about the products, practices, and perspectives of Chile. It is suggested that they evaluate one product and/or practice and the respective perspective. Students can record themselves for this task in **Explorer**.

 ¡Tu opinión cuenta!

Students connect to the former hilo on *Ciudadanía global* by answering the questions in their journals or in an interpersonal debate forum described below. They should be specific and use examples to justify their answers.

 Optional: Students could do a U shape debate forum:

Many teachers are replacing the adversarial, closed-minded debate format with more open-ended discussions where students are encouraged to see the merits of all sides and to accept positions along a continuum. To facilitate this approach, class discussions may be configured in a "U-shape." Students with polar views (either strongly agreeing or strongly disagreeing with the proposition) seat themselves at either tip of the "U;" students with mixed opinions sit at appropriate spots along the rounded part. At varying stages in the discussion, students are encouraged to move along the spectrum as their intellectual positions on the issue change. In this way, less dogmatic attitudes are encouraged: the implicit messages of the traditional debate – black or white, fixed opinions with the objective of winning the argument – are supplanted by different messages of the "U-shaped" discussion – provisionally held positions as one tries to figure out the most defensible personal stance from a continuum of options.

¿Cómo se entiende el ocio desde la perspectiva local?

Actividad 5 ¿Cómo puedes pasar un día tranquilo en familia?

Student book page 105
Time estimate: 1 60-minute period with homework

Throughout this activity encourage students take their time to view and read the pamphlet, and guide them to think about what they would do with this kind of print information given to them in a Spanish-speaking country. While many times there will be English translations of information for tourists, that is not always the case!

 B A good online resource is images.google.cl with the search term "Parque Metropolitano Santiago."

 Culture box: "La gastronomía de Chile" video is the last of the Fuentes in **Explorer** for hilo 4 and provides a delicious look at the culinary specialties of Chile. There are comprehension questions that accompany it. Tell students not to be worried about understanding everything that is said! You might encourage them to look up recipes for a dish they find interesting in the culinary tour.

 4b This is a chance to connect back to hilo 3 *cuidadanía global,* students can refer to the characteristics of a global citizen found there.

 1. This is a good chance to check students' use of the preterit and imperfect, which will be important in the next hilo for the final project. Review and discuss proper use as necessary. Make sure that students understand the writing prompt which is to journal about a day that they just *had* (using the past tenses), not one that they *would have* (which would be the conditional).

 2. This interpersonal writing prompt can be given as homework as well; an email template is available in **Explorer**.

3. This is the kind of oral presentation prompt given on the new AP Language & Culture exam: after getting to know the cultural products, practices, and perspectives of a Spanish-speaking country, compare it to your own culture. You may want to treat this as a formative assessment and collect it. In the next activity students will have to do something similar but record it as an oral presentation, similar to the AP exam task.

¿Cómo se entiende el ocio desde la perspectiva local?

Actividad 6 ¿Qué piensan los chilenos sobre el ocio?

Student book page 110
Time estimate: 60 minute class with A tejer! and/or ¡Tu opinión cuenta! assigned for HW

 A **2.** and **3.** Have students take the necessary time to really understand and practice using this vocabulary, since it will make them feel more comfortable hearing the audio selection for this activity. If you wish, you can go back over the words for each section of the audio recording before listening to that section.

B For all parts of this audio, remind students that they may not understand every word being said (the Chilean native speaker speaks quickly) but can still get a lot of the content in context. They will recognize many words that they already know. Also, they will hear everything twice! This is all "active listening" – there is always something for students to do as they listen and the activities are meant to help them know what to focus on.

Audio script

PRIMERA NARRACIÓN

Hola, mi nombre es Fabiola Moraga y soy chilena.

Les quiero contar algunas cosas típicas de nuestra cultura para que si algún día desean viajar, se sientan cómodos y disfruten de nuestro país. Esta es mi perspectiva de nuestra cultura en la adolescencia.

Se dice que como latinos llevamos sabor en nuestra sangre, somos afectivos, cálidos y nos gusta demostrar nuestro cariño sin importar si lo hacemos en público o en privado. Da lo mismo. Si estamos en pareja, pololeando como decimos en Chile, caminamos de la mano con nuestro pololo o polola e incluso podemos besarnos en público sin pudor. Asimismo, si nos presentan a alguien por primera vez, siempre vamos a saludar con un beso en la mejilla, y si ya somos amigos o familiares, podemos agregar un abrazo a este saludo, y para despedirnos, repetimos el mismo acto. Esto lo hacemos desde que somos bebés.

SEGUNDA NARRACIÓN

En nuestra cultura el compartir con la familia es muy importante ya que lo tenemos arraigado desde pequeños, de hecho, cuando salimos del colegio a los 18 años y vamos a la universidad, podemos seguir viviendo con nuestros padres toda la etapa universitaria. Eso es algo normal, aun si tenemos incluso 30 años de edad, hay hijos que se quedan a vivir con sus padres por costumbre y comodidad.

Hay cosas en nuestra cultura que pasan de generación tras generación sin darnos cuenta de ello. Por ejemplo, los domingos son dedicados a la familia y generalmente se hace un asado para compartir a la hora del almuerzo acompañado con un buen vino chileno. En estos almuerzos se pueden reunir abuelos, tíos, sobrinos, etc. para pasar un rato agradable, conversar y descansar de la rutina del trabajo. Estos almuerzos son largos ya que hacemos una extensa sobremesa y luego, algunos duermen una siesta para reponerse de la comida y la bebida, que a veces es en exceso.

TERCERA NARRACIÓN

A los jóvenes en Chile les gusta salir a "carretear" los fines de semana, por lo que el viernes o sábado se reúnen en la casa de algún amigo o amiga alrededor de las 9 o 10 de la noche, para luego ir todos juntos a bailar a una disco *bakán* alrededor de las 12 e incluso la 1 de la madrugada. La gente sale tarde a bares y clubes nocturnos porque las fiestas en Chile duran hasta las 4 de la mañana y todos los locales nocturnos están abiertos hasta esa hora. Es como costumbre pasar a comer algo después del carrete, por lo que hay locales de comida rápida abiertos también hasta las 4 o 5 de la mañana. Hay gente que incluso sigue el carrete después de las 5 de la mañana en la casa de alguien y a esto se le llama After Hour. Por esta razón, todos duermen hasta tarde a la mañana siguiente. Yo creo que a los jóvenes chilenos les encanta salir, compartir, conocer gente y pasarlo bien, y salen tarde porque todos se demoran en llegar a la hora porque innatamente saben que la salida es tarde, o porque se arreglan, se maquillan, se perfuman y en otras ocasiones cenan antes con su familia, y luego salen a carretear.

CUARTA NARRACIÓN

En Chile pasamos a ser mayores de edad a los 18 años y como en muchas culturas del mundo, a los jóvenes les gustan muchas cosas similares al resto de los jóvenes. Por ejemplo, algunos cuando están en el colegio o liceo, crean bandas musicales y ensayan por las tardes o los fines de semana siguiendo a alguna banda famosa y *bakán* como Metallica o Guns N' Roses, y algunos siguen con la misma banda, incluso después de salir del colegio. A las adolescentes les gusta la moda, o siguen y leen sobre actores y actrices famosos, a otros les gustan los video juegos y la computación.

QUINTA NARRACIÓN

Finalmente, una cosa negativa que puedo decir sobre mi cultura, es la impuntualidad que tiene gran parte de los chilenos de cualquier edad para llegar a los compromisos, especialmente cuando se trata de compromisos más informales con amigos o familia. Es costumbre, por ejemplo, que si se planea un carrete de cumpleaños a las 10 de la noche, todos comienzan a llegar a las 11. Es aceptable y todos lo saben, por lo que es difícil aún cambiar esta costumbre. Es por esto que cuando vienen visitantes "gringos" a nuestro país, deben acostumbrarse a la hora chilena, que siempre será media o una hora más tarde de lo planificado.

Espero que algún día visiten Chile, sus paisajes y sobre todo conozcan la cultura que de seguro les va a encantar, ¡Chile es bakán!

¡A tejer!

This is the kind of oral presentation task that students will be asked to complete on the Advanced Placement Language & Culture exam. A place to record themselves is available in **Explorer**.

¡Tu opinión cuenta!

Students need to read to comprehend the email already written, and then respond appropriately; this also mirrors a possible Advanced Placement Language & Culture exam task. Some students may want to plan out their response beforehand. Students can use the email template provided in **Explorer** if they wish.

Essential questions:
- ¿Cómo se planifica un viaje a un país donde se habla español?
- Como viajero, ¿cómo se puede experimentar la vida cotidiana de otro país?
- ¿Cómo se entiende el ocio desde la perspectiva local?

Hilo 4 Evaluación Final - *Un viaje virtual*

Student book page 114

Time estimate: About 1 week outside of class to collect information and begin working on folleto and presentation, about 2 days in class if you would like to give them time to work on the project, 1 or 2 days for presentations

Grammar in context: Conditional (p. 93), future (p. 99), present subjunctive (p. 133)

We suggest that students work in pairs for this activity as it has many parts and is very detail-oriented. You may want to have students of differing skill levels work together; remember that some students may have stronger technology skills and others a higher level of Spanish! Keep in mind that this checklist can be shortened or expanded per your students' abilities and as time permits. Go to your **Explorer** course for additional resources for students.

This summative assessment is all about giving students the opportunity to immerse themselves in a virtual travel experience, not only their own, but to imagine the trips their classmates have planned as well. We have provided the context and checklist for the presentations in the book, and a step-by-step guide can be found in **Explorer** to help students research the information they should include in their final project.

Students' access to technology will determine the options they have for their presentations. The following options are suggestions to save time for in class presentations but still holding students accountable:

1. PowerPoint: Have students compile the information for the oral presentation in a PowerPoint presentation that they will present to the class. To save time have them record their voices in the program and share the presentations digitally. Students can listen to their classmates' presentations either at home or in class.

2. Google Earth: Using this free program either on the computer or on a mobile device, have students take their classmates into the streets of the places they will visit, demonstrate 360 degree photos, or photos other tourists have shared on the program. If they use computers they can actually create a virtual tour, record their voice and share the entire presentation with a Google Group.

3. PhotoStory: This option functions much like PowerPoint does, however it allows for more customization by adding effects to images and text to the final video. Students can share these files digitally or play them for the entire class.

4. Prezi: This website would allow students to create online digital presentations that can be shared easily. They would need to present in front of the class however, as customization of audio is difficult with this program.

Presentación oral: Encourage students to practice what they will say and give them guidelines for what you expect from their oral presentations. For example, you may want to specify that they can only have a brief outline or key words noted for use during their oral presentation instead of the entire script written out. This could also be differentiated for students based on ability level.

Presentación escrita: The folleto can be done on construction paper, digitally with Word or Publisher, or even more digitally with a final PDF being emailed to the teacher and classmates or shared through iBooks.

MANTA 2 Vida contemporánea

Hilo 5 Educación y carreras

Essential questions:
- ¿Cómo son los sistemas educativos en varias partes del mundo hispanoamericano?
- ¿Cómo nos prepara la educación para nuestra vida futura?
- ¿Cómo se elige una carrera profesional?

Student Learning Objectives

Interpersonal Communication: Speaking and Writing
- Exchange information about educational systems and careers in Spanish-speaking countries.
- Express opinions about school, selecting colleges, and careers.
- Exchange messages such as emails, blogs, or social media posts about school life, selecting colleges, and careers.
- Engage in discussions about the purpose of education.
- Explain how education prepares people for the future.

Interpretive Communication: Print, Audio, Audiovisual, and/or Visual Sources
- Demonstrate comprehension of educational systems and careers in Spanish-speaking countries from authentic texts, governmental documents, websites, blogs, audio, and audiovisual resources.
- Analyze and evaluate education and career options in Spanish-speaking countries.
- Describe and analyze significant details from audio and audiovisual sources about education in Spanish-speaking countries.
- Research and evaluate a professional from a Hispanic culture.
- Interpret, discuss, and evaluate information from authentic resources on graduation rates in Spanish-speaking countries.

Presentational Communication: Spoken and/or Written Presentations to a Variety of Audiences
- Create and produce a personal narrative about past experiences related to a current career/profession.
- Develop a professional resume.
- Analyze and evaluate educational systems in different Spanish-speaking countries.
- Present a history of a professional career.
- Produce reflections and journal entries to demonstrate understanding of educational systems, practices, and perspectives in Spanish-speaking countries.

Relating Cultural Practices to Perspectives:
- Investigate, explain, and reflect on the relationship between the practices of choosing career options to perspectives (beliefs/values/attitudes) of Hispanic cultures.

Relating Cultural Products to Perspectives:
- Investigate, explain, and reflect on the relationship between the products (educational options) to perspectives (beliefs/values/attitudes) of Hispanic cultures.

Connections: Connect with Other Disciplines
- Make connections to content knowledge about professional careers, K-12 and higher education.

Connections: Acquire New Information
- Apply new information from authentic sources about education and careers in Hispanic cultures.

Comparisons: Language
- Make linguistic comparisons of cognates, passive voice, past tenses, indirect and direct object pronouns, and subjunctive uses when giving advice.

Comparisons: Culture
- Compare similarities and differences of public and private K-12 and/or higher education in the U.S. and in a Spanish-speaking country.
- Compare cultural similarities and differences about selecting colleges and careers in the U.S. and Spanish-speaking countries.

School and Global Communities:
- Interact with Spanish speakers about education and careers in Hispanic cultures.

Lifelong Learning:
- Set goals and reflect on progress in using Spanish for enjoyment, enrichment, and advancement.

Suggested Lesson Plan Sequence/Pacing Guide

Manta 2: Vida contemporánea
Hilo 5: Educación y carreras

Focus according to Essential Question Pages in SE	Day (based on 60 min class)	Classroom Activities	Homework/ Formative assessment/ Exit pass
Los sistemas educativos aquí y en el mundo hispanohablante pp. 120–128	1	* Introduce unit with cartoon, reflection, and conversation * Practice with vocabulary and tweeting * Prepare for Activity 1 with Four Corners activity	* Response to tweets
	2	* Viewing and listening activities about schools in Argentina * Comprehension activities on audio * Cultural comparison and reflection	* Cultural comparisons and/or Reflexión activities
	3	* Share out cultural comparison work from the previous day * Watch video on dropout rates in Latin America * Have students reflect on Tu opinion cuenta * Reading and viewing activities on drop-out rates * Group conversation and individual reflection	* Reflexión journal prompt
La preparación que nos da la educación para una vida futura pp. 129–138	4–5	* Email and vocabulary exercises * Note-taking for comparison of two texts * Comprehension activities * Role-play as student/guidance counselor * Culture box video and discussion * Reflection questions	* Email task * Reading can be assigned outside of class with T-chart notes * True/False comprehension check * Reflexión prompt
	6–7	* Group conversation about choosing a college * Reading while note-taking and prioritizing * Cultural comparisons * Looking at college entrance exams in Mexico and Spain * Reflection and evaluation exercises * Formative assessment	* Reading can be assigned outside of class with notes * Venn Diagram comparison * Reflexión * ¿Qué aprendiste? Formative assessment (1 of 3 options)
Elegir una carrera profesional pp. 139–149	8–9	* Imagining your ideal job activities * Preparing for and taking online aptitude test * Reflecting on and sharing results * Analysis and comparison of example results, including formal paragraph * Email task	* As needed, online test can be completed at home, as well as follow-up journal prompt * Synthesis paragraph * Email task
	10–11 + possible Workshop day	* Pre-reading reflection and vocabulary categorization * Guided reading with comprehension questions * Reflection activities to share out in class * Groupwork: Internet research, prepare and give persuasive presentation to class (if students need time to work in class)	* ¿Qué entendiste? Questions (can be assigned in full or partially as HW) * Reflexión * Groupwork and presentations
	12 + Workshop day(s)	* Present summative assessment – **you want to guide students through the "pasos" list as early as possible in the unit so they are ready to begin at this point** * Students prepare written narratives and curriculum vitae * Extra days to work in class as possible/desired	* Students develop and polish their projects outside of class
	13 (+ 1?)	* Students present to each other and interview each other at Career Fair	

Hilo 5 La educación y carreras profesionales

Introducción ¿Qué significa aprender?

Student book page 120
Time estimate: 15 minutes

A Have students look at the cartoon. Either as a class, individually, or in pairs have students come with up adjectives or actions that might describe the two students depicted in the cartoon. Tell students to use a T-chart to make the comparison and to emphasize the juxtaposition.

B Once students have brainstormed the vocabulary that will enhance the conversation activity, pair students up to respond to the themes in the "Conversa con un compañero" activity in the text.

Antes de empezar *Tuiteando sobre #educación*

Student book page 120
Time estimate: 30 minutes

A Choose 3 to 5 words like education, school, classes, future and study. Pair students up and explain the activity to them. You will say one word, like education, and students will take turns going back and forth saying words or phrases they associate with that word. They cannot repeat what their partner says and they have to say as many words as they can in 30 seconds until you tell them to stop. After each round have students share out their favorite words that came out during the game. Repeat for each word. This is a great way to have them review vocabulary they already know associated with this theme and to get them practicing their new vocabulary.

B As they read the tweets the first time advise them to pick 5 tweets to rewrite in "amix", in hilo 2, pp. 55-56 of the textbook. You could have them do these on sentence strips and post them around the room or you could have them share their "amix" tweets with the class using PollEverywhere.com. While students are reading the tweets a second time have them choose the 5 tweets that relate most to school, classes, and studying. Students can share these in the forum in **Explorer**.

C Using the tweets they just chose, have students write out replies in Twitter format (140 characters or less). They should give a shout out to the person they are responding to by including their username @____. They can also hash tag (#) important themes in their message like #escuela. Students can either turn these in for you to read; post them around the room, grouping them by their responses to specific tweets; or electronically using one of the sites mentioned in hilo 2, *Redes sociales*. The second option here allows for the class to see trends in how other students in their class feel about school. In the final part of this activity have them pair up with another student in the class and talk about the prompting themes in Part C 2. It is always helpful to then open the discussion up to the class afterward, to see what your students discussed in their pairs.

¿Cómo son los sistemas educativos en varias partes del mundo hispanoamericano?

Actividad 1 ¿Educación pública o privada en Argentina?

Student book page 122
Time estimate: 60 minutes + comparaciones culturales and reflexión the following day
Grammar in context: Passive voice with *ser* and *se*

A 1. Divide your class into groups of four. You can have them move all four of their desks into a square table with a student sitting at each desk. Provide each group with an 11 x 17 piece of paper divided into four parts as indicated on p. 122 of the textbook, or print an 11 x 17 copy of the organizer in **Explorer.** Put the sheet of paper in the middle of the group. Set a timer for 20 seconds and tell students to write as many vocabulary words or phrases they know and can associate with the four types of schools they have chosen (**public, private, charter, technical, magnet,** etc.). When the 20 seconds is up have them rotate the paper, reset the timer, and repeat. Continue this process until students have a wide variety of words and phrases to aid in their comprehension and production activities associated with this lesson.

3. The Y chart for this activity can be found in **Explorer.**

4. Before students hear the recording, have them guess if these words refer to public or private education based on their previous knowledge. This chart is available in **Explorer.** Answers follow on the next page.

Answers to Part 4:

es gratuita	PUB	hay escasos recursos	PUB
se debe abonar inscripción y cuotas mensuales	PRI	se brinda el servicio de copa de leche y comedor	PUB
ofrece competencias que les beneficiarán para competir en el mercado laboral	PRI	hay paro frecuente de docentes por razones salariales y otros derechos	PUB
se nota que el perfil de los alumnos es bajo	PUB	hay días reiterados sin clases	PUB
hay carencia (falta) de cosas necesarias para estudiar	PUB	se requiere el uso de guardapolvos	PUB
existen problemas económicos para afrontar gastos como pasajes de ómnibus y útiles	PUB	hay el temor de encontrarse con gente que tenga otro estilo de vida	PRI
fueron fundadas por inmigrantes	PRI	le cuesta mucho estudiar porque debe ayudar a su familia	PUB
las escuelas atravesaron etapas de desprestigio	PUB	hay conformación social	PRI

 B Students will listen to the audio in **Explorer** - Fuente for Actividad 1. Have them listen to see if they hear any of the expressions in the chart in order to verify their predictions.

« | » | Audio script

Vas a escuchar una grabación sobre la educación pública y privada en la República Argentina. Hay dos partes de la grabación, la primera parte se trata de la educación pública y la segunda parte se trata de la privada. Se escuchará cada parte dos veces.

Soy Viviana Allegri, Directora de una Escuela Pública de Educación Primaria y Profesora en Institutos de Formación Docente. Vivo en Villa Gobernador Gálvez, Provincia de Santa Fe, República Argentina.

Les voy a hablar sobre la EDUCACIÓN PÚBLICA y PRIVADA de la zona en que vivo.

La educación pública- primera parte

LA EDUCACIÓN PÚBLICA por ser gratuita es elegida en su mayoría por la población de escasos recursos. En estas escuelas, fundamentalmente en las de nivel primario, se brinda el servicio de copa de leche y comedor.

El perfil de alumno de la escuela pública, por lo general, es humilde, con carencias, le cuesta mucho estudiar porque debe ayudar a su familia, tiene problemas económicos para afrontar gastos como pasajes de ómnibus, compra de útiles escolares, libros, etc. En muchos casos abandonan antes de finalizar sus estudios, especialmente aquellos cuyas familias no los ayudan o exigen.

Los alumnos de la escuela primaria usan guardapolvos y los de la escuela secundaria visten con ropa común, preferentemente de colores blanco y azul.

La Educación Pública atravesó etapas de desprestigio por reiterados días sin clases por medidas de paros docentes por reclamos salariares y por no actualizar su propuesta pedagógica. El Estado no la priorizó y todo esto impulsó que muchos alumnos de familias que podían pagar se cambien a la educación privada.

La educación privada- segunda parte

LAS ESCUELAS PRIVADAS fueron fundadas por inmigrantes de distintas nacionalidades preocupados por transmitir su idioma y mantener su identidad cultural a través de las generaciones. También hay escuelas religiosas con una larga tradición.

Para asistir a las Escuelas de Educación Privada las familias deben abonar inscripción y cuotas mensuales, por lo tanto la población que la elige es de nivel socio-económico medio o alto.

Los alumnos deben usar en forma obligatoria uniforme, el que es diferente para cada escuela.

Se supone que frente a una educación pública desprestigiada, la educación privada ofrece competencias específicas que beneficiarán a futuro a los educandos para competir en el mercado laboral (computación, idiomas, otros) o para continuar estudios superiores.

Si bien hay escuelas públicas que ofrecen una buena calidad educativa, a los padres de clase media y alta les preocupa la conformación social. Se buscan escuelas con un estilo de vida parecido al de la familia. El temor es encontrarse con muchas diferencias en la convivencia, con gente que tenga otro estilo de vida o pertenezca a un estrato social diferente. En realidad ningún sistema garantiza de por sí calidad. Los padres deberían elegir escuela para sus hijos despojados de prejuicios y en función del proyecto de cada institución y de cómo este es llevado a cabo.

C Here students show their comprehension through a fill in the blank activity.

Answers to Part C:

1. Los alumnos en las escuelas públicas en la región de la directora en la grabación representan en su mayoría la población de __escasos recursos__.
2. En las escuelas públicas se brinda el servicio de __copa de leche y comedor__.
3. Al alumno en la escuela pública le cuesta mucho estudiar porque __debe ayudar a la familia y tiene problemas económicos con gastos escolares__.
4. Los alumnos de la escuela primaria pública usan __guardapolvos__ encima de su ropa.
5. Los alumnos faltan días reiterados sin clases debido al __paro de docentes por razones salariales__.
6. Las escuelas privadas fueron fundadas por __inmigrantes de distintas nacionalidades preocupados por transmitir su idioma y mantener su identidad cultural__.
7. Las familias cuyos hijos asisten a las escuelas privadas deben __abonar inscripción y cuotas mensuales__.
8. Las escuelas privadas ofrecen competencias como __idiomas y computación__ para que los alumnos estén preparados para el mercado laboral.
9. Los padres de clase alta y media les preocupa __la conformación social__ y temen que sus hijos se encuentren con diferencias en __la convivencia__.
10. Los padres deberían elegir escuela para sus hijos __despojados (libres) de prejuicios__ y en función del proyecto de cada institución y de cómo este es llevado a cabo.

Reflexión

Based on what they heard in the audio, this question may generate some interesting opinions from the students. The idea presented was that no one system can absolutely guarantee a quality education, therefore it depends on each institution to carry out its work. In **Explorer** students can submit their journal responses to a forum and respond to each other's ideas. For students who are having difficulty answering the question, seeing others' responses may help them formulate their own.

¿Cómo son las escuelas en varias partes del mundo hispanoamericano?

Actividad 2 ¿Qué causa la deserción escolar?

Student book page 125
Time estimate: 45 minutes

Before beginning this activity, take three minutes to watch the video from Univisión about dropout rates in the United States in the **Explorer** Enlaces for Actividad 2. This video can be a way to preface this activity so that students have background knowledge about statistics on graduation rates in the US before they begin discussing the information in the article and the infographic in the student text. After students view the video they can share what information they learned. It would be interesting to have students write down the most surprising thing they learned in the video, for example that 1 in 3 students doesn't graduate from high school, or the amount in US dollars that high school dropouts earn in their lifetime versus students who graduate high school and college.

Summary: Respecto al tema de la deserción escolar, hay estudiantes que abandonan prematuramente sus estudios, principalmente por motivos económicos, para entrar al mercado laboral sin haber adquirido las habilidades necesarias para conseguir un empleo bien remunerado. Cabe destacar que los apoyos a estudiantes con bajos recursos son muy pocos y su deserción es aún mayor.

  A Have your students converse with a partner, responding to the topics given. Then, ask them to define the terms in part 2 about levels of education.

   B As students read through the text for the first time have them highlight the statistics mentioned in the text. Then in part 2 have them make note of things that surprise them, things that they do not understand, any information they already knew before reading the text and any vocabulary they don't know.

  C After students have read through the text twice, open up the class to discussion by having students answer the opinion questions in the student text. You can have them write answers to the questions first if you feel they need the scaffolding, or you can ask one question at a time and encourage several different students to share their opinions.

D Before students look over the graphs, have them read the small text on p. 127 in the graphic. Then have students answer the questions given. Finally, have students look through the graphs and process the statistics they represent.

> **Answers for Part D:**
> - el porcentaje de graduados según los niveles económicos en América Latina
> - los colores diferentes representan los niveles económicos: Q1 representa la porción más pobre y siguen sucesivamente hasta Q5 que representa la porción más rica.

 E After your students have looked through the graphs, have them break into pairs to discuss the questions presented in the student text. You may also encourage students to think about some possible causes that might explain the statistics on graduation rates in Latin America. You can have them refer back to the reasons listed in the text in part B to help aid in their discussion.

> **Answers for Part E:**
> - Chile y Argentina
> - Guatemala y Honduras
> - El porcentaje de graduados aumenta con el nivel económico en cada país.
> - El nivel económico influye directamente si un estudiante se graduará de la secundaria.

 Reflexión

To wrap up this activity, have students write what they have learned about dropout rates in Latin America in the text and in the graphs and then have them give two recommendations to improve graduation rates.

¿Cómo nos prepara la educación para nuestra vida futura?

Actividad 3 ¿Cómo sirve la educación secundaria en la preparación para la universidad?

Student book page 129
Time estimate: 2 60-minute classes and reading assigned for homework
Grammar in context: Indefinite articles, present subjunctive and "si" clauses with past subjunctive-conditional

    A Divide students into pairs or a group of three for the conversation about secondary school in the U.S. Have them take notes in Spanish to share. As students share out, have them record their info on chart paper posted on the wall/board. When the information is on the board, have students add

HILO 5 La educación y carreras profesionales

to their own notes so that they can compose an e-mail to the student to inform him/her about your school. An email template is in **Explorer**. The email could be assigned as HW or as an exit card at end of class.

Vocabulary box: While students read, they should infer the meaning of these words and as they go along, choose the word that is NOT a synonym of each word in this context. This is also available as a Vocabulary quiz in **Explorer**.

Vocabulary Answers:
The word in bold is not a synonym of the others.
1. *preparatoria*: media superior/**graduado**/secundaria
2. *vínculo*: **separación**/puente/conexión
3. *etapa*: época/**escalera**/tiempo
4. *ingresar*: inscribirse/matricular/**abandonar**
5. *egresado*: graduado/**principiante**/licenciado
6. *encargarse de:* asumir/responsabilizarse/**comprender**
7. *gama*: **escala musical**/variedad/repertorio
8. *abarcar:* incluir/**excluir**/contener
9. *corroborar*: confirmar/**alejar**/apoyar
10. *proporcionar*: facilitar/**repartir**/aportar

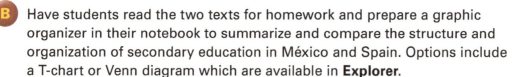

B Have students read the two texts for homework and prepare a graphic organizer in their notebook to summarize and compare the structure and organization of secondary education in México and Spain. Options include a T-chart or Venn diagram which are available in **Explorer**.

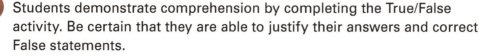

C Students demonstrate comprehension by completing the True/False activity. Be certain that they are able to justify their answers and correct False statements.

Answers to Part C:
1. Falsa- España: hay 3 modalidades- general, preparatoria y orientadora. México: hay 3 modalidades: general, profesional técnico y tecnológico.
2. Cierta- Se encarga de una formación para el trabajo y educación especializada- industria, salud, comercio, administración y comunicaciones.
3. Cierta- Prefieren hacer el general porque piensan ir a la universidad.
4. Cierta- Hay materias especializadas y el estudiante puede corroborar si su gusto por dicha área es la que se quiere enfocar.
5. Falso- El bachillerato es de carácter voluntario pero la ESO es obligatoria y abarca 4 cursos
6. Cierta- En España, las actividades en el bachillerato les prepara para que tengan efectos laborales y académicos.
7. Cierta- Les permite acceder a la educación superior.

¡Tu opinión cuenta!

Divide students into small groups of 3 or 4 students and give them one of the three questions to answer and then share out.

D Tu perfil de estudiante can be assigned as homework a day or two in advance of the interview in *¿Qué aprendiste?*

 ### ¿Qué aprendiste?

Options for the interview: 1) students can record themselves on the space provided in **Explorer**; 2) have them interview with you or possibly with another Spanish teacher; or 3) students can interview each other. Consider having students role-play the interview for practice before it is graded. Use the interpersonal speaking rubric to provide feedback or a grade.

 ### ¡Te toca a ti!

Students are now imagining themselves as the counselor who interviewed them, as they write follow-up e mail with advice for the student. Suggest that they give at least three recommendations to the student. Students should use the present subjunctive expressions in the grammar strategy box as well as "si" clauses with present and future tenses as featured in hilo 3 (pages 68 and 69). There is a space in **Explorer** for students to record themselves if you want to check each student's completion of this task; in this case you could use the presentational speaking rubric to give them feedback or a grade.

 Culture box: This video on education in Nicaragua is well worth watching; the questions in the culture box will guide students regarding what to focus on and discuss afterward.

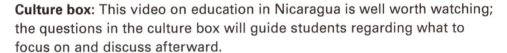
¿Cómo nos prepara la educación para nuestra vida futura?

Actividad 4 ¿Cómo se elige una institución de educación superior?

Student book page 134
Time estimate: 2 60-minute classes with reading for homework

 A Prepare for this activity with the following materials: 4 sheets of chart paper, 4 different colors of markers, stop watch or clock (with seconds) to limit the time for each group.

1. and 2. Divide students into small groups of 3 or 4 students to discuss the topic on how to select the best university. Each student needs to take notes for the next part of the activity. Important factors do NOT include going to a "party school".

Another option for Part 1 and 2: Give these instructions **before** dividing the class into 4 larger groups (you can assign each group a name of a country, a number, letter, etc.). Give each group a different color marker.

Each group will have a limited amount of time to discuss factors to consider when choosing a university. Then each group will post their findings on the chart paper in the 4 corners of the room. Give them a limited amount of time (1 minute 7 seconds) before moving to the next station to add more factors to the existing chart without repeating anything that is already there. They have to read what the other groups write because they cannot repeat. At the conclusion students sit down and one or two people can read off the factors on each list. The class can decide if it is an important consideration to include on a master list. The scribe will circle it on the chart paper. They continue to the next group and repeat the process without any repeats. Have the scribes check off what has been contributed on their charts. You can have someone recording the factors on a laptop or other device.

 B Have students read the text in class and rank each factor by their personal priority in their journal. In class discussion, students could explain why certain factors are more or less important to them.

 C This is a cultural comparison regarding the factors that the students brainstormed before reading the text. Are their factors similar or different from the information in the text? They can use the Venn Diagram or a T-chart (both available in **Explorer** or they can make their own). Have them summarize the results in their notebook or journal to reference later in this activity.

 D Only 3 out of 10 students in México have access to higher education. Share this fact with students before reading and in a quick Think-Pair-Share, have students think about how that impacts their outlook on secondary education.

 Culture box: Educación Superior en España: Tell students that they will be reading to find out why Spain changed their university system. Encourage students to do additional research on the change. In **Explorer**, under Apoyo adicional they can see what the admissions exams are like in Mexico and Spain; discuss as a class how this is different than the tests required for college admissions in the U.S.

 ¿Qué aprendiste?

 Options 1 and 3: Have students write one paragraph using the sentence starters. They can present to their classmates (presentational speaking) or this can be collected as a presentational writing formative assessment. **Option 2** can be a presentational speaking task or an interpersonal writing task such as an email. All options have a place in **Explorer** for students to record their answer as a presentational speaking task.

¿Cómo se elige una carrera profesional?

Actividad 5 *¿Cómo puedes discernir una carrera apropiada y atractiva para ti?*

Student book page 139
Time estimate: 2 class periods with 2 days of homework
Grammar in context: Familiar commands and present subjunctive (in final email task)

 A 1. Depending on the size of your class, you may want to ask students to introduce their partner and his/her career interests to the class. This involves presentational speaking as well as interpersonal.

 B Students go online to take a digital aptitude test, found under Fuentes. The vocabulary can help guide them through the questions. You may want to allow them to help each other during this time.

 C 3. Students analyze sample results (of one of the *Tejidos* authors!) and give advice. This is good practice for informal tú commands; review as necessary.

4. Students view the other set of results and write a formal paragraph comparing the two. (On the first bullet point of the instructions here, note the use of the verb "deber" – many students do not know this is how they can say "should.") This is a synthesis-level task, excellent practice for the AP Language & Culture exam! Refer students to the lists of connectors and previous examples of synthesis between two or more sources of information at the end of hilo 1. They could complete a Venn Diagram first to help themselves organize their thoughts.

 ¡Te toca a ti!

Students write an email using the present subjunctive (to give recommendations) based on their experience, hopefully a positive one, using the online aptitude test. An email template is available in **Explorer** if you would like, or encourage students to send the email to a Spanish-speaking friend to help them out!

¿Cómo se elige una carrera profesional?

Actividad 6 ¿Qué factores influyen al elegir una carrera?

Student book page 143
Time estimate: 2 class periods with HW and a possible workshop day to prepare presentations

A **3.** Encourage students to talk about each word (separated into nouns/adjectives/verbs) in Spanish, although they can note the exact cognate in English in writing if they would like. This helps students identify words that they can already recognize before seeing them in context.

B The "Qué entendiste" questions can be completed individually, then reviewed as a class. Alternatively, you can pair students in high-low pairings to read the text together and find the answers to the questions. Direct students to return to the text when they are unsure, because these are questions whose answers can be encountered directly in the text.

Of the careers listed in the third reading selection, many are cognates. None of these words are glossed so you might want to take questions from the class and provide some translations of key careers ("informática" = computer science, for example).

C Assign students to mixed-level groups of 3 or 4. Assign roles like Lead Researcher, Secretary, Timekeeper and Lead Presenter. Students will conduct Internet research to see how college graduates in the U.S. fare in their assigned field; average salaries are not hard to find online. Students then prepare a persuasive presentation to the rest of the class, as if they were at a Career Fair trying to convince young people to enter this profession because of its experiences, pay and benefits. Go to your **Explorer** course for a graphic organizer to help guide students in their work. All students should participate in the final oral presentation; you can use the presentational speaking rubric to give them feedback and/or a grade.

Essential questions:
- ¿Cómo son los sistemas educativos en varias partes del mundo hispanohablante?
- ¿Cómo nos prepara la educación para nuestra vida futura?
- ¿Cómo se elige una carrera profesional?

Hilo 5 Evaluación Final - *Exposición de carreras profesionales*

Student book page 148
Time estimate: Depending on how much time you have spent preparing some of these tasks earlier (see note below), 2–3 days preparation and 1–2 days Career Fair
Grammar in context: Past tenses (preterit, imperfect, past perfect) and the present and past subjunctive

Note: Do everything you can to scaffold this summative assessment for students beforehand, so that they have already completed some or many of the different "pasos" before they reach this point in the hilo. There is a checklist in **Explorer** summative assessment document.

Pasos para preparar tu presentación: These are important steps for students to know what they will focus on for this project. Encourage students to journal their answers, which both helps them stay organized and also accountable to you on their progress.

1. Students should do this project on something that they are truly interested in – this is not the moment for career counseling so if students say that they want to be a famous athlete or musician, they should go ahead and do so!

2. Here again you will need to decide how pair students with Spanish-speaking countries, as in the previous hilo 4 evaluación final. It would not be a problem to have more than one student assigned to a country, since they will be investigating different interests and people. If it turns out that you have multiple students who want to be lawyers in Spain in the future, you may want to reassign countries so that they will be working with different material.

3. Here, students have to find someone who would be able to tell a similar story to the one that they will imagine and share: someone from that country (native to that country, not who just happens to live there now). While students will find different information, ideally they will find something in that person's voice, either autobiographical or an interview online. It should be someone relatively recent, probably still living. When students do research for this section it is a good opportunity to practice appropriate use of the Internet, reliable sources of information, etc.

4. While students have a "role model" that they are using, their story of "how they arrived at their dream" should NOT be an exact copy of this other person's. (The comparison activity should help remind students of this.) Have them research professional programs and opportunities online, with the Google site for that country (ie. google.es, google.ar, google.cl, etc.) as a good starting point. It is fine for them to study in one city, then move to another for further education or a job.

5. The partial model provided below may help students with the language use expectation: they are telling this story in the PAST tense. (This might take some explanation and an example, so that they do not tell the imaginary path that they could take in the future, from this point forward.) Perhaps highlight with them the verbs in the past tenses in this model.

> **Example of student work: Telling life story in past tense**
> Siempre **me había interesado** todo lo que es cocinar y comer. **Solía** invitar a mis amigos y familiares a una cena especial y les **preparaba** platos nuevos cada vez. Recuerdo que una vez mi tía me **dijo** que mi comida era la mejor que **conocía**. En ese momento **decidí** desarrollarme como chef. **Quería** seguir disfrutando de la preparación de platos interesantes y **quería que** la gente siguiera disfrutando de comerlos. Así **solicité** a varios institutos culinarios en Perú y al final **terminé asistiendo** al Instituto Gastronómico en Lima.

Parte I: See the notes and sample above regarding students' personal narratives about past experiences related to a current career/profession of interest.

Parte II: Professional resume: Students will research how to write a professional resume in Spanish and write one for the professional they have chosen to represent and role-play at the Career Fair. There are many resources online to guide students, easily located by searching in google.es, for example www.modelocurriculum.net .

Parte III: To prepare students for their interaction with each other in the Career Fair, we suggest:

1. Ask students to prepare the questions that they will ask the professionals at the career fair. What would they be curious to know?

2. Put students in pairs to practice asking and answering each other's questions.

3. Do at least one mock interaction in front of the class: Ask a student (high-level) to come to the front of the room and pretend that it is the career fair. Ask them the sort of questions one would field at a career fair.

4. Decide what your requirements will be for the career fair and communicate this clearly to students. The document in **Explorer** for a visitor to the career fair may help as a way to guide and motivate students to fully participate.

5. For the Career Fair, have students take turns playing professional and visitor (1–2 days).

MANTA 2 Vida contemporánea

Hilo 6 Relaciones personales

Essential questions:
- ¿Cómo afecta la comunicación a nuestras relaciones personales?
- ¿Cómo nos definen nuestras amistades?
- ¿Cómo influyen nuestras expectativas en el noviazgo?

Student Learning Objectives

Interpersonal Communication: Speaking and writing
- Exchange information about communication in family relationships.
- Express opinions about friendship.
- Exchange messages such as emails, blogs, or social media posts about the influence of social media on relationships.
- Engage in discussions about making good choices when selecting friends.
- Collaborate to give advice to others on solving problems regarding social relationships.

Interpretive Communication: Print, Audio, Audiovisual, and/or Visual Sources
- Demonstrate comprehension of relationships in Spanish-speaking countries from authentic texts, literature, websites, blogs, audiovisual, and audio, including songs.
- Interpret, analyze and evaluate the parent-child relationship in audio and literary sources from Hispanic cultures.
- Analyze and evaluate artwork from a Hispanic culture that depicts a relationship.
- Describe and analyze significant details from audio sources about friendships.
- Interpret and analyze poems from Hispanic cultures about friends and romantic relationships.

Presentational Communication: Spoken and/or Written Presentations to a Variety of Audiences
- Create and produce a scenario that provides advice on problematic relationship situations.
- Convince others to make good choices regarding friends.
- Write a letter or a poem to a special person.
- Describe an ideal friend or soul mate using figurative language.
- Interpret, analyze, and evaluate a poem from a Hispanic culture.
- Produce reflections and journal entries to demonstrate understanding of practices and perspectives of relationships in Hispanic cultures.

Relating Cultural Practices to Perspectives:
- Investigate, explain, and reflect on the relationship between practices and perspectives (beliefs/values/attitudes) about friends, family, and romantic relationships in Hispanic cultures.

Relating Cultural Products to Perspectives:
- Investigate, explain, and reflect on the relationship between products (songs, poems) and perspectives (beliefs/values/attitudes) about friends, family, and romantic relationships in Hispanic cultures.

Connections: Connect with Other Disciplines
- Make connections to content knowledge about poetic terms and literary devices.

Connections: Acquire New Information
- Acquire and apply new information from authentic sources about relationships in Hispanic cultures.

Comparisons: Language
- Make linguistic comparisons of cognates, *si* clauses using imperfect subjunctive in a hypothetical situation, and use of commands vs. present subjunctive when giving advice.

Comparisons: Culture
- Compare cultural similarities and differences of traditions and customs regarding special holidays for family and friends in the U.S. and in a Spanish-speaking country.

School and Global Communities:
- Interact with Spanish speakers about friendships, family, and romantic relationships in Hispanic cultures.

Lifelong Learning:
- Set goals and reflect on progress in using Spanish for enjoyment, enrichment, and advancement.

Suggested Lesson Plan Sequence/Pacing Guide
Manta 2: Vida contemporánea
Hilo 6: Relaciones interpersonales

Focus according to Essential Question Pages in SE	Day (based on 60 min class)	Classroom Activities	Homework/ Formative assessment/ Exit pass
Relaciones familiares: la comunicación pp. 154–167	1	* Introduce unit with viewing, discussion and brainstorming activities * Note to someone you appreciate * Listening prompt for *Antes de empezar* * Comic strip activity: view, summarize, and respond	* Informal letter * Write/draw and defend your own ending to the comic strip
	2	* Listening activities and comprehension checks * Grammar foci for audio source * Write your own letter to the psychologist	* ¡A tejer! formal letter
	3–5	* Pre-reading activities: Prediction, vocabulary, charades * Active reading with note-taking: "No oyes ladrar los perros" * Comprehension checks and discussion * Formative assessment: presentational writing	* Reading and note-taking can be partially assigned outside of class * ¡A tejer! Formative assessment – writing in response to literature
Amistades: cómo nos definen pp. 168–176	6	* Grammar practice: present subjunctive to describe the ideal friend * Poetry reading and response * Reading and responding to popular sayings about friendship	* Reflexión activity
	7	*Pre-reading: brainstorm how to celebrate Friendship Day *Infer vocabulary from context Reading about Friendship Day in Paraguay	* Debate * Creative product for a friend- assigned for later date
	8–9	*Pre-reading: Culture box regarding Don Quijote * Brainstorming about influences friends have on others *Reading "El caso de Jaime" and comprehension questions from text	*Reflexion activity: presentational writing * Te toca a ti interpersonal role-plays
El noviazgo: nuestras expectativas pp. 176–183	10–11	* Pre-viewing discussion activities * Artwork discussion using Y chart, and critiques * Making connections to how art and society influence our ideas and expectations of "love" * Leave a voicemail and write a letter to your soulmate	* Artwork critique and responding to others' forum postings can be HW * Presentational oral and presentation writing tasks
	12–13	* Pre-reading discussion and grammar foci * Listening and reading poem "Me gustas cuando callas" * Literary analysis * Analyzing theme of communication or lack thereof * Following poem structure to write your own	* Part C questions * Reflexión * ¡A tejer! Poem activity
	14–15	* Introduce summative assessment * Students in groups and organizing: choose topic, etc * Student work time	* Students develop and polish their projects outside of class
	16	* Students present summative assessment * Students hand in written reflection * Audience work for students watching	

Hilo 6 Relaciones personales

Introducción ¿A quién amas tú?

Student book page 154
Time estimate: 30 minutes

 A Start by having students view the images and describe what they see to a classmate. After giving students some time to work in pairs, discuss as a class the types of relationships they see demonstrated in the images, the emotions of the characters in the images and what it makes students think about those types of relationships.

 B To build on the vocabulary they already know and prepare them for using it during this hilo, have students fill in the empty house, hand and heart with vocabulary words and phrases that describe the types of relationships students have with family, friends and boyfriends/girlfriends. This organizer is available to print in **Explorer**. You can also do this with small groups or as a class by creating a template on large paper of a house, hand and heart and asking students to fill them in the same way they might do the individual activity. This can be set up like a graffiti activity with each student having a different color marker to make the final products more visually appealing. Obviously students cannot repeat the same word as another classmate. You can leave the posters hanging up on the walls of your classroom throughout this hilo.

 C As an extension activity, have your students write a thank you card to someone who has had a positive impact on their lives.

Antes de empezar *Amor adolescente*

Student book page 155
Time estimate: 30 minutes

 A Before viewing the cartoons Have the class listen to the scenario give in **Explorer** (audio script below). You may want to listen to it twice as a class. Students will then talk with a partner about what kind of advice to give each student and then share out with the class. You could come up with additional scenarios on your own or ask students to do so, if you would like further discussion of this sort.

Audio script

Vas a escuchar un escenario sobre dos amigos que tienen una amistad especial pero… algo está pasando. Después de escuchar la fuente auditiva dos o tres veces vas a conversar con unos compañeros para determinar qué consejos le darían a Elena.

Elena y Paco han sido amigos desde la niñez. Viven en la misma vecindad y siempre han pasado mucho tiempo juntos. Además asisten a la misma escuela y tienen el mismo horario. Después de las clases Paco siempre camina con Elena a la casa. Recientemente Elena ha empezado a pensar que posiblemente Paco puede ser más que un amigo. Paco es su mejor amigo y no quiere arriesgar su amistad, pero tampoco quiere perder la oportunidad de ser su novia. ¿Qué le aconsejarías?

 B 1. As students read through the comic, have them write out definitions or other ways of expressing the sayings that the characters use.

 2. Then have students read through the cartoon and write a one to two sentence summary of what happens in each strip in the series.

 3. Finally, have students discuss the questions with a partner and get students to comment on why Baldo looks different in the last strip than he does in the rest. Is Baldo dreaming? Does he actually meet up with Estella in the park?

 D Have students write the final scene of this cartoon strip. What does Estella say? Then have students write a paragraph in which they explain why they chose that ending.

¿Cómo afecta la comunicación nuestras relaciones familiares?

Actividad 1 ¿Son normales los conflictos entre los hermanos?

Student book page 156
Time estimate: 60 minutes
Grammar in context: stem changing present tense verbs (o-ue, e-ie, e-i), *cuanto más* + present subjunctive, *deber* and its meaning, present subjunctive to request advice

 A 1. Having students complete the Venn Diagram (available in **Explorer**, Recursos, Organizadores gráficos) holds them accountable to the successful completion of this task.

 2. These vocabulary exercises are meant to get students interacting with the vocabulary and with each other, so that when the words come up in this activity's audio source they are ready. You could choose to do a vocabulary quiz or have students complete a homework assignment using these for extra practice as you deem best.

3. In pair and whole-class conversation here, have students practice using the target vocabulary in their answers to the questions.

B This audio source is under Fuentes for this hilo in **Explorer**. Students will hear it twice and can take notes. After listening for the first time, they have the chance to compare what they understood with a classmate.

« | » | Audio script

Este informe que se titula "La rivalidad", se emitió por la emisora Radio Araucano en junio de 2005.

Doctora Anselmo: Buenos días. El tema de nuestro programa hoy es la rivalidad entre hermanos. El otro día recibí esta carta de una madre obviamente agitada y agotada. Me escribió lo siguiente:

Brotes de Roscos: Querida doctora Anselmo: Mis dos hijas siempre se pelean. Ya tienen doce y nueve años y hace años que no se llevan bien. Casi siempre es algo sin importancia: Mami, me hizo una mueca. Mami, me pellizcó. Mami, Sarita tiene mi muñeca. Estoy harta y desesperada. No sé qué hacer. ¿Esto es normal?

Teresa Brotes de Roscos

Doctora Anselmo: Muchos padres me han escrito preguntando lo mismo. Esta conducta es una realidad donde hay niños que están obligados a compartir espacio, juguetes y padres. Esto es algo básico en el desarrollo infantil.

La rivalidad entre hermanos regularmente comienza mucho antes de la preadolescencia, con el nacimiento de un nuevo bebé. El proceso de resolver el conflicto de separación de los padres se interrumpe con la llegada de un hermanito. El hermano mayor percibe al nuevo bebé como un invasor.

Afortunadamente hay factores culturales en las familias latinas que pueden aliviar esta rivalidad. Las familias latinas suelen ser muy unidas y esperan la mejor colaboración entre todos, incluyendo los abuelos. Esta intimidad favorece mucho a la familia latina con su deseo de minimizar los conflictos entre los hermanos.

Una de las causas principales de rivalidad surge cuando los padres muestran preferencia por uno de los hijos a expensas del otro y cuando los padres no son sensibles a las diferencias de edad y personalidad.

Por ejemplo, un hijo mayor siente la presión de ser perfecto y es muy exigente consigo mismo y con su hermano menor. Los padres no deben estereotipar a sus niños. Deben darse cuenta que algunos de ellos no van a poder alcanzar sus esperanzas. Cuanto más les den a los niños la oportunidad de crear un sentido positivo de sí mismos, más sanos serán. Proporcionarles responsabilidades que concuerdan con su edad y personalidad ayudaría a darle un sentido del valor de su propia personalidad. Hasta la oveja negra necesita saber que sus padres le aprecian por quien es.

A veces estos conflictos no desaparecen y siguen hasta que son adultos. Generalmente estos conflictos perpetuos se deben al hecho de que los padres nunca ayudaron a sus niños a enfrentar las rivalidades. Desgraciadamente muchas veces se deben estos conflictos severos al hecho que algo anda mal en la familia. En estos casos los padres y los niños deben buscar la ayuda de un profesional.

Pues, ya es la hora. Hasta mañana. Señora Brotes, recuerde Ud. que siempre hay esperanza.

As students listen a second time, have them complete the sentences according to what they hear. This is to guide their listening; it is OK if they are not able to correctly complete every one! The worksheet with the questions for part C is in **Explorer**, in the Apoyo adicional para actividades section for this hilo.

Answers for Part C:
1. Los conflictos entre hermanos son parte del **desarrollo** infantil.
2. La rivalidad entre hermanos empieza **mucho antes de la pre adolescencia** cuando el hermano mayor percibe al bebé como **un invasor**.
3. Las familias latinas suelen ser **muy unidas** y como resultado minimiza **los conflictos (entre los hermanos)**.
4. Una causa principal de la rivalidad es **cuando los padres muestran preferencia por uno de los hijos/cuando los padres no son sensibles a las diferencias de edad y personalidad**.
5. El hijo mayor se siente la presión de **ser perfecto**.
6. Los niños necesitan la oportunidad de tener sentidos **positivos de sí mismos**.
7. Es buena idea proporcionarles **responsabilidades que concuerdan con su edad y personalidad**.
8. Si no pueden resolver los conflictos, pueden **buscar la ayuda de un profesional**.

¿Qué aprendiste?

This is a separate audio fuente in **Explorer** for this activity, with only the questions, not the audio script; there is a 20-second pause between each question. This is important listening practice for students, as questions are not printed! You may play the audio source two or three times. Encourage students to treat this like a test; for example, if they have time, students read ahead to see what the answer choices are for the next question even before hearing the question. Students can complete this task on the same worksheet as they started for Part C; they can also take this as a multiple-choice quiz online in **Explorer**.

« | » | Audio script

"La rivalidad" questions

1. ¿Qué tipo de carta acaba de recibir la doctora?
2. ¿Por qué dice la doctora que estos conflictos suelen ser normales?
3. ¿Cuándo empieza la rivalidad entre hermanos?
4. ¿Qué factores favorecen a las familias latinas en aminorar estos conflictos?
5. ¿Cuál es uno de los modos de resolver estos conflictos?
6. Si no pueden resolver los conflictos, ¿qué pueden hacer los familiares?

Answers for ¿Qué aprendiste?:
1. B   4. C
2. B   5. D
3. A   6. B

D The grammar review here is an excellent way for students to focus on specific grammatical points in the audio source. You may want to listen to it one more time for both grammatical points, or once through for each grammatical concept. Discuss and take questions. Note that questions for part D. follow on p. 160 of the textbook.

¡A tejer!

Students practice formal writing skills in this task and also make a personal connection. Emphasize that this can be a fictitious situation and does not require students to share anything that makes them uncomfortable. The strategy boxes give sentence prompts for how to structure the letter and maintain the formal register. Note the use of present subjunctive with the prompts *Necesito que… Qué me recomiendas que…* After students write e-mails as a homework or in-class task, extend the interpersonal writing task to include students exchanging emails and responding as the doctor to the problems in the e-mail they receive. Students can use the email template available in **Explorer** and respond to each other's letters on the digital forum there.

¿Cómo afecta la comunicación nuestras relaciones familiares?

Actividad 2 ¿Cómo afectan a los padres las decisiones de sus hijos?

Student book page 160
Time estimate: 3 classes with reading assigned for HW
Grammar in context: perfect tenses using haber: present perfect, present perfect subjunctive, past perfect, past perfect subjunctive, and conditional perfect

A **3.** The idea of giving a selection here is so that students familiarize themselves with some key vocabulary (the vocabulary italicized in this selection is glossed in student text). It also allows them to have a glimpse into the story and predict what might be happening. The black-and-white image on p. 161 should help with comprehension of the reading selection and the prediction task.

4. Students can now read the definitions for the italicized words in the reading selection. Vocabulary box is on the following page in the student textbook. With a partner, they should go back to re-read the selection and make sure they understand, again using the image for assistance.

5. This second set of vocabulary includes words that have to do with physical movements. There are different ways that you can teach this vocabulary: with images, or with motions (Total Physical Response/TPR is an appropriate method here). If possible have students do something other than, or in addition to, writing the translation of the word in English in their notebooks. Playing charades is a great way to check for comprehension and have fun! Divide the students into two or more teams and see who can guess the word the fastest, or assign them turns and use a timer to give them ten seconds to decide as a team. If they don't get the right answer, the turn (and the point) goes to another team. You can also do charades in small groups of three or even two students each, and there is more chance of everyone being engaged. There are picture flashcards for this activity in **Explorer** as well.

B This graphic organizer, available to edit and/or print in **Explorer**, is an opportunity for students to record their findings and then afterwards, be ready to constantly refer back to the text when discussing the story with their classmates. Encourage them to not forget the last column where they note the corresponding line in the text! It is a long story so they will be glad to know where to go back to in the text.

C **2.** Use this as a comprehension check along with the complete graphic organizer and ensuing student conversations to see that students understood the text and to clarify any misunderstandings.

Answers for Part C:
1. Falsa – No lo acompañó porque está muerta/se falleció.
2. Falsa – Iban a Tonaya para buscar ayuda médica.
3. Cierta
4. Cierta
5. Falsa – Explicó cómo y por qué su hijo le había decepcionado.
6. Cierta
7. Falsa – Ignacio estaba muerto cuando llegaron a Tonaya.

¡Tu opinión cuenta!

These questions are scaffolded up the levels of Bloom's Taxonomy. You may choose to assign certain questions to some students and all questions to other students, as best fitting their skills and abilities. After students have time to converse in pairs or groups of three, call on specific individuals or groups to report back to the class on what they discussed.

¡A tejer!

These options are tiered and meant to be assigned to different students based on ability, or students could choose based on their interest. Option 3 might be extended to a presentational oral activity, since students could read their monologues to the class. Students can complete this assignment in **Explorer** if you choose.

¿Cómo nos definen nuestras amistades?

Actividad 3 ¿Por qué son los amigos valiosos en nuestra vida?

Student book page 168
Time estimate: 1 60-minute class plus another 30 minutes
Grammar in context: Subjunctive after the indefinite antecedent

A Students should write about 5 sentences using "Busco un amigo/a que…" Use the vocabulary from the list at the end of the hilo as needed. Refer the students to the Apoyo adicional para actividades for this hilo in **Explorer**. There is a link to a Laura Pausini song on "La amistad."

B Have a student read the poem aloud. Then individually students will identify words or expressions in the poem that define a friend and record the vocabulary in their journals.

 C Have students add words to their list of "cualidades de un amigo." Discuss the words or expressions and comment on the rhyme (a, b, a, b/a, a, b, b) and overall meaning of the poem. At this time students should be able to compose their own definition of an ideal friend or friendship. Have them write one with a classmate and post to a forum in **Explorer** or to their favorite social media site.

D Have students read the quotes from famous people aloud and discuss the meaning of one or two. Ask them if they have any other "refranes" to contribute. Working in pairs, have them choose one refrán in the activity, discuss what it means, draw a representation of it, and share with the class.

  Reflexión

 This can be assigned as HW or uploaded to the class wiki or blog: have students write a message in their journal to a friend about why they appreciate them, using the new vocabulary. They can also do it as an exit card for the end of class.

¿Cómo nos definen nuestras amistades?

Actividad 4 ¿Sabes que hay un Día Mundial de la Amistad?

Student book page 170
Time estimate: one 60-minute class then 30 minutes day 2 for debate

A Students activate their background knowledge and vocabulary about celebrations such as celebrating a Friendship Day. Students can complete this task in **Explorer**.

B Have students interpret the meaning of the italicized words in the text from the context by making inferences, and then explain their answers to a classmate.

> **Answers to Part B:**
> - A la usanza tradicional de antaño = las costumbres tradicionales del pasado
> - Crudo invierno, con 32 grados centígrados de temperatura a la sombra = en el invierno, el 30 de julio, era 32°C = 89.6°F, es decir que hacía mucho calor aunque fuera invierno en el hemisferio del sur!
> - Los especialistas ya hablan de "tecno autismo", incapacidad de expresar las emociones personalmente = como son tan "enchufados" los jóvenes, se dice que son como autistas (sin habilidades sociales e incapaces de expresar emociones)
> - Las relaciones humanas en cambio, son impredecibles = no se puede predecir cómo se van a interactuar los humanos
> - para esta generación salir a la realidad puede resultarle un proceso "estresante" = los jóvenes que tienen que socializar cara a cara se ponen muy estresados.
> - Los padres deberían de estar alerta y ayudarles a establecer las fronteras entre estos dos mundos, el personal y el virtual = es la responsabilidad de los padres de poner límites entre lo personal y lo virtual (en línea)

C Students will debate the content in the reading about the Día de la Amistad en Luque (Paraguay) when the journalist says that "specialists are concerned about *tecno autismo*" among the young people who are stressed about meeting face to face. Divide the class into two groups, and debate their thoughts about that declaration. The debate strategies are in the student text.

 Culture box: Have students read and discuss similarities and differences in customs between U.S. and Paraguay. What would U.S. students do to celebrate the day of friendship in their community? Talk with a classmate and then share with the class.

 ¡Te toca a ti!

 This can be a fun formative assessment having students creating something special in Spanish for a friend who speaks Spanish!

Links in Explorer include:

Canciones de la amistad y el amor:

    a. "La amistad" de Laura Pausini

    b. "Amigos" de Juan Luis Guerra

    c. "Amigos" de Los Enanitos Verdes

    d. "Me enamoré de ella" de Juan Luis Guerra

    e. "La llave de mi corazón" de Juan Luis Guerra

Have students research other songs about friendship in Spanish!

¿Cómo nos definen nuestras amistades?

Actividad 5 ¿Cómo nos influyen los amigos?

Student book page 173
Time estimate: 2 90-minute class periods if you assign the reading for homework; Use the first day to get students to choose a scenario to act out the 2nd day.

 To introduce this activity, have students read the introduction and culture box about Don Quijote and Sancho Panza. Do they think the proverbs on friendship mentioned in the introduction are still true today, 400 years later? Depending on your time frame, you may want to have students read some of Don Quijote or access more information online.

 A Students have the opportunity to talk about the influence of friends. You may want to assign one question to 3 different groups of students to answer more in depth or form groups of 4–5 students to answer the questions. Students can also discuss this online in the **Explorer** discussion forum. A discussion should arise from the answers in which the whole class will participate. Ask for specific examples of influences friends have on each other, both positive and negative, in regard to their social lives and behaviors.

B As students read the texts, have them think about what they would do in similar situations or if they know others who have been in similar situations. Please note that the text from Spain reflects a cultural difference about the use of marijuana, since it is legal throughout the country to smoke in public. This is not the stereotype of a typical teenager.

 C The answers to these questions can also be found in **Explorer, Recursos, Sólo para los profesores**.

Actividad 5

¿Cómo nos influyen los amigos?

C Respuestas:

1. Se ve en seguida cómo son las personas por la forma que tienen de pasar el rato.
2. Se portan tontos, dicen bobadas, te ríes con ellos, todo es muy superficial, no se puede ser íntimos con ellos porque si te descuidas, te dan en las narices (te pegan en la cara).
3. Si "los colegas" te llaman todos los días cuando estás estudiando, acabas saliendo con ellos y en vez de estudiar, te pones perezoso también.
4. Cuando Jaime tenía catorce años, sus amigos fumaban porros e iban a los discos; era difícil no enviciarse y seguir lo que hacían ellos.
5. Lo más difícil era cuando no quería fumar porros, lo excluyeron del grupo y no tenía adónde ir.
6. Jaime tuvo suerte porque encontró otros amigos que hacían mucho deporte, iba a jugar con ellos a sus casas y venían a la suya, se aficionó a la bicicleta y a leer. También jugaba partidos a las diez de la mañana los domingos.
7. El Profesor Aguilar quiere que todos los jóvenes entiendan que seleccionar amigos es sensatez, porque rodearse con amigos que tienen un bien mutuo y con quienes quieres codearte es lo que realmente importa en una amistad.

 Reflexión

 Students will write a reflection using the imperfect subjunctive and conditional tenses. They can complete this task in **Explorer** if you wish.

 ¡Te toca a ti!

 Students will role play how they can influence or advise others when it comes to selecting friends. There are several options and at the end they can give advice on how to avoid "bad company."

¿Cómo influyen nuestras expectativas en el noviazgo?

Actividad 6 ¿Cómo formamos nuestras ideas y expectativas del amor?

Student book page 176
Time estimate: 30 minutes with HW (presentational speaking task)

 A 1. Before students turn in the book to see the artwork, have them complete the first part of activity A by drawing a picture of what they think of when they hear the words "love," "dating," or "romance." Examples might be a mother hugging her child or a couple enjoying a candlelit dinner. Have students share these with a partner and then put some up around the room so that students can discuss, as a class, similar themes or images that appear in their artwork.

B 1. Give your students a few minutes to look at the artwork (on page 178) without talking or sharing anything with a partner or the class. Then pair them up and have them work through the questions together. A Y chart is available in **Explorer** under organizadores gráficos. As a class you may want to discuss certain questions to see how well students were able to respond to the prompts.

2. For the critique students can use the vocabulary in an upcoming hilo, as mentioned in the student textbook. Go over these words and phrases together; if students are unsure they can work in pairs or groups of three. You can have students write these in class or for homework. You could also have them post these on the discussion forum provided in **Explorer** so that other students can interact with them.

C 1. This activity is meant to help students realize how what they see and hear about relationships impacts their perspectives on love and dating. A copy of the graphic organizer is in **Explorer**. An example might be:

Obras	Cómo ha influido tu perspectiva	Características de tu futura alma gemela
Comedias románticas	Las chicas son dependientes en hombres guapos para ser felices.	Mi alma gemela va a ser feliz consigo mismo sin depender en nadie más.

3. Have your students record their messages using the space provided in **Explorer**.

4. In the Actividad opcional provided in **Explorer** students can learn how to write a "love letter" in Spanish! If you want to share these as a class, you might ask students to write to a famous person from history or a celebrity instead of someone their age.

¿Cómo influyen nuestras expectativas en el noviazgo?

Actividad 7 ¿Cómo influyen las expectativas en una relación romántica?

Student book page 179
Time estimate: 2 class periods with homework
Grammar in context: the verb *gustar* when used interpersonally, the past subjunctive with como si

Teacher Note: The connections to English Language Arts curricula are descriptive and figurative language (metaphors), poetry analysis. This activity features a poem by Pablo Neruda, "Me gustas cuando callas." Refer back to the culture box on Pablo Neruda – hilo 4 act 3, page 98.

 2. This use of the verb *gustar* will probably be new to most students. Review it and if students like, they could come up with short skits using the verb in an interpersonal way.

 1. The idea here is to give students the chance to hear the poem first, before reading it. We have provided a link in **Explorer** but there are many versions available online so you might find your own! It is also possible to find a YouTube version of Pablo Neruda reading his own poem.

 2. Read the poem aloud while students read along in the text. You could do this more than once, the second time the poem is read, pause briefly to clarify certain words or ideas. However, make sure you read the poem in its entirety two or three times before getting deeper into the details.

Vocabulary answers for Part C 1:

Verso del poema	Palabra en español	Cognado en inglés
1	ausente	absent
6	emerges	emerge
7	pareces (del verbo aparecer)	appear
10	distante	distant
14	silencio	silence
16	lámpara/simple	lamp/simple
17	constelada	constellation

Vocabulary answers for Part C 2:
1. Eres como la noche, callada y constelada
2. simple como un anillo
3. mariposa de sueño
4. claro como una lámpara

Text interpretation answers for Part C 3:
a. 1) Habla un narrador que está enamorado de una mujer. Dirige el poema a ella.
   2) Hay cinco estrofas y 24 versos. Cada estrofa contiene 4 versos.
b. 1) ausente, llena (del alma mía), distante, quejándote, callada, constelada, distante, dolorosa
   2) Tu silencio es "claro como una lámpara, simple como un anillo... es de estrella, tan lejano y sencillo" (líneas 16, 18)
c. 1) te pareces a mi alma; te pareces a la palabra melancolía; eres como la noche
   2) Mariposa de mi alma; mariposa en arrullo
   3) Parece que los ojos se te hubieran volado; parece que un beso te cerrara la boca; Distante y dolorosa como si hubieras muerto
   4) Variarán las respuestas.
   5) Variarán las respuestas.

5. This is the kind of writing task that again connects to English Language Arts standards and the Common Core. Students need to be able to state what their main idea is before they start; you might ask them to note this for you as well as textual evidence from the poem before they begin. This increases their chances for success! You can grade this using the presentational writing rubric if you would like, preferably after students have the chance to receive feedback on their first draft from you and/or peers and rewrite.

In **Explorer**, there is a poem template to guide students in structuring their creative piece. You could choose to give students the options of a more free-form poem, if they would like; however, some students will really need the structure the poem template provides to be able to complete this activity. If there are students resistant to writing a love poem perhaps there are alternative products they could create to show their comprehension and creativity! You know your students best!

Essential questions:
- ¿Cómo afecta la comunicación a nuestras relaciones personales?
- ¿Cómo nos definen nuestras amistades?
- ¿Cómo influyen nuestras expectativas en el noviazgo?

Hilo 6 Evaluación final — *Jóvenes de hoy*

Student book page 184
Time estimate: 2 90-minute class periods over a period of at least one week; one class period for students to work together for planning the role plays and another for them to present or show the filed product to the class so other students can respond.
Grammar in context: past perfect subjunctive ("si" clauses), present subjunctive, familiar and plural commands

This summative assessment aims to have students work collaboratively to develop a script for a "public service announcement" type video that will be uploaded to a website, *Jóvenes de hoy*, to provide advice to teens from teens on topics relating to relationships. Go to your **Explorer** course for details and checklists.

Suggestions: While the grammar needed for the summative assessment is outlined earlier in Tejidos, you may want to review the grammar (si clauses with imperfect subjunctive, present subjunctive and familiar or plural commands) necessary to successfully participate in Parts II & III of this summative assessment, perhaps by modeling with the whole class.

In order for students to be placed in a group where they will work well and be motivated, consider asking students for their preferences (1–3) for family/friendship/relationships. This way, you can take this into consideration as well as aiming for mixed-level groups.

While group work can be challenging to assess at the individual student level, you can rate students' presentational oral skills based on their individual participation in the role play (Part I). Also, Parts II & III were designed to be able to individually assess students' writing abilities and grammar usage.

Parte I: Un escenario, presentado en grupo

You may wish to assign roles or ask students to decide them among themselves and report back to you: a Secretary is definitely necessary to take notes and write the script, and a Director is usually a very good idea with group skits. A Timekeeper may also be helpful to keep the group on track. Consider breaking the group work up into discrete parts and assigning a deadline to each: "I need your skit idea and roles by the end of class;" "I need a complete script handed in by…" etc.

Paso 1: You may have to assist students in brainstorming ideas here but hopefully the list of "possible topics" will help! Review the options for the topics in the student text with the groups.

Pasos 2 & 3: Insist that all students participate in the creation of the script as well as having a speaking role, however minimal.

Paso 4: These suggestions or advice for young people make this video like a Public Service Announcement for a website that aims to share advice for teens from teens. Review scripts and advice they provide with each group so that they are appropriate. If you wish you can make this part of the requirements optional.

Paso 5: Options for the presentation of the role-plays: Act them out in class and have someone film, or have students film them outside of class and hand in their video to you, then watch videos with the whole class. Remember that students must see each other's skits to respond to them (Part III.)

Parte II: Trabajo individual

This is an individual 100 word written reflection where students come up with an alternative situation for one of the characters in the role-play. If…. were to have done…., then…. Students use the appropriate grammatical structures (imperfect subjunctive with conditional tenses.)

Parte III: Trabajo de la audiencia

Students will view all the class role-plays live or in video format. The goal is that they will provide advice to one or more of the characters using two familiar commands, one in the affirmative and the other negative. They will do this for a minimum of three presentations that they see.

MANTA 3 Belleza y estética

Hilo 7 Belleza y moda

Essential questions:
- ¿Cómo varían las definiciones de la belleza en otras culturas?
- ¿Quién tiene el poder de definir la belleza y la moda?
- ¿Cómo se puede concientizar a la gente de una definición más amplia de la belleza?

Student Learning Objectives

Interpersonal Communication: Speaking and Writing
- Describe how beauty is defined in other cultures.
- Exchange information about beauty and fashion throughout history and in different cultures.
- Discuss and demonstrate knowledge about beauty and fashion products, practices and perspectives from different cultures.
- Express opinions about the ideal concept of beauty imposed by society and how that definition can be expanded.
- Exchange messages such as emails, blogs, or social media posts about beauty and fashion preferences, including the influence of celebrities' preferences.
- Engage in discussions on self-esteem and stereotypes related to beauty and fashion.
- Explain the influence of the fashion industry, media, and celebrities on beauty and fashion.

Interpretive Communication: Print, Audio, Audiovisual, and/or Visual Sources
- Demonstrate comprehension of concepts of beauty in Spanish-speaking countries from a variety of authentic texts, literature, websites, blogs, and audiovisual sources.
- Interpret, analyze, and evaluate information from authentic texts, promotional materials, audiovisual, and websites about beauty and fashion.
- Analyze and evaluate an article from a Hispanic culture on the importance of "image."
- Describe and analyze significant details about beauty from promotional audiovisual sources.
- Interpret and analyze perspectives on beauty and fashion preferences from indigenous Hispanic cultures.

Presentational Communication: Spoken and/or Written Presentations to a Variety of Audiences
- Collaborate to create, produce, and present a fashion product inspired from an indigenous culture.
- Develop a written and oral promotional product featuring a healthy concept of beauty.
- Write and record a personal definition of beauty, including how it is connected to a culture.
- Describe concepts of beauty and/or fashion throughout history and in indigenous Latin American cultures.
- Interpret, analyze, and evaluate how the concept of beauty changes and continues to change over time in various cultures.
- Produce reflections and journal entries to demonstrate understanding of practices and perspectives about beauty and fashion in Hispanic cultures.

Relating Cultural Practices to Perspectives:
- Investigate, explain, and reflect on the relationship between fashion and beauty practices and perspectives (beliefs/values/attitudes) about beauty and fashion of Hispanic cultures.

Relating Cultural Products to Perspectives:
- Investigate, explain, and reflect on the relationship between fashion and beauty products and perspectives (beliefs/values/attitudes) about beauty and fashion of Hispanic cultures.

Connections: Connect with Other Disciplines
- Make connections to mathematics and art about Da Vinci's concept of human perfection.

Connections: Acquire New Information
- Acquire and apply new information from authentic sources about beauty and fashion in Hispanic cultures.

Comparisons: Language
- Make linguistic comparisons of cognates, ordinal and cardinal numbers, relative pronouns, and use of "let us"/*nosotros* commands.

Comparisons: Culture
- Compare beauty and fashion in Western cultures with those of indigenous cultures in Latin America.

School and Global Communities:
- Interact with Spanish speakers about products, practices, and perspectives of beauty and fashion in Hispanic cultures.

Lifelong Learning:
- Set goals and reflect on progress in using Spanish for enjoyment, enrichment, and advancement.

Suggested Lesson Plan Sequence/Pacing Guide

Manta 3: Belleza y estética
Hilo 7: Definiciones de la belleza

Focus according to Essential Question Pages in SE	Day (based on 60 min class)	Classroom Activities	Homework/ Formative assessment/ Exit pass
Varias definiciones de belleza en diferentes culturas pp. 192–202	1	* Introduce unit with word splash and discussion activities * Critical reading of quote and response	* Paragraph response
	2–3	* Pre-reading activation activity with critical response to quotes * Reading while making connections with vocabulary and time periods * Graphic organizer to show comprehension * Formative assessment: three paragraph written composition	* Reading and graphic organizer can be assigned as HW in part or in full * ¿Qué aprendiste? Formative assessment: 3 paragraphs
	4–5	* Pre-reading activity: Infer vocabulary * Active reading of first text with graphic organizer for cultural analysis * Reflexión and pie chart group activity before moving onto second text * Complete cultural analysis with reading of second text * ¿Qué aprendiste? 4 paragraph essay *(you may want an extra Writer's Workshop day for this)*	* Reading and note-taking can be partially or fully assigned outside of class * Reflexión response to first text * ¿Qué aprendiste? Formative assessment – 4 paragraph essay
El poder de definir la belleza y la moda pp. 202–207	6	* Brainstorming and conversation pre-reading activities * Annotating text	* Text annotation * Timeline activity can be assigned as homework
	7	* Comprehension checks from yesterday's reading: Timeline activity and conversation * ¡Tu opinión cuenta! extension activity (can be finished for HW) * Viewing and responding to celebrity photographs	* ¡Tu opinión cuenta! Formal interpersonal writing task * Journal prompt after seeing photos
Hacia una nueva definición de belleza pp. 207–217	8 – 9 + optional workshop day	* Discussion and vocabulary exercises activators * Viewing, discussion, and active reading of first text source * Interpersonal writing formative assessment * Viewing activities for video and discussion response * Vocabulary preview and reading of second text * Debate in class * ¡A tejer! projects could be done in class (Workshop day)	* Reading and graphic organizer may be assigned or completed as homework * Interpersonal writing task (tiered formative assessment) * Vocabulary in context fill-in-the-blank exercise * ¡A tejer! projects
	10 + optional workshop day	* Reflection, discussion and vocabulary pre-reading exercises * Guided reading with paragraph-by-paragraph guiding questions * Discussion of text and sharing out * Two formative assessments: presentational speaking and presentational writing	* Reading and note-taking could be assigned in part or in full for homework * ¡Tu opinión cuenta! And ¡A tejer! Formative assessments
	11	* Present summative assessment	* Students develop and polish their projects outside of class

Hilo 7 Belleza y moda

Introducción ¿Puedes tú definir la belleza?

Student book page 192
Time estimate: 30 minutes

A Before your students start this unit on definiciones de belleza, have them brainstorm their ideas about beauty. You can use the large bubble letter handouts in **Explorer** if using technology for this activity would be difficult. Another way to do this and incorporate technology is to use a website like Wordle.net or Tagxedo.com (much like Wordle, but allows you to create word clouds in the shape of words) to create a word cloud for "Belleza." They should include synonyms, similar words, words they associate with beauty, quotes or song lyrics in the text of their word cloud. Students can send these to you electronically, they can print them out, or they can embed them in a class blog, wiki or webpage. Students can do this for homework one night and bring it to class to begin the discussion the next day.

B Have students work in pairs to share their word clouds, the Venn diagram and then talk about their similarities and differences. Once students have had time to work with a partner on this you can have students share out three of the similarities in each pair's word clouds and write them on the board or on a large poster (or digitally in a wordle) to show the themes all students agree belong with the idea of beauty. You can discuss some of the most distinct differences in the word clouds to talk about how ideas of beauty differ among individuals.

C Students can turn these in on paper, submit them via Todaysmeet.com, Polleverywhere.com or Cel.ly. Instead of 140 characters or less you can make it "en 30 segundos…" and have students record their voices using Audioboo.com, vocaroo.com, or Google Voice telling you in 30 seconds or less how they define beauty.

Antes de empezar ¿Por qué es difícil definir la belleza?

Student book page 192
Time estimate: 30 minutes (assign paragraph to finish as HW)

Refer to the introduction included in the activity to describe the Barrio de las Letras, and/or you can have students visit their website to learn more about this area of Madrid (http://www.barrioletras.com/).

A After reading the quote, you may want students to answer the questions for homework. These questions are easy to answer and there might be better discussion among pairs if students have time to prepare in advance.

B You can tailor this writing activity to best fit the needs of your class. You can provide more specific directions on how students should write this short paragraph, or you can use the directions in the text to guide their writing. Students can submit questions on paper or can post them electronically to a class blog or website

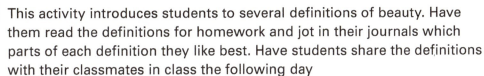

¿Cómo varían las definiciones de belleza en otras culturas?

Actividad 1 ¿En qué se ha basado la belleza a través de la historia?

Student book page 193
Time estimate: 2 60-minute class periods, you may want to assign the reading and graphic organizer for homework
Grammar in context: Agreement of ordinal and cardinal numbers

  A This activity introduces students to several definitions of beauty. Have them read the definitions for homework and jot in their journals which parts of each definition they like best. Have students share the definitions with their classmates in class the following day

 B Have a class discussion on what they might already know about earlier beauty prototypes throughout history; you might have them come to the board and write what they know. The vocabulary text box indicates words that they will encounter in the reading; have them complete a chart that is available in **Explorer** to infer the meaning of the word and which period of history it represents.

 C Have students infer meanings of italicized words from the text and state the corresponding historical period. Complete the chart in **Explorer** (electronic or print.)

  ¿Qué aprendiste?

Formative assessment: How have concepts of beauty over the ages influenced our present day concept? Have students draft three paragraphs following the strategies and examples indicated in the strategy box. They need to include evidence from the *fuente* and add images/drawings or names of people who are considered beautiful according to today's standards of beauty and how those characteristics are influenced by beauty concepts in two or three other periods of time.

Culture box: "Hombre de Vitruvio" de Leonardo da Vinci

Math and beauty connections:

The culture box gives an explanation of the *número áureo*. In English it refers to the golden number/ratio/the divine proportion. Have students research "the golden number" or "*número áureo*" in art.

Here is some background information in Spanish to provide to the students:

Se trata de un número algebraico, que posee muchas propiedades matemáticas y algebraicas interesantes, que fue descubierto en la antigüedad, no como "unidad" sino como relación o proporción. Es el número de oro, Φ (FI), también conocido como la proporción áurea. Es uno de los conceptos matemáticos que aparece una y otra vez ligado a la naturaleza y el arte.

DaVinci propone un hombre perfecto en el que las relaciones entre las distintas partes de su cuerpo sean proporciones áureas (perfectas). Estirando manos y pies y haciendo centro en el ombligo se dibuja la circunferencia. El cuadrado tiene por lado la altura del cuerpo que coincide, en un cuerpo armonioso, con la longitud entre los extremos de los dedos de ambas manos cuando los brazos están extendidos y formando un ángulo de 90° con el tronco. Resulta que el cociente entre la altura del hombre (lado del cuadrado) y la distancia del ombligo a la punta de la mano (radio de la circunferencia) es el número áureo.

¿Cómo varían las definiciones de belleza en otras culturas?

Actividad 2 ¿Qué otros conceptos de belleza hay en otras culturas?

Student book page 197
Time estimate: 2 60-minute class periods with an additional possible Writer's Workshop day; reading and graphic organizers can be assigned as HW

A This is a preview of vocabulary from the first *fuente* to review key words needed for reading the text; have students complete the organizer in **Explorer** (under Vocabulario) or print it for them to do in class/HW.

B While reading they can complete the organizer that is in **Explorer**. Suggestions for reading the first article:

- **Option 1:** In class: Read the first paragraph together and summarize it, then assign small groups to read specific sections of the article: Asia, Africa, Western culture (North America, Latin America or Europe.) This way it is like a jigsaw activity and less reading for everyone; have groups report out at the end. Review the 3 P's (in **Explorer** in *hilo* 1) and an example of each "P" is provided in the student text. Have students complete the organizer in **Explorer** or base it on the abbreviated table in the student book.
- **Option 2:** Homework- read the article and complete the organizer

C This is the second *fuente* for this activity on indigenous cultures. To find out what students already know about Latin-American indigenous cultures, have them complete the pie chart in groups of four. The chart is accessible in **Explorer** in the Apoyo adicional section for this hilo. Then have them read the article.

> Examples of indigenous groups: aztecas, mayas, incas, guaraníes, araucanos, mapuche (hilo 4), quechua, etc.
> 1. Características: físicamente generalmente son bajos, morenos, fuertes, de pelo negro/moreno liso; viven de la tierra: agricultores, cazadores; artesanos,
> 2. Mujeres indígenas: más gorditas, cargan niños en la espalda mientras trabajan, tienen menos oportunidades que las mujeres de la ciudad
> 3. Vestimenta: tejidos, faldas, bordados (embroidery), chales, pieles
> 4. Influencias en la cultura occidental: música, bailes, comidas, palabras, prácticas médicas

D After they have read the article, continue to add to the chart organizer that they started in part B with information from the first reading.

¿Qué aprendiste?

This is a formative assessment on cultural comparisons between cultural perspectives from Western and indigenous cultures from Latin America. Using the information in the chart from parts B and D, they will write a four-paragraph culture comparison between perspectives of beauty in the western cultures and the indigenous cultures of Latin America. Follow the guidelines in the student text and the additional support in **Explorer**.

¿Quién tiene el poder de definir la belleza y la moda?

Actividad 3 ¿Quién decide lo que está de moda?

Student book page 202
Time estimate: 90 minutes

A 1. You can have students brainstorm based on what they know, or you can have them use popular magazines or the web to do some research about what trends are currently popular. The second option would be helpful for students who may not be particularly interested in fashion. They could also create collages in which they illustrate the fashion trends that seem to be showing up consistently in their research. Access the graphic organizer available in **Explorer** so students can individually organize their thoughts, then follow-up with a class graphic organizer using a large poster or a digital tool like Prezi.com. Prezi allows you to search for Google images and YouTube videos relevant to the topic that you can insert into your graphic organizer, which can transform this experience into a truly interactive group graphic organizer.

2. These speaking prompts are targeted to engage students to think about why they wear or don't wear certain articles of clothing. This would also be a great activator for a class discussion once students have had the chance to talk with a partner and organize their ideas.

B 1. This reading strategy will give your students a task to complete while reading that encourages them to reread certain sentences, to ask questions about what they are reading, and bring their attention to the parts of the text they don't understand. You can have students work with a partner to compare their markings or you can have students share out what they marked as a way to ensure that all students are able to comprehend the text. The text is available in **Explorer** to print out or annotate digitally.

2. You can also do this as part of the first reading activity if you do not want students to spend class time reading the text twice. Another option is do this as one of the "Después de leer" activities. You can go over this as a class to make sure that all learners understand the main concepts discussed in the article.

C 1. In this section of the activity you can have students create their timelines on paper or electronically. This could be a homework assignment and then you can start the next class having students compare their timelines. Students can also share their timelines and comment on one another's on the digital forum provided in **Explorer**.

2. You can scaffold this activity however you see fit. If you think your students can respond to these questions without any preparation, pair them up and let them start chatting. If you think your students might need some time to organize their thoughts in response to the questions, have them look in the article and mark where they find the answer. Then have students write some ideas (not write out complete sentences) that will help them answer the questions when they are paired with a friend.

 ¡Tu opinión cuenta!

This is be an optional extension activity based on your timing of the activities in this unit. Alternatively use it as a homework assignment to close out the activities students have been working on in class. An email template is provided as part of the Resources in **Explorer**.

¿Quién tiene el poder de definir la belleza y la moda?

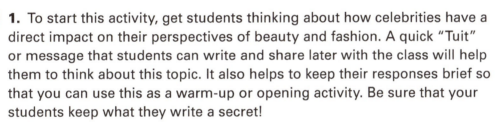

Actividad 4 ¿Cómo influyen los famosos en nuestra moda?

Student book page 205
Time estimate: 45 minutes

 1. To start this activity, get students thinking about how celebrities have a direct impact on their perspectives of beauty and fashion. A quick "Tuit" or message that students can write and share later with the class will help them to think about this topic. It also helps to keep their responses brief so that you can use this as a warm-up or opening activity. Be sure that your students keep what they write a secret!

 2. The second part of the pre-viewing is to be played like 20 Questions. In pairs, students interview their partner asking a variety of interrogatives (Not just yes or no questions!) Students should ask as many questions as they can until they are able to guess which celebrity most inspires their partner.

 Have students do this in pairs or you open it up as a class discussion. The goal of this section is to get students thinking about what they see and build a foundation for the post-viewing activities.

 1. The Think/Pair/Share aspect of this activity gives your students the opportunity to think about their responses before talking with a partner. It also gives you a chance to assess how students are able to respond to these topics in the class discussion.

 2. For the final part of this activity have students complete a written response, or if you have students with strong enough verbal skills you could have them record a message and make it a presentational speaking formative assessment.

¿Cómo se puede concientizar hacia una definición más amplia de belleza?

Actividad 5 ¿Pueden los productos culturales cambiar nuestras perspectivas sobre la belleza?

Student book page 207
Time estimate: 2 60-minute class periods, possible additional workshop day for projects
Grammar in context: Nosotros commands

Note to teachers: In the end even though it's girls here who have body image issues (as highlighted in the Dove video) it's a bigger issue, one that affects boys and it is important for them to know about and be aware or critical about it.

A **2.** Depending on the level of your class you may wish to spend more or less time with these vocabulary words. Some in the right-hand column may not be new to all students but are critical to their comprehension of the text. Allow students to say the cognates for the first set of words in English even if you do not. An exit slip or homework assignment could be to use some of these words in original sentences; it is best to practice using them in context so you may want students to read the article first before having them practice using the words.

B **1.** This link is available in **Explorer**, in the Fuentes auditivas y audiovisuales section for this hilo. This is not something to approach as "look at these pretty new dolls" but rather an academic experience and one that does not connect to students' gender, previous experiences, or likes or dislikes. As such redirect students to the questions at hand as necessary.

C These note-taking exercises are important practice for students to decide what's most important and paraphrase the article in their own words. The graphic organizer is available in **Explorer**.

D **2.** This formative assessment can be assigned for homework and has tiered options of increasing difficulty; consider assigning students Option 1, 2 or 3 depending on their writing level and where they need more practice.

E **1.** Watch the video once so students understand the gist of the content and language. Have students share the message communicated in the video with a partner.

2. In **Explorer** there is a space for students to watch the video and respond with the cause-effect ideas in a digital forum. This could be assigned as a homework assignment.

4. This is a chance for students to practice using vocabulary in context. It is available as an online vocabulary quiz in **Explorer** as well.

> **Vocabulary answers for Part E 4:**
>
> **Estalló** una discusión en mi familia cuando yo **revelé** que quería ser modelo. Mi papá quiere averiguarlo todo y tenía la **hipótesis** que la idea de ser modelo se debía a que yo miraba tantos programas de belleza en la tele. Él suele echarle la culpa a los **medios de comunicación** por todo. Mi hermana mayor se sentía orgullosa de mí porque yo tenía la **confianza** en mí misma para hacerlo, aunque le confesé que me daba miedo la idea de **desfilar en las pasarelas** donde todos estarían mirándome, ¿y si tropiezo? Mi interés en el modelaje coincidió con un **furor mediático** anunciando que las modelos ahora ganaban más dinero que antes. De pronto, mis padres mostraron un **aumento** en su interés por el modelaje y aceptaron mi plan. Me dieron ánimo para que yo no lo viera como algo **inalcanzable**; como siempre dice mi mamá, ¡nunca se sabe lo que es posible hasta intentarlo!

Note to teachers: While there is no "Al leer" for the second text, on page 212, students can find the vocabulary words from the previous exercise and understand their use in the context. To accompany the Dove "Campaña de Dove por la Belleza Real" text you can view the "Evolution" video referenced in the article, available as a Fuente in **Explorer**. Additionally, keep in mind that this text leads to the next activity which is a debate. Between viewing and reading about the new line of dolls, the Part E video, and this write-up from Dove.com.es about their campaign, students have the chance to form an opinion in response to the activity title question: *¿Pueden los productos culturales cambiar nuestras perspectivas sobre la belleza?*

F 1. You want this debate to be a chance for students to express their reactions – positive or negative – to the cultural products that they saw. To that end, while there is always the option to assign students to different sides of a debate, these questions are designed to be more open-ended and invite students to participate with authentic opinions. As the teacher you can play "devil's advocate" and push students to defend their opinions or give evidence from one of the fuentes. If the class is so large that it seems difficult to have everyone participate, consider splitting the class into two circles and have another adult or responsible student help you keep track of participation and play timekeeper to pose the next question.

Here are some suggestions for the student-created products: a collage, a poster, an online ad, a Facebook page, an illustrated slogan, a Power Point/Photostory/video with a slideshow of images. There is a space for students to record themselves in **Explorer**, if they do a presentational oral task for this assignment. You might want to publish or share these products in your school or community in some way!

> ¿Cómo se puede concientizar hacia una definición más amplia de belleza?

Actividad 6 *¿Eres más que una imagen?*

Student book page 213
Time estimate: 1 60-minute class period with homework, possible additional workshop day for projects

A **3.** Word associations help students develop their language abilities and vocabulary. For the exercise on the left, you may need to go over "sustantivo – adjetivo – verbo" with students before beginning. For the cognates exercise on the right, be prepared for students to not know all of these words in English – good SAT practice!

> **Vocabulary Answers for Part A 3:**
>
> **Familias de palabras: Completa la relación entre palabras que comparten la misma raíz.**
> La **belleza** es el sustantivo del adjetivo **bello**.
> La **delgadez** es el sustantivo del adjetivo **delgado**.
> La **juventud** es el sustantivo del adjetivo **joven**.
> El adjetivo **corporal** viene del sustantivo **cuerpo**.
> La **difusión** es el sustantivo del verbo **difundir**.
> La **aparición** es el sustantivo del verbo **aparecer**.
> El **consumidor** es el sustantivo del verbo **consumir**.
> El adjetivo **alimentaria** viene del verbo **alimento** y el sustantivo **alimentar**.
>
> **Cognados: Anota las palabras en inglés.**
> modificar = **modify**
> maleable = que se puede cambiar = **malleable**
> se moldea = **mold**
> el prototipo = un modelo = **prototype/model**
> eterno = **eternal**
> primordial = primitivo, primero, fundamental = **primordial**
> erróneo = equivocado, incorrecto = **erroneous**
> mero = insignificante, no importante = **mere**
> el receptor = la persona que recibe el mensaje = **receptor**
> los medios de comunicación = medios informáticos (la tele, la radio) = **(the) media**

B Students should use this list of guiding questions to focus them on each part of the text. Encourage good note-taking skills during this process. This could be assigned or completed as homework. Afterwards, in Part C, students share out with each other and then as a class. **Note:** Some students may not have seen the use of @ to represent a/o as appears in this text, for example "l@s model@s" to say "los/las modelos/as." You may wish to go over one example together as a class.

¡Tu opinión cuenta!

 Students can access the link to record themselves in **Explorer**. Alternatively, have students give their presentations in class, even if it is a short activity with time to plan their responses and present them orally to a partner or small group. In all cases, they are using presentational oral skills and starting to prepare their ideas for the **¡A tejer!** activity.

 ¡A tejer!

 The graphic organizer in **Explorer** should help students get their thoughts ready before writing. Options for format include: poem, narrative format like a "This I Believe" statement about beauty, Powerpoint slideshow with text and voiceover or Photostory, "word splash" or graffiti-style poster with accompanying paragraph explanation. Direct your students toward one or two options or give them all of these (or more) as you would like. In all cases students should be using presentational writing skills and you can set it up to have them use presentational speaking skills as well. (In this case students would present in front of class or to a group, or record themselves speaking.)

Essential questions:
- ¿Cómo varían las definiciones de belleza en otras culturas?
- ¿Quién tiene el poder de definir la belleza y la moda?
- ¿Cómo se puede concientizar hacia una definición más amplia de belleza?

Hilo 7 Evaluación final — ¿Puedes diseñar un nuevo look para los jóvenes inspirado en una cultura indígena?

Student book page 216
Time estimate: 2 60-minute class periods for presentations; allow some class time every day the week prior to the presentations for students to work in pairs.
Grammar in context: si clauses with imperfect subjunctive and conditional tenses, familiar commands, subjunctive, relative pronouns, past tenses

Note to Teacher:
Students will work in pairs to design clothing (2 articles of clothing and 2 accessories) for young people inspired by clothing and accessories from an indigenous Latin American culture. Announce what the summative assessment entails at beginning of the *hilo* so students can think about who they want to work with and what they want to do. Pp. 216–217 of the student edition introduce the summative assessment in detail. The research on an indigenous group can be done outside class but students will need to meet with their "co-designer" about 15 minutes a day after activities 3 and 4 have been completed. The presentations will take one to two 60-minute class periods. They can present to other groups for practice if some finish before others. Have students do peer assessments to make them accountable for listening to others, then they can vote on the best design to be reproduced on the cover of the company catalog!

Explorer has detailed checklists for this summative assessment. The communication modes are indicated on the summative assessment rubric in the appendices. The link in **Explorer**, polyvore.com directs students to a site that can give them some ideas of what to include in an outfit even though they have to design their own for this summative assessment.

Fuentes for this activity:

Students will choose one fuente from the hilo plus an additional two fuentes of their choice depending on the indigenous culture they want to research. There are several sites that sell indigenous clothing made from sustainable materials.

Some suggestions are:

1. Mapuche – el chamal, adornos de plata, sandalias de cuero, chiripa, ponchos tejidos

2. Hombre quechua – sombreros negros de paño, poncho de lana, alpargatas (sandalias),

3. Mujer quechua- bordados florales, encajes, colores fucsia o turquesa

4. Gauchos de las pampas – botas, ponchos

5. Mayas- huipil

6. Incas- uncu, plumas de aves, lana de vicuña o alpaca

7. Aztecas- pieles de animales, plumas, diversidad y colorido

8. Guarani (Paraguay)

MANTA 3 **Belleza y estética**

Hilo 8 **Artes escénicas y visuales**

Essential questions:
- ¿Cómo interpretan los artistas la realidad y la fantasía en sus obras?
- ¿Cómo refleja el arte una perspectiva cultural?

Student Learning Objectives

Interpersonal Communication: Speaking and Writing
- Exchange information about a variety of art forms and artists from Hispanic cultures.
- Express opinions about how artists interpret reality and fantasy in their artwork.
- Exchange messages such as emails, blogs, or social media posts about art preferences and/or favorite artists.
- Engage in discussions about how artwork reflects cultural perspectives about history.
- Ask and respond to questions about a variety of art forms and their artists.

Interpretive Communication: Print, Audio, Audiovisual, and/or Visual Sources
- Demonstrate comprehension of content from authentic sources about art forms, including music and dance, from Hispanic cultures.
- Interpret, analyze, and evaluate visual arts, musical arts, and theatrical or literary arts from Hispanic cultures.
- Analyze and evaluate cultural perspectives reflected in music and dance from Hispanic cultures.
- Interpret and critique significant details from a work of art from a Hispanic culture.
- Interpret and analyze cultural perspectives reflected in street art from Hispanic cultures.

Presentational Communication: Spoken and/or Written Presentations to a Variety of Audiences
- Retell and/or summarize a story, from a Spanish-speaking country, with the support of student-created illustrations.
- Recreate and interpret a work of art.
- Collaborate with others to present information on a form of art not featured in the student text.
- Describe and analyze the purpose and meaning of street art, such as a mural, from a Hispanic culture.
- Analyze and evaluate a work of art and artist from a Hispanic culture.
- Produce reflections and journal entries to demonstrate understanding of cultural perspectives about forms of art in Hispanic cultures.

Relating Cultural Practices to Perspectives:
- Investigate, explain, and reflect on the relationship between practices (art, dance, music) and perspectives (beliefs/values/attitudes) about art forms of Hispanic cultures.

Relating Cultural Products to Perspectives:
- Investigate, explain, and reflect on the relationship between products (artwork, dance, music) and perspectives (beliefs/values/attitudes) about art forms of Hispanic cultures.

Connections: Connect with Other Disciplines
- Make connections to content knowledge about a variety of visual art forms, literature, dance, and music from Hispanic cultures.

Connections: Acquire New Information
- Acquire and apply new information from authentic sources about a variety of art forms in Hispanic cultures.

Comparisons: Language
- Make linguistic comparisons of cognates, use of gerunds with reflexive pronouns, and the use of impersonal *se* + 3rd person verb forms.

Comparisons: Culture
- Analyze and compare artists and artwork representing different genres from the U.S. and a Spanish-speaking country.

School and Global Communities:
- Interact with Spanish speakers about art and artists in Hispanic cultures.

Lifelong Learning:
- Set goals and reflect on progress in using Spanish for enjoyment, enrichment, and advancement.

Suggested Lesson Plan Sequence/Pacing Guide
Manta 3: Belleza y estética
Hilo 8: Artes visuales y escénicas

Focus according to Essential Question Pages in SE	Day (based on 60 min class)	Classroom Activities	Homework/ Formative assessment/ Exit pass
Interpretaciones artísticas de la realidad y fantasía pp. 222–233	1	* Introduce unit with 4 corners activity and categorizing images * Cultural perspectives * Sharing out of favorite kinds of art	* Cultural analysis graphic organizer
	2	* Y chart and viewing activities around flamenco murals * Practice describing art * Email to artist	* Email to artist * Extension activity: describe art
	3	* Think, Pair, Share on Lady Gaga and Dalí * Vocabulary to describe artists while reading first text * Facebook pages for both artists	* Facebook pages for both artists
	4	* Comparison of artists' work using second text; viewing of their work online * Response to artwork via conversation and 3-paragraph formal analysis	* ¡Te toca a ti! 3-paragraph response
	5–6	* Review of reading strategies * Active reading of "La continuidad de los parques" with visual and written summaries for each section * Artistic retelling of the story	* Visual and written summaries * ¿Qué aprendiste? retelling of the story
La conexión entre el arte y la perspectiva cultural pp. 233–243	7	* Pre-viewing activities about previous knowledge of public art * Viewing of first mural with focus on vocabulary and message * Reading of César Chávez text and response (may be assigned or completed for homework)	* Synthesis activities between first mural and César Chávez text: D 2 and D 3
	8	* Viewing of second mural with focus on visual description and symbols * Bloom's taxonomy tasks – some may be assigned for homework	* Higher-level Bloom's taxonomy tasks
	9	* Vocabulary and conversation around previous knowledge of dance * Reading and viewing activities on Caribbean dances * Comparison of dances and written response	* Graphic organizer and Tweets on different dances * ¡Te toca a ti! as HW/which would need extra time to present in class
	10–11 (or more)	* Present summative assessment * Students research and choose artist and artwork * Students develop their final projects * Presentation of final projects – can be a day for art gallery presentation	

Hilo 8 Artes visuales y escénicas

Introducción ¿Qué tipo de arte te gusta más?

Student book page 222
Time estimate: 45–60 minutes

A   **Graffiti 4 corners instructions**: Have a piece of chart paper in each corner of the room representing the 4 types of art indicated in Part A. Then divide the class into 4 groups. Each group starts in one corner of the room with a different color marker for each group. One student is the scribe and will write the art forms found in that category (Ex: arte aplicado- cerámicas para la comida). After 90 seconds, call time (maraca, bell etc.) and each group moves to the next corner (clockwise) with their marker. The next group cannot start writing until you say BEGIN. next three rounds about 60 seconds per station. At each station they will read what the other groups have written so they will not repeat.

B   In groups of 3 or 4, have students categorize and identify the 12 images according to the three bulleted criteria using the word bank on page 222. They may need to research the artist and the cultural practices. This can be assigned as homework or researched in class by students to then share out. The images are in **Explorer** in an editable graphic organizer. The answers follow on the next page.

Answers from top left to right 2nd row left to right, etc.

1.	escénico	baile- flamenco	Origen en Andalucía, sur de España, popularizado por los gitanos para contar tragedias de la vida y entretenerse
2.	visual	obra de arte de Pablo Picasso	es famoso por el estilo cubista,
3.	visual	tejidos	sirven para ropa, mantas, alfombras, bolsas, etc.
4.	visual	escultura surrealista de Dalí	expresión de la sociedad de esa época
5.	escénico	Mexican mariachi	canciones tradicionales y música de celebraciones
6.	visual	Parque Güell in Barcelona de Antoni Gaudí	un lugar para ir a pasear
7.	visual	esculturas pre-colombianas	representan la gente poderosa de la época
8.	escénico	ballet de Cuba	expresión de movimiento y música
9.	visual	Las Meninas- Velásquez	arte del renacimiento, la familia real
10.	visual	cerámica	arte aplicado- bonito y útil
11.	escénico	el tango- baile de origen argentino	expresión de sentimientos románticos
12.	escénico	la zarzuela (como la ópera)	relata un cuento con música

 ¡Te toca a ti!

Write your name, favorite form of art and an example of that type of art. When everyone has finished, tell them to crumple it into a snowball and when you signal them, students will throw it into the air, not at each other. You may want to model this first. After they have fallen to the floor, everyone picks up one, opens it and reads the information to share with the class.

Antes de empezar *¿Cómo se describe el arte?*

Student book page 224
Time estimate: 45 minutes
Grammar in context: *ser/estar* with descriptions

A As an opener before they read the culture box regarding the artist's life and paintings, use a large poster of the Y chart. (This graphic organizer is available in **Explorer**, Recursos, Organizadores gráficos.) Have students describe what they see, think and want to know. This can be done as a class with a student scribe recording the student responses. Only work on one section of the Y at a time and, staying focused on what they see, describe both murals (no interpretations, etc., just descriptions). Leave the charts up on the board/wall. Students can record a conversation with a friend in **Explorer** in which they discuss the information in their Y Charts.

B Have students read the culture box and take notes in their journals to use when they describe the painting formally and in more detail.

C **1.** In groups of 3 or 4, have students use the expressions in the strategy boxes to describe each of the murals in detail. They take turns saying something but cannot repeat what has already been said. A scribe records what is expressed in order to share out with the class. This may take 5–6 minutes.

2. Share out each group's descriptions with the class again, not repeating what has been said. The purpose is to use the vocabulary expressions and their own thoughts to describe the art in preparation to write an e mail to the artist!

There are numerous resources in Spanish regarding the origin and demonstration of the flamenco art- dance, music and song. Some links are under Enlaces for Antes de empezar in **Explorer.**

> ¿Cómo interpretan los artistas la realidad y la fantasía en sus obras?

Actividad 1 ¿Cómo inspiran las obras surrealistas de Salvador Dalí a Lady Gaga?

Student book page 226
Time estimate: 2 60-minute class periods with homework (Facebook pages for artists the first night; 3 paragraph analysis the second night)

A This Think, Pair, Share activity will give students time to process what they already know about these famous artists. Once students have time to think individually, share with a partner and add any additional information to their charts, give them a chance to share out. Have one student from each pair pretend to be Lady Gaga and the other to be Salvador Dalí. You may want to bring in a blond wig or big pair of sunglasses for the person pretending to be Lady Gaga and a mustache for the person pretending to be Dalí. Then have students introduce their partner to the class, giving a brief description using the information they collected in their T-chart. In **Explorer**, it is possible to have students complete this activity in a digital forum, so that students see each other's responses and learn from one another.

B The first reading activity is designed to have students gather information as they read about each artist, focusing on nouns, adjectives, and verbs in the text. The second reading activity is designed to have students make a comparison about the two artists based solely on their short biographies. This graphic organizer and a Venn Diagram template are available in **Explorer**.

C **2.** This activity can be done electronically, on paper or on poster board. Students will take the information presented in the article and create a Facebook-style page for each artist. Based on the time you have, students can choose one artist, work in pairs or small groups, or complete these for homework. There is a template available for use in **Explorer**.

D In this activity that accompanies the second reading, we want students to be able to identify the specific Lady Gaga performances and the Dalí works that inspired them. On the second reading of the text, students should be able to identify what specific objects or characters of the Dalí works are being imitated in the Lady Gaga performances. Even if students haven't seen either of these before they should be able to identify these from the text. This graphic organizer is available in **Explorer**.

Sample student work for Part D:

Nombre de la interpretación de Lady Gaga	...asociada con qué obra de Dalí	Lo que Gaga emula
Speechless	La tentación de San Antonio	las piernas de los elefantes
gorra de langosta y gorra de teléfono	"teléfono-langosta"	el teléfono y la langosta
nació de un huevo en los Grammy's	"Niño geopolítico observando el nacimiento del nuevo hombre" y la actuación en que Dalí y su esposa salieron de un huevo	el huevo y el nacimiento

E Now it is time for students to start doing a little comparing and contrasting of their own. There are links provided in **Explorer** for the works mentioned in the article; you can either show the links to your students in class or you can give students the links to view the works on their own. If you want to scaffold this, you can assign students to the different pairs of artwork or they can be assigned to view all of them. You can provide learners with a Venn Diagram to help them start the process of analysis and aid them in the conversation.

¡Te toca a ti!

For this three-paragraph essay you can provide your students with more scaffolding by giving them time to complete a Venn Diagram comparing the two works of art and giving them sentence starters for comparing and analyzing artwork. You can also make it more challenging by choosing one of the three comparisons, and giving students a limited time to write their essay, much like the AP Exam.

¿Cómo interpretan los artistas la realidad y la fantasía en sus obras?

Actividad 2 ¿Quiénes serán los amantes?

Student book page 230
Time estimate: 2 60-minute classes
Grammar in context: use of the gerund with reflexive pronouns

A This is meant to activate the students' background knowledge about types of strategies to use when reading a story or novel and how to infer meaning if they don't know all the words. In this activity, students will read one part of four at a time. You can start reading the first part in class and assign the other parts as homework. Whether students work in groups in class or individually, they need to draw a sketch of each scene and then write a summary using key words that they choose from each selection. Model this with part 1 in class. The idea is that each group will post their four visuals to compare interpretations and then points of view on what happened and who was involved.

B From the description of the protagonist have students infer what type of person he may be considering his professional & social position. What do they think is his motive for reading, to pass the time or avoid problems?

C After each part the students will follow this same process:

Visualiza, dibuja y titula: In a group of 2 or 3 have students draw a representation of each part I- IV, give it a title, determine 5-6 words that will help them to recall the details of that part, and then write a brief summary of that part of the story.

D Have students notice the view from his window, does it have any connection to the title? What is the character focusing on in the that novel he is reading?

F Notice the intense and quick series of actions. Is there a reference to the fate of the protagonist?

H Notice the lovers' quick movements as if they were on a film set as they left the cabin and headed in different directions: where did they go, who are they, who entered the house, were they familiar with the house and the area, what is the evidence to support the answers? The idea is that students debate, defending their answers.

¿Qué aprendiste?

There are 3 options for students to demonstrate what they have learned about this story as it relates to the arts. Students can show the images to the class or take a photo with a smart phone and upload their images in **Explorer** for all students to view online.

¿Cómo refleja el arte la perspectiva cultural?

Actividad 3 ¿Qué se puede ver "detrás de" un mural?

Student book page 233
Time estimate: 2 60-minute periods with homework both nights
Grammar in context: Se impersonal and use of the past subjunctive in the last paragraph of the César Chávez text

1. The goal of this Think-Pair-Share is to have students naming what they see in the mural: nouns, actions, and what's happening. The goal is not to make any inferences or conclusions yet, or give opinions. At first, let them work with the vocabulary they have and utilize circumlocution to start talking about what they see.

Reflexión

This is an opportunity to have students write about what they think this mural is trying to say: what is the message? What are we supposed to feel or think as a "take-away"?

Culture box: A good source of information on **César Chávez** is his foundation, a link to which is provided in **Explorer**.

3. At this time, encourage students to prepare some kind of oral presentation, based on availability of time and resources. Students could record themselves speaking (podcast or video style) and while there is a space to do this in **Explorer**, it is preferable to do this in person, if possible. By teaching a classmate, the goal is that the student has to explain their interpretation, defend and justify it, giving examples. If the presentation is in person, have the "student" ask questions of the "teacher." Have students switch to other pairs before switching roles so that the same pair of students does not present to each other. You may want to do peer evaluation with a simple rubric for how well your peer taught this material.

Note to teachers regarding "Rescate": On the right, the two men represent a pre-Columbian agricultural laborer (slave) harvesting corn and modern migrant farm worker in the grapes. The image seems to evoke the Diego Rivera murals in Palacio Nacional in D.F., which depict the history of Mexico. A link in **Explorer** takes you to see this image and the repeated symbol of corn.

E 1, 2 & F 1–4 These steps follow Bloom's taxonomy and are meant to guide students through a progressively more advanced viewing of the second mural and comparison of the two. Step F 4 can also be completed as a presentational writing exercise instead of speaking.

2 b can be completed in **Explorer** in the space provided.

Culture box: As an optional homework assignment you could ask students to search online and find a Diego Rivera mural that they like; they could describe this to the class or a small group of students.

¿Cómo refleja el arte la perspectiva cultural?

Actividad 4 ¿Qué tienen en común los bailes del Caribe?

Student book page 239
Time estimate: 1 60-minute class period with homework (¡Te toca a ti!)

A 2. A good reference here is the Map of Central America available in **Explorer**. Many students need to review when it comes to geography! You could make a quick quiz or game out of this.

D 3. Have students work on this individually or in pairs as you wish. This could be a homework assignment or an in-class activity. The links are in **Explorer** and encourage students to find others that they like as well. Assign each student or pair a dance to research its origins, rhythms and instruments, and famous artists. Have students present their findings to the class in a short oral presentation accompanied by a video of the dance. This could be done online by students posting their videos and voice recordings on the forum provided in **Explorer**, along with the graphic organizer.

¡Te toca a ti!

This is a personalized activity meant to have students share about one of their favorite kinds of art (that they enjoy and perhaps produced themselves) in Spanish to the rest of the class. Students can work together to perform a skit or piece of music but need to each speak and write presentationally in Spanish on their own. This should be open-ended in order to include all students' interests; refer back to the Teacher's Edition page for the introduction to hilo 8 for various examples of types of art. If students need an online resource to find vocabulary relevant to their topic that is not included in the list at the end of the hilo, we recommend www.wordreference.com.

As time and resources allow, you may choose to have students present their kinds of art in person to the class or online. For ways to do this online consider the forum in **Explorer** or a class blog or wiki. Students could record themselves presenting their kind of art and include this as a voice-over to a Power Point file, Photostory or video. Some guidance on what to include in their presentations is included under Opción 1 and Opción 2 for this activity in **Explorer**.

Essential questions:
- ¿Cómo interpretan los artistas la realidad y la fantasía en sus obras?
- ¿Cómo refleja el arte las perspectivas culturales?

Hilo 8 Evaluación final — *Bienvenidos al Museo Tejidos*

Student book page 242

Time estimate: you can allow as little as two days to as much to one week with students working outside of class and during class. Depending on your time frame, schedule the way in which you wish to implement this assignment, and choose a timeframe that works best for you and your students. There is a detailed checklist and outline in **Explorer**.

Pasos para seguir:

1. Elige al artista y obra de arte del mundo hispanohablante que vas a usar: If students are unsure of what constitutes "art" that they could choose for their project, direct them back to the Antes de empezar activity. They could choose a dance, film, a play, a comic strip or cartoon, etc. – anything that could be presented to the class along with the original. If it is a dance, students will need a computer or phone to show their classmates the original dance and their interpretation.

2. Investiga en línea: Make sure that students use legitimate sites for this part, and check for plagiarism. You could require a list websites used of "Sitios usados" to make them accountable.

3. Analiza la obra de arte: Remind students that this is a collection of their ideas and thoughts – there is no one correct answer!

4. Haz tu propia interpretación de la obra: Suggestions: There are many digital resources for creating art, videos, and presentations. Adobe programs for editing video, and animating images are great resources if your school has these in a computer lab. Other options are the simple Paint program, PowerPoint, Keynote, iMovie, Windows Movie Maker, Animoto, Garage Band, Audacity, Vocaroo, etc. Students who want to work offline could use traditional arts and crafts materials, including collage or found objects. The goal is to do your own version of the artwork – some will mirror them much more obviously, other students will choose to do something more abstract. Encourage their creativity!

5. Presenta tu interpretación personal: Here students are doing two things: describing and comparing. The presentation of this information may depend on the format of their own artwork.

The presentation of the museum project is adaptable to your needs and that of your school. Suggestions for creating your museum follow on the next page. In all cases, consider inviting other world language or social studies classes, or other students as you wish!

1. Use the hallway in your school! This is very under-used space in most schools. Have the students post their work and walk around to see that of others.

2. Have a "museum day" in your classroom, rearrange the furniture and have students put their work up on the walls or tri-fold posterboards.

3. Create a digital museum by using a site like blogspot.com or wordpress.com. Students can scan or upload their work, and comment on each other's.

The interactive piece of this project can be interpersonal speaking or writing:

- Students can leave each other questions (on Post-it notes, or in a "guestbook" left by each piece of artwork) and then the artist can respond in writing to several of his/her choice.

- Have two rotations around the museum; have half of the class stand by their artwork. As the other half of the students walk around to view the art, they can ask questions in Spanish of the artist, who need to respond on the spot. If you walk around with a clipboard to take notes on everyone's participation, they will be sure to ask and answer questions in Spanish! Then switch and ask the other half of the class to stand by their artwork and answer questions.

MANTA 4 Identidades personales y públicas

Hilo 9 Héroes y personajes históricos

Essential questions:
- ¿Cómo expresan los seres humanos su identidad en diversas situaciones?
- ¿Cómo puede un individuo contribuir a definir la identidad de una nación?

Student Learning Objectives

Interpersonal Communication: Speaking and Writing
- Exchange information about contributions from heroes and historical figures from Spanish-speaking countries who influence their culture.
- Express opinions about what defines a hero.
- Exchange messages such as emails, blogs, or social media posts about individuals from Hispanic cultures and their contributions to politics, society or culture.
- Engage in discussions about personal and public identities of an individual from a Hispanic culture.
- Ask and respond to questions about individuals from Hispanic cultures who influence and make significant contributions to society.

Interpretive Communication: Print, Audio, Audiovisual, and/or Visual Sources
- Demonstrate comprehension of content from authentic texts and audiovisual sources about heroes, literary, and historical figures from Hispanic cultures.
- Interpret, analyze, and evaluate the contributions of an individual who defined the identity of a nation.
- Analyze and evaluate cultural perspectives reflected in an individual's contributions to society.
- Interpret and summarize significant details about the life of a historical figure from Hispanic culture.

Presentational Communication: Spoken and/or Written Presentations to a Variety of Audiences
- Synthesize and present the political, social, or cultural contributions of a historical figure from a Hispanic culture.
- Write a letter to a hero or historical person from a Hispanic culture.
- Collaborate with others to interview and present information on an individual who has made a significant contribution to politics, society, and/or culture.
- Describe and analyze the political, social, and cultural challenges that individuals face when making changes to a nation.
- Analyze and evaluate the contribution of a historical figure from a Hispanic culture.
- Produce reflections and journal entries to demonstrate understanding of the challenges that individuals overcome to make contributions to society.

Relating Cultural Practices to Perspectives:
- Investigate, explain, and reflect on the relationship between practices (how they are remembered) and perspectives (beliefs/values/attitudes) about heroes, historical, and literary figures from Hispanic cultures.

Relating Cultural Products to Perspectives:
- Investigate, explain, and reflect on the relationship between products (monuments/film) and perspectives (beliefs/values/attitudes) about heroes, historical, and literary figures from Hispanic cultures.

Connections: Connect with Other Disciplines
- Make connections to content knowledge about professions, history, poetry, politics, and culture.

Connections: Acquire New Information
- Acquire and apply new information from authentic sources about heroes, literary, and historical figures from Hispanic cultures.

Comparisons: Language
- Make linguistic comparisons of cognates, adverbs, and irregular past tense forms.

Comparisons: Culture
- Analyze and compare individuals who make significant societal and cultural contributions from two different Hispanic cultures.

School and Global Communities:
- Interact with Spanish speakers about heroes, literary, and historical figures from Hispanic cultures.

Lifelong Learning:
- Set goals and reflect on progress in using Spanish for enjoyment, enrichment, and advancement.

Suggested Lesson Plan Sequence/Pacing Guide

Manta 4: Identidades personales y públicas
Hilo 9: Héroes y personajes históricos

Focus according to Essential Question Pages in SE	Day (based on 60 min class)	Classroom Activities	Homework/ Formative assessment/ Exit pass
Las expresiones de la identidad humana pp. 250–261	1	* Introduce unit with game on famous people in the Spanish-speaking world * Online research on further individuals	* Homework can be further research online, completing graphic organizer
	2	* Finish activity from yesterday with conversation about your response to these individuals * Begin "Julia de Burgos" activity with conversation, listening to poem, first time reading through	* Radioemisión activity as optional homework * Comparison graphic organizer for two sides of Julia de Burgos
	3 + optional workshop day	* Review of poem, comprehension and analysis activities * Artistic representations of Julia de Burgos * ¡A tejer! formative assessments could use a workshop day in class, as time allows	* Artistic representation and explanation * ¡A tejer! formative assessment
	4–6	* Previous knowledge of Federico García Lorca * Active reading and completion of timeline of Lorca's life * Written evaluation of the end of Lorca's life * Listening and reading of "La guitarra" * Analysis of poem: questions and journal prompt	* Completed timeline * Written evaluation (Part C) * Comprehension questions * ¡Tu opinión cuenta! journal response
La contribución de un individuo a la identidad de una nación pp. 262–271	7–8	* Active reading of Eva Perón biography with choosing titles for paragraphs * Viewing of documentary with completion of timeline, Myth or Fact comprehension check * ¡Te toca a ti! tribute to Evita	* Completed timeline * ¡Te toca a ti! formative assessment
	9	* Finishing of any Evita-related activities, sharing of tributes * Preview of Rigoberta Menchú interview * Documentary viewing with foci on imagery, vocabulary, then comprehension check	* Classwork on documentary * Some of tomorrow's reading could be assigned for homework
	9	* Annotated reading of Rigoberta Menchú biography and conversation * Simulated conversation with Rigoberta Menchú * Final activities: Introduction and journal response	* Formative assessments: Simulated conversation (interpersonal oral) and Introduction (presentational oral)
	10–11 (or more)	* Present summative assessment * Students research and choose historical figure * Students develop their final projects * Presentation of final projects	

Hilo 9 Héroes y personajes históricos

Introducción ¿Reconoces a estos íconos del mundo hispanohablante?

Student book page 250
Time estimate: 30 minutes

A In this intro students will be tested to determine what they know about famous people from the Spanish-speaking world. You can give students a time limit and can offer a prize to add to the excitement of the game. The goal is to win the most points. Students will look at the images of the famous people and come up with as much information as they can remember for each person. Any additional information not mentioned in the rules can also count as an additional point (for example if they give the name of a work of art or song they get an additional point). Students can work in pairs, small groups or individually.

In **Explorer**, our tech consultant created a timed slideshow of these images, for a ready-made game for your class!

Answers for Part A:

1. Celia Cruz: Cuba, Cantante, Popularizó la música cubana
2. César Chávez: Estados Unidos, Líder campesino, Fundó la Asociación Nacional de Trabajadores del Campo - después se convertiría en la coalición Trabajadores del Campo Unidos.
3. Don Quijote: Miguel de Cervantes, España, nació en España, escribió esta novela clásica del siglo 17, inspirándose en las novelas de caballería de la Edad Media en las cuales los caballeros andantes tuvieron muchas aventuras con el fin de acabar con las maldades del mundo.
4. Eva Perón: Argentina, Primera Dama de la Nación Argentina, Presidenta del Partido Peronista Femenino, Presidenta de la Fundación Eva Perón, Feminismo, trabajadores
5. El Greco: Creta, República de Venecia; España, Pintor, Contrarreforma, Doménikos Theotokópoulos
6. Frida Kahlo: México, Pintora, Feminismo
7. Madres de la Plaza de Mayo: Argentina. La organización fue creada con el fin de recuperar con vida a los detenidos desaparecidos, y luego establecer quiénes fueron los responsables de los crímenes de lesa humanidad y promover su enjuiciamiento.
8. José Martí: Cuba, Político, escritor y periodista, Revolución Cubana
9. Pablo Picasso: España, Pintor, Protocubismo, Cubismo, Surrealismo, Pacifismo
10. Sandino: Augusto César Sandino, Nicaragua, Revolucionario, Parte del Ejército Defensor de la Soberanía Nacional (EDSN), Ejército Liberal Constitucionalista. Luchó contra los ocupantes estadounidenses.
11. Simón Bolívar: Simón Bolívar, Venezuela, Militar y político, Libertador de Bolivia
12. Pancho Villa: México, Leñador, agricultor y comerciante, La Revolución Mexicana

Antes de empezar ¿Cómo han influido en la historia los héroes y personajes públicos?

Student book page 251
Time estimate: 60 minutes

A After the intro, which engaged students in recalling their background knowledge of famous Spanish-speakers in history, this activity is to help broaden the depth of that knowledge. Students will use a variety of web-based resources to discover a better understanding of famous people throughout the history of the Spanish-speaking world. First have them complete the research. This can be done individually or in pairs. The organizer and a forum are in **Explorer**.

B Group either the individuals into pairs or the pairs into quads to look at their organizers, compare the information they found and complete the discussion.

C Have students record a message on the space provided in **Explorer**, in which they share a brief biographical radio clip about one of the people they learned about either in the intro or in this activity.

¿Cómo expresan los seres humanos su identidad en diversas situaciones?

Actividad 1 ¿Cómo cambiamos nuestro comportamiento para cumplir con las expectativas de los demás?

Student book page 252
Time estimate: 2 60-minute class periods + 1 optional workshop day; comprehension questions and artwork assigned as homework

B 1. Read the poem first in a way that students can hear the overall tone and repeated structures: "Tú... Yo no..." This is a conversational poem, a voice speaking directly "to" someone: read it as such!

2. This poem juxtaposes or gives a contrast between two parts of the author – the inner and outer Julia de Burgos. For this critical reading, have students focus on the most obvious or basic differences between the two, that is scaffolded for them on the graphic organizer; this organizer is available in **Explorer**. You may want to have students work together on this part or give them the option to do so; some students may need more time.

¡Tu opinión cuenta!

Students have the opportunity to analyze the poem together at this point, their "opinion" being valid because there are always various ways to interpret poetry! Encourage them to justify their answers and refer back to the text.

1. These are more direct questions and can be assigned as homework to give time for students to work independently before sharing their ideas with one another.

3. What words, phrases, symbols and/or images could students put on the two sides of the face to represent the two parts of Julia de Burgos? This template is available in **Explorer**; some artistically inclined students might want to start from scratch!

¡A tejer!

These options give students a way to interact with the poem; they are not tiered in terms of difficulty but rather each give a different creative point of approach. You might consider letting students choose what is most interesting to them! It is worth the time to have students share this kind of creative, open-ended work with their classmates in small groups rather than with the whole class, you might put them in groups of three or four and have them share their projects with just those classmates.

Note to teachers: The following are helpful literary terms (in anticipation of AP Literature and Culture, perhaps! This is one of the assigned texts on the new reading list!) which should also connect to students' Language Arts curriculum:

- **La voz poética** – who is speaking in the poem?
- **Apóstrofo** – when the "voz poética" or voice in the poem is speaking directly to someone or a group of people. This is a classic example of the use of this technique.
- **Alusión literaria** = literary allusion – in this poem, references to Don Quijote and the Bible
- **Metáforas** – as noted in the student book
- **Antítesis** = antithesis – a comparison of two things that are directly opposed to one another
- **Paralelismo** = parallel structure – a repeated structure in the poem; in this case, "Tú eres… Yo no…"

¿Cómo expresan los seres humanos su identidad en diversas situaciones?

Actividad 2 ¿Cuál es el legado que nos dejó Lorca?

Student book page 257
Time estimate: 3 60-minute class periods; assign biography reading for homework

Have students access the organizer in **Explorer** or provide a print copy. They can work in small groups of 3 or 4. The red vocabulary box has information that goes in the organizer (similar to a matching exercise). They need to talk about what they know about Garcia Lorca connecting to the names, places, and dates on page 257 in the student text. Students will not be able to complete the time line yet; inform them more information is coming! A timeline of Lorca's life is in **Explorer, Recursos, Sólo para los profesores.**

MANTA 4 Identidades personales y públicas

B As they read the biography, have students add more items and details to the same organizer with the four categories from Part A.

C Have students evaluate Lorca's end of life situation and contribute their opinion on **one** of the topics given in the student text, writing about 8 sentences. This activity is provided as a forum in **Explorer** as well.

D "La guitarra" is one of Lorca's earlier poems from *Cante jondo,* that includes poems relating to Andalucía, Granada and *los gitanos*. Have students skim/scan the poem looking for words that repeat, jotting them in their journals.

E The audio of the poem set to guitar music is accessible in **Explorer** as a Fuente for this activity. Have students close their books and close their eyes while they listen to an audio of the poem to get a sense of how they feel regarding the tone (sadness, pain, happiness) and the rhythm.

F These questions may need to be researched or you can reference a detailed analysis of the poem in **Explorer, Recursos, Sólo para los profesores**. Students can be divided into 5 groups (questions 3 and 4 are simpler to answer without research so they could be one group) to answer the questions. Next, jigsaw so that one person from each of the 5 groups forms a new group to share out all the answers.

> **Answers to Part F:**
>
> 1. ¿Qué importancia histórica o cultural tiene la guitarra? (¿qué sabes de la música y danza de Andalucía?) *Cuando se toca la guitarra en reuniones de cante jondo y flamenco, cantan hasta la madrugada. La guitarra expresa las emociones de los gitanos- su pena, angustia, muerte, sentimientos y pasiones de la vida real. Muchos poemas del "Cante jondo" de Lorca se convirtieron en cantes jondos de flamenco porque Lorca es la voz de los gitanos. Según el diccionario de la RAE, el "cante jondo" es "el más genuino cante andaluz, de profundo sentimiento". Manuel de Falla consideraba que el cante jondo era el cante antiguo, mientras que el cante flamenco era el moderno.*
> 2. Qué puede simbolizar la guitarra? ¿Por qué es la guitarra una metáfora apropiada?
>   a. La guitarra es personificada, tiene carácter humano, es el corazón de la gente de España, los gitanos.
>   b. en el primer verso la metáfora "llanto" para referirse al sonido de la guitarra, que representa la protesta de la gente.
>   c. El sonido o el "llanto" de la guitarra se repite tanto que ya "es imposible callarla", las emociones no pueden aguantar más opresión.
> 3. ¿Cuál es la diferencia entre versos y estrofas? *Versos son como "lines" en inglés, una palabra o un conjunto de palabras que tienen medida y cadencia Estrofa se refiere a cada una de las partes en que está dividida el poema, ej: cuatro estrofas de seis versos.*
> 4. ¿Cuál es el tono del poema y qué palabras o versos crean ese tono en tu opinión?
>
>   *El tono es uno de dolor, tristeza, y expresión de la angustia que sufren los gitanos. Los versos varían de un estudiante al otro.*

5. Lorca no expresa el dolor explícitamente sino que usa metáforas para comunicar su mensaje. Explica: "llora flecha sin blanco" y "la tarde sin mañana", "primer pájaro muerto sobre la rama

   a. *Lorca mezcla recuerdos de su niñez ("arenas del Sur"), con la incertidumbre del futuro ("flecha sin blanco, tarde sin mañana")*

   b. *El presentimiento de un final trágico ("primer pájaro muerto sobre la rama").*

6. ¿Cómo es una guitarra un "corazón malherido por cinco espadas" en un sentido literal y en un sentido metafórico? ¿Cómo puedes conectar esta última imagen con los gitanos?

En los dos últimos versos, conecta a quien toca la guitarra ("corazón malherido") con los cinco dedos del guitarrista ("cinco espadas"), que indica la presencia de la muerte. Los dedos son los que hieren al corazón de España. Los gitanos emplean la guitarra como instrumento de comunicación para expresar sus dolores de sus corazones. Representan a la gente humilde de España que es oprimida y no tiene voz. Pero en una escala aun más grande, se puede decir que es presentimiento de todos los españoles que sufren por la situación política represiva.

¡Tu opinión cuenta!

This can be a formative assessment reflection connecting the poem to Lorca's identity and life five years later. What are some predictions of the political climate in the poem?

Note to teachers: This activity is a great preparation for the poem by Lorca, also about *los gitanos,* on the revised Advanced Placement Literature & Culture reading list. You could read it at the close of this activity if you want to expose your students to that work at this time.

¿Cómo puede un individuo contribuir a definir la identidad de una nación?

Actividad 3 ¿Cómo se convirtió Eva Perón en una leyenda?

Student book page 262
Time estimate: 2 60-minute class periods with homework (complete timeline and comprehension activities on documentary) and another day for students to present one of their "homenajes" options
Grammar in context: Irregular preterit

Before beginning this activity, do a quick background knowledge check of what associations students already have with the name "Evita."

  As students read the biography, have them choose a descriptor of Eva that best fits one of the paragraphs in the reading.

Possible answers for Part A: There is no one correct answer but they should be able to justify their choice. Possibilities include:

(1) atrevida, ambiciosa
(2) carismática, manipuladora
(3) luchadora por justicia social, motivadora
(4) abanderada de los pobres
(5) luchadora por derechos de mujeres, benefactora, humanitaria
(6) luchadora por justicia social
(7) polémica, controversial
(8) inmortalizada, eterna

B Students will create a chronology of Eva Peron's life based on the reading. It is available to complete digitally in **Explorer**.

C Students will watch the documentary and will hear the dates noted in the student text and record what happened on those dates on the same time line.

Answers for Timeline:
- junio, 1947- gira por Europa: Madrid- fue recibida por Generalísimo Franco, Italia- el papa la recibió, Francia y Suiza. A su vuelta a Buenos Aires fue recibida en triunfo por su esposo.
- 3 de septiembre, 1947 – el congreso aprobó el voto para la mujer
- 22 de agosto, 1951 – el partido Peronista- le pidieron a Evita que aceptara el honor de ser parte del partido (vice-presidente)
- 30 de agosto, 1951 – anunció que no podía aceptar el honor de ser vice-presidente de la república debido que estaba enferma con cáncer
- 28 de septiembre, 1951 – hubo una tentativa (golpe de estado) contra Perón pero fue sofocada
- 11 de noviembre, 1951 – realizaron las elecciones- la primera vez que las mujeres pudieron votar
- 1° de mayo, 1952 – su último discurso en público
- 26 de julio, 1952 – se falleció del cáncer

D Students will watch the documentary a second time and note what happened. Following, this is a comprehension "quiz" of the documentary: Myth or Truth? Have students correct myths with facts. The comprehension quiz is in **Explorer**.

Answers for Part D:
1. Verdad
2. Mito – También fue motivada por las ancianas- todas las mujeres sin recursos.
3. Mito – Ella se falleció después de las elecciones.
4. Verdad
5. Mito – No pudo aceptar al final porque se enteró de que tenía cáncer.

¡Te toca a ti!

Students work in pairs to research the tributes to Eva and choose among 3 options: 1) write a critique of a song, poem, movie, Broadway theatre, novel, etc. 2) create an activity for the class to complete such as a cloze passage to one of the songs or poems with a word bank 3) create their own tribute to her. There is a detailed guide to writing a "crítica" for all three options in the Apoyo adicional para actividades section for this hilo of **Explorer**.

¿Qué aprendiste?

Based on the commemorative 100-peso bill that came out in 2012, dedicated to Eva Perón, students will explain three contributions that Eva Peron made to Argentina during her lifetime. They can record themselves in **Explorer** or submit their work then share with a group of students. There is a link on the **Recursos solo para Profesores** for more information on her contributions.

> ¿Cómo puede un individuo contribuir a definir la identidad de una nación?

Actividad 4 ¿Cómo puede el testimonio de una persona transformar la situación política de una nación?

Student book page 266
Time estimate: 1 60-minute class period and 30 minutes; can assign some of biography reading for homework and recorded presentational oral task as homework the second night

A For this brief text students can read silently or you or a student can read the selection aloud to the class. Then give students the opportunity to converse with a partner to answer the questions in the book. You can encourage them to take turns asking the questions so that each person has the opportunity to answer two of the questions. After students have chatted in pairs, it would be helpful to go through the questions as a whole class to ensure that student were able to infer from the text the correct answers. After reading this short excerpt, show the video two times. The first time have students make a list of images that they see in the video. While viewing the second time have students write a list of vocabulary and cognates that they recognize. Once students have seen the video twice, have them write out answers to the questions in complete sentences. Ask the questions to the class after students have had time to prepare their answers and go over them as a whole group. The three fuentes used in this activity give pieces of Rigoberta's story, so it is important that students fully understand both texts and the video to get a better understanding of her life and what she has accomplished.

B While watching the documentary on Rigoberta Menchú, students will use the strategies indicated in the text and record the notes in their journals. They can also complete this task via the digital forum provided in **Explorer**.

C After watching the documentary students can work in pairs to answer the following questions.

> **Answers to Part C questions:**
> 1. Rigoberta Menchú extrañaba a sus padres y a sus hermanos en la ceremonia porque se habían fallecido y esperaba que pudiera recibir este honor sin haber perdido a su familia.
> 2. 10 años
> 3. Menchú utilizó el símil de un tejido para describir su exilio debido a que las historias de la gente indígena de América Latina forman un "tejido" de su existencia.
> 4. Su gran deseo es que los indígenas siempre vivan y sean parte de la sociedad y la identidad de América Latina.
> 5. En esta época los indígenas habían hecho progreso en la organización de las comunidades políticas, pero, a la vez, el gobierno militar también había aumentado su poder sobre los políticos del país.
> 6. Menchú espera que algún día los indígenas puedan participar en un congreso mixto, haciendo las decisiones económicas, militares y políticas que influyen en la sociedad guatemalteca.
> 7. La misión de la fundación Vicente Menchú tiene la meta de ayudar con la resolución de los conflictos políticos en América Latina.

D As students read her biography, they should use the reading strategies outlined for the first and second reading to help them find important information in the text. The text is available in **Explorer** to print out and annotate or mark up digitally. Students can also accomplish the same task by using sticky notes and attaching them in the book where they found the key information.

E 1. Work with a partner to discuss the questions that address the key themes of the text. You can give students time to look for the answers and mark them in the text, or you can have them do that in their pairs. Afterwards, discuss the answers they shared in their small groups as a class.

2. This is a simulation of the interpersonal task on the Advanced Placement Language and Culture Exam. Read all instructions carefully and set it up beforehand so that you have everything ready and will know how it will work.

- As a teacher, go to your **Explorer** course to play the audio recording for this task, which includes both instructions (in Spanish), time for students to preview the outline for the interpersonal task, and a recording of one side of the conversation – Dra. Menchú's voice. Audio must be played for the whole class from the teacher computer and it will appear on students' recordings as well.
- Students will go to **Explorer** to view the outline for the simulated interpersonal conversation that they will have with Dra. Menchú.

Students are provided time to preview it before the recording starts, and then follow it for the length of the conversation. Students will follow the instructions on the audio and will record their voices in **Explorer** to submit their recording. Students press record at the beginning of the audio task and KEEP RECORDING the entire time, so that the audio includes their own voices as well as the recording of Dra. Menchú.

- Instructions to the students on the recording are in Spanish. Here are the English instructions: *"You will participate in a conversation. You will have 90 seconds to read the preview of the conversation and an outline of each turn in the conversation. Each time it is your turn to speak, you will have 30 seconds to record each response so that you get used to the recording process."*

- **Note**: We suggest that you model the process with the whole class so they understand the format and see what you do. Students are encouraged to say one or two complete thoughts but they do not have to speak the entire 30 seconds. Whatever they can say that is on-task is excellent; at the Advanced Placement level they will need to speak the entire time! You could use the interpersonal oral rubric to grade and give feedback on students' recordings.

« | » | Audio script

Description students will read in Explorer prior to and while listening to the audio

Llamada telefónica a la Dra. Menchú:

La organización del gobierno estudiantil va a patrocinar un programa sobre los derechos humanos el próximo mes. Estás encargado/a de organizar el programa y quisieras invitar a la Dra. Rigoberta Menchú para que les hable a los estudiantes de las clases de español. Entonces te toca a ti llamarla e invitarla a la escuela. Antes de hacer la llamada, piensa en lo que vas a decir cuando ella conteste el teléfono. Si quieres ver un ejemplo de un esquema para este tipo de conversación, visita la guía digital.

Vas a participar en una conversación. Primero vas a tener 90 segundos para leer la introducción y el esquema de la conversación. Después, comenzará la conversación, siguiendo el esquema. Cada vez que te corresponda participar en la conversación, vas a tener 30 segundos para grabar tu respuesta. Debes participar de la manera más completa y apropiada posible pero no hay que llenar el tiempo completo en la grabación.

Tienes 90 segundos para leer la introducción y el esquema de la conversación.

El esquema de la conversación entre tú y la Dra. Menchú:

Dra. Menchú:	Te saluda.
Tú	Salúdala y dile quién eres.
Dra. Menchú	Te responde y te hace una pregunta.
Tú	Explícale el evento que estás organizando y el propósito de tu llamada.
Dra. Menchú	Te responde y te hace una pregunta.
Tú	Contéstale con más detalles.
Dra. Menchú	Te responde.
Tú	Contéstale con los detalles del viaje
Dra. Menchú	Te responde y te hace una pregunta.
Tú	Contéstale afirmativamente y despídete de ella.

Audio script

Instructions will be heard two times in Spanish: *Vas a participar en una conversación. Primero vas a tener 90 segundos para leer la introducción y el esquema de la conversación. Después, comenzará la conversación, siguiendo el esquema. Cada vez que te corresponda participar en la conversación, vas a tener 30 segundos para grabar tu respuesta. Debes participar de la manera más completa y apropiada posible.*

Introducción

La organización del gobierno estudiantil va a patrocinar un programa sobre los derechos humanos el próximo mes. Estás encargado/a de organizar el programa y quisieras invitar a la Dra. Rigoberta Menchú para les hable a los estudiantes de las clases de español sobre su lucha por los derechos humanos en Centroamérica. Entonces te toca a ti llamarla e invitarla a la escuela. Has leído sobre Menchú y su lucha por los derechos humanos y civiles de los indígenas de Guatemala.

El esquema de la conversación entre tú y la Dra. Menchú:

Dra. Menchú	Hola, muy buenas tardes, habla la Dra. Menchú
Tú	((Salúdala y dile quién eres.))
Dra. Menchú	El placer es mío, siempre me gusta conocer a los jóvenes que estudian español como segundo idioma, ¿en qué puedo servirte?
Tú	((Explícale el evento que estás organizando y el propósito de tu llamada.))
Dra. Menchú	Me honra tu invitación. ¿Hay algún tema específico en el cual quieres que concentre mi presentación?
Tú	((Contéstale con más detalles.))
Dra. Menchú	Voy a consultar mi calendario para ver si puedo viajar a tu escuela durante esas fechas.
Tú	((Contéstale con los detalles del viaje.))
Dra. Menchú	Bueno, acepto con placer tu invitación, ¿me haces el favor de escribirme un correo electrónico para confirmar los detalles de la presentación?
Tú	((Contéstale afirmativamente y despídete de ella.))

  3. This presentational oral formative assessment is a follow up to the interpersonal conversation with Rigoberta Menchú. Students can record themselves in **Explorer**. Have students prepare a written introduction to Dra. Menchú for the school visit, then they record it and submit it to you. Make sure they include: 1) a brief biography, 2) political ideals, and 3) most impressive contributions and achievements. I would limit it to 150-200 words, one paragraph for each aspect.

Reflexión

Have your students take a few minutes, either in class or at home, to respond to the questions in this reflection activity.

 Note to teachers: There is also another video (12 Minutes) about the political situation and individual struggles that Rigoberta Menchú faced. Summary in Spanish follows. The link is in **Explorer, Recursos, Sólo para los profesores.**

"La voz indígena (Rigoberta Menchú)" 13 oct 2012

Repasamos la figura de la líder indígena guatemalteca Rigoberta Menchú. Con cinco años empezó a trabajar en plantaciones de café y algodón. A la explotación laboral a la que fue sometida le siguió la muerte de cinco miembros de su familia, fruto de la violencia rural en un país dominado por terratenientes y militares. Fue entonces cuando se comprometió de lleno con la lucha por la libertad, la justicia y los derechos humanos, en especial de los pueblos indígenas. En 1992 recibió el premio nobel de la paz en reconocimiento a su trabajo. Entonces, Informe Semanal emitió este reportaje. Histórico de emisiones: 17/10/1992

Essential questions:
- ¿Cómo expresan los seres humanos su identidad en diversas situaciones?
- ¿Cómo puede un individuo contribuir a definir la identidad de una nación?

Hilo 9 Evaluación final — ¿Con quién cenarías, si pudieras elegir a alguien famoso del mundo hispano?

Student book page 270
Time estimate: 1–3 days; this will depend on how much is completed in class and if students do research outside class.
Grammar in context: conditional, future, and subjunctive tenses

The starting point for this project is the question, *Who would you dine with if you could have dinner with one person (real or fictional) from the Spanish-speaking world?* The goal is to have students complete a research project in which they locate two resources (one written and the other can be visual, audiovisual or audio) that will provide information to describe the person and analyze their impact on society. This is one framework for how you can have students complete this assignment, but based on your students and your teaching style, please modify as you see fit.

Investigación:
Have students research a person or character from the Spanish-speaking world. The Antes de Empezar activity might be a good place to go back and remind students of the wide variety of people they could choose to research. They will need to find one reliable written text that either describes the biography of the person or their impact on society. Based on the information students will need to include in this assessment, they may need to find two reliable text resources. Students should also look for an audio, audiovisual or visual resource to include in their project as well. This could be one of the most influential paintings of an artist, a song that transformed a nation by a famous performing artist, a documentary of a political figure or an audio interview with the person being described in the project. Students may need more than just two fuentes, but the goal is to require them to find at least two.

Ensayo:
Before students begin the oral presentation portion of the project, they should use the resources they found to write a well-articulated essay about their person of interest. In that essay they should give a brief biographical background, a description of the person's character or personality, an analysis of his/her impact on society and the reasons they would like to dine with this person. The goal of writing the essay first is so that students have a firm understanding of the person they will be presenting to the class before they begin work on the more interactive pieces of this assignment.

Sesión de preguntas y respuestas:
If the students were to have the captive audience of a famous person during dinner, what would they ask him/her? This is the real-life application of our context. What would you say? What would he/she say? Students should think about this and write ten questions to which they would love to know the answers. Then they should select five and write an answer from the perspective of the person with whom they are dining What would his/her answer be?

Presentación:
This is the part of the project where we encourage students to synthesize what they have learned and produce an interesting and meaningful oral presentation to the class. For the monologue they will compile the information they think would be most interesting to the class to present as if they are the person they have been researching and writing about. They can dress up in costumes or bring props to help their classmates feel more like they are meeting that person in real life. For the dinner interview students can work individually or in pairs. Each student is responsible for his or her own presentation, but they can ask a partner to help them with the interview if they would like. Other students might choose to act both as themselves and their persons of interest in the dinner interview. The documentary option is for the technology enthralled students in your class who would like to create a video of the life and impact of their famous person. They should be sure to include a clip at the end in which they explain why they want to dine with this famous person.

MANTA 4 Identidades personales y públicas

Hilo 10 Identidad nacional e identidad étnica

Essential questions:
- ¿Cómo se expresan los varios aspectos de la identidad?
- ¿Cómo se unen distintas culturas para formar una identidad étnica?
- ¿Cómo influye el idioma en la identidad de una persona?

Student Learning Objectives

Interpersonal Communication: Speaking and Writing
- Exchange information about national and ethnic identities.
- Exchange opinions on how people express their identity.
- Collaborate to develop a definition of identity.
- Exchange messages such as emails, blogs, or social media posts about preserving mother tongue languages.
- Engage in discussions about the influence of language on identity.
- Explain and provide examples of how cultures unite to form an ethnic identity.

Interpretive Communication: Print, Audio, Audiovisual, and/or Visual Sources
- Demonstrate comprehension of content from a variety of authentic sources about ethnic and national languages in Spanish-speaking countries.
- Interpret, analyze, and evaluate the individual and national identity of an individual from a Hispanic culture.
- Analyze and evaluate the diversity of Latin American culture reflected in a variety of authentic materials, including poems, songs, and other audiovisual sources.
- Interpret and summarize significant details of the linguistic variation in Spain and Latin America.
- Interpret and analyze cultural perspectives of *mestizaje* as reflected in literary works from Hispanic cultures.

Presentational Communication: Spoken and/or Written Presentations to a Variety of Audiences
- Present information about the relationship between the mother tongue and identity.
- Collaborate with others to present information on an ethnic group that maintains the language and culture of their ancestors.
- Describe and analyze the Latin American ethnic identity from the lyrics of a song.
- Analyze images and metaphors about identity in poems from Hispanic cultures.
- Produce reflections and journal entries to demonstrate understanding of the influence of language on ethnic and national identities.

Relating Cultural Practices to Perspectives:
- Investigate, explain, and reflect on the relationship between the ways Spanish is spoken and the perspectives (beliefs/values/attitudes) of Hispanic cultures.

Relating Cultural Products to Perspectives:
- Investigate, explain, and reflect on the relationship between the Spanish language and the perspectives (beliefs/values/attitudes) of Hispanic cultures about identity.

Connections: Connect with Other Disciplines
- Make connections to content knowledge about the history of *mestizaje* in Latin America.

Connections: Acquire New Information
- Acquire and apply new information from authentic sources about ethnic groups and languages in Spanish-speaking countries.

Comparisons: Language
- Make linguistic comparisons of cognates, *si* clauses with past perfect subjunctive and conditional perfect tenses, and possessive pronouns

Comparisons: Culture
- Analyze and compare ethnic languages in Spanish-speaking countries.

School and Global Communities:
- Interact with Spanish speakers about ethnic languages in Spanish-speaking countries.

Lifelong Learning:
- Set goals and reflect on progress in using Spanish for enjoyment, enrichment, and advancement.

Suggested Lesson Plan Sequence/Pacing Guide

Manta 4: Identidades personales y públicas

Hilo 10: Identidad nacional e identidad étnica

Focus according to Essential Question Pages in SE	Day (based on 60 min class)	Classroom Activities	Homework/ Formative assessment/ Exit pass
La expresión de las varias partes de la identidad pp. 276–283	1	* Introduce unit with brainstorm on parts of your identity * Vocabulary game and exercises with nationalities	* Part B representation of your identity for homework * Reflexión
	2	* Pre-reading discussion and vocabulary * Active reading of "Mi nombre" with notes on inferences * Comprehension questions and discussion and journal prompts	* Notes on inferences * Name poems for homework
	3	* Finish yesterday's remaining activities and share out name poems * Discussion of previous knowledge of Frida Kahlo * Two times reading of text with guiding focus (can be completed as homework)	* Assign as homework Internet research on Frida Kahlo self-portraits
La unión de distintas culturas para formar una identidad étnica pp. 284–293	4	* Share out notes from yesterday's reading * Present ¡Te toca a ti! assignment (to do at home and present in class on a future day) * Think-Pair-Share on vocabulary for "Balada de los dos abuelos" * Preview reading of poem and cognates activity * Listening and first reading of poem	* ¡Te toca a ti! individual self-portrait to complete outside of class * First round of graphic organizer (imagery) – can be completed as homework
	5	* Finish graphic organizer with inferences from poem * Analysis, vocabulary, and historical connections exercises * Begin writing ¡A tejer! essay – to finish outside of class (you could do an additional workshop day if students need more support with this writing task)	* Application of vocabulary * ¡A tejer! essay
	6	* Think-Pair-Share on Latin American identity using visuals * Two readings of lyric with metaphor graphic organizer * Discussion of song and cultural analysis * ¡A tejer! closing activity	* Reflection can be assigned for homework
La influencia del idioma en la identidad pp. 294–305	7–8	* Pre-reading activities with famous Spanish speakers' favorite words * Think-Pair-Share on Spanish-speaking countries' languages and dialects * Active reading of text with note-taking on objectives of **El Día E** * Answer email from director * Two viewings of video with spoken summary * Present ¡Te toca a ti! task – to complete outside of class and share with the class on a future day * ¡Tu opinión cuenta! debate	* Interpersonal writing task * Presentational speaking task * ¡Te toca a ti! formative assessment to complete outside of class * ¡Tu opinión cuenta! debate
	9–10	* Spain map activity * Active reading with graphic organizer * Written cultural comparison * Documentary viewing, questions, and discussion	* 3-paragraph written cultural comparison * Reflexión
	11–12	* Present summative assessment * Students choose and research linguistic group * Students prepare presentations and share with class	* Different parts of summative assessment

Hilo 10 Identidad nacional e identidad étnica

Introducción ¿Cuáles son las partes de mi identidad?

Student book page 276
Time estimate: 20 minutes part A, assign part B for homework

  A The organizer is available in **Explorer** to complete. Here are sentence prompts for those who may need them:

- rol en la familia   *Yo soy...*
- religión/creencias   *Yo (no) creo.../Yo soy...*
- lugares/países   *Yo soy...   Yo soy de...*
- idioma(s)   *Yo hablo...*
- género (hombre/mujer)   *Yo soy...*
- intereses   *Yo soy... (atleta/artista/soñador/escritor, etc)*
- esperanzas para el futuro   *Yo seré... Espero ser...*

  B Have students work on Part B for homework for the next day, then you can move on to antes de empezar This can be an oral presentation grade if you have students present their tasks to the class, or to a small group of classmates depending on time and resources. Give them specific instructions: Can they read their paragraph to the class or do they need to speak extemporaneously?

Antes de empezar ¿De dónde eres?

Student book page 277
Time estimate: 30–45 minutes with homework
Grammar in context: adjective agreement for nationalities

 A **1.** You could run this review activity in a variety of ways:

  B **1.** Option 1: Divide the class in half, into two groups: A and B. Have students in Group A read their lines out loud in unison, one by one, and see if Group B can respond "in unison" (some students will know the answers before others and some will repeat). Perhaps do the call-and-response a few times so that students practice saying the words; if there is deafening silence give that group of students a hint or write the word on the board. Be sure to check for correct answers before moving on!

Option 2: Facilitate this more as a team activity with points. Group A can present their question then Group B can confer before one person giving their answer (as a "spokesperson") or all of the students giving the answer together in unison. If the group answers correctly on the first try, they win a point.

Option 3: Students could do this in pairs: Student A and Student B instead of groups. Be sure to go over the correct answers as a class to check for comprehension.

2. These are "irregular" nationalities, perhaps more challenging for students to remember. Encourage them to infer the country name from the adjective given – and then remember both!

There is a link to countries, cities & nationalities from the Real Academia Española in **Explorer**.

At the close of both of these exercises you could do a review game or an activity with flags or a map to give students more practice, as you see necessary based on their demonstrating their knowledge thus far.

Vocabulary Answers:

porteños – de Buenos Aires, Argentina
salteños – de Salta, Argentina
sevillanos – de Sevilla, España
bogotanos - de Bogotá, Colombia
gallegos – de Galicia, España
madrileños – de Madrid, España
habaneros – de la Habana, Cuba
asunceños – Asunción, Paraguay
vascos – del País Vasco, Euskadi, España
catalanes – de Cataluña, España
canarios – de las Islas Canarias
mallorquines – de Mallorca, España
santiaguinos – de Santiago, Chile y Santiago de Compostela, España, ¿hay más?
sanjuaneros – de San Juan, Cuba
tegucigalpenses – de Tegucigalpa, Honduras
caraqueños – de Caracas, Venezuela
andaluces – de Andalucía, España
limeños – de Lima, Perú
aragoneses – de Aragón, España

Culture box: You may wish to take this chance to talk about events like the Puerto Rican Day Parade and other festivals and events that celebrate specific country groups' identity and pride in the United States.

Have students share the countries they are from and what that nationality is in Spanish: Australia- **australiano**, Japan- **japonés**, etc.

As time allows, have students complete this as a short homework activity and present their findings to class: a few sentences and perhaps a visual to accompany the term.

Reflexión

This question tries to get students thinking about their identity: would you call yourself "American"? some other nationality? How would other generations in your family identify themselves? When does it switch from the country of origin to the country where you have moved? **Note:** When someone from the U.S. is traveling in Latin America, people will often correct you if you say you are "americano" – since "las Américas" include where you are traveling, thus you are all "americanos"! The word *estadounidense* is a helpful word to learn and certainly a good one to use to describe yourself, when people ask!

¿Cómo se expresan los distintos aspectos de la identidad?

Actividad 1 ¿Cómo se puede expresar la identidad a través de la literatura?

Student book page 278
Time estimate: 1 60-minute class period with homework, including time for writing and revising name poems
Grammar in context: You may wish to highlight the following language features for your students before reading or upon completion of reading the text:

- The verb *gustar*/the present subjunctive: "a los chinos, como a los mexicanos, no les gusta que sus mujeres sean fuertes."
- The conditional perfect: "Me habría gustado conocerla"
- The use of "como si" and the past subjunctive: "como si fuera un candelabro elegante"

  B Have students create a simple three-column organizer for this activity in their notebooks: When does the author seem to feel these emotions? This asks students to "read between the lines" or make inferences, so you can accept different answers, as long as students can defend them!

 ¡Te toca a ti!

 Have students interview each other in pairs and then present their classmate to either the rest of the class, or to a small group of classmates. Additionally have students take notes while listening to the presentations and then write an Exit Slip that compares a few classmates: similarities and differences. Students can also complete this task by recording themselves in the digital forum provided in **Explorer**.

 D You could have students share these with the class or in small groups as a presentational oral activity as well. Consider asking students to include some kind of visual or symbol to accompany part of what they wrote and hang them in your room.

¿Cómo se expresan los distintos aspectos de la identidad?

Actividad 2 ¿Qué conexión hay entre los distintos aspectos de Frida Kahlo al ver sus retratos?

Student book page 282
Time estimate: 60 minutes

A By this point in their study, most Spanish students are least minimally familiar with Frida Kahlo. This is your opportunity to help them activate their background knowledge before they begin the reading. You could start by showing a photograph of Frida Kahlo to help them recall what they know.

B As students are reading you want to help them focus on the vocabulary used to describe the way that Frida Kahlo expressed her identidad—both personal and ethnic—in her paintings. After each reading you can have students share out some of the information from the text that helps them create that framework for understanding. Students can share their ideas in the digital forum provided in **Explorer**.

C After reading give your students time to find portraits of Frida Kahlo. There are resources provided for this activity in **Explorer**, in the Enlaces section of this hilo. You can do this a few ways:

a. Set this up as a jigsaw activity by dividing students into groups and having them work on one painting and then putting together groups made up of one member from each of the original groups to discuss what they identified in the paintings.

b. In advance, locate several of her self portraits in a book or art history book and assign them to students.

c. Give them time to find one at home and print it out to bring in to class.

d. Assign them time in class to use a computer or iPad to locate Frida's self-portraits and choose a few to study.

Provide time to students to do the individual assignment of identifying the distinct elements of Kahlo's identity in the paintings. Once that has happened pair students with a partner and give them a chance to discuss and compare what they have found.

¡Te toca a ti!

The desired outcome of this activity is that students will be able to express the diverse elements of their personal identities (including elements of their national/ethnic identities.) You can use your creativity to refine this to best serve your students and their interests. It can become a presentational oral activity if you would like students to present their *autorretrato* to the class or a small group of classmates.

¿Cómo se unen distintas culturas para formar una identidad étnica?

Actividad 3 ¿Cómo ha influido el mestizaje en la cultura latinoamericana?

Student book page 284
Time estimate: 2 60-minute class periods with homework
Grammar in context: si clauses with imperfect subjunctive and conditional from poem

Note to teachers: "Balada de los dos abuelos" is included on the revised Advanced Placement Literature & Culture reading list. Another poem that could go well as additional reading for this activity is "Mujer negra" by Nancy Morejón, which addresses similar themes.

A **2 a.** This selection of the poem offers students the ability to practice the visualization reading strategy highlighted to the right. Students can also answer the questions on the next page and begin making predictions about the content of the poem.

B Before analyzing the poem, read the poem aloud at least once or find a narration that you like online. This is a poem with a very clear cadence and rhythm. Students could respond to both the poem's flow and content and ask questions before continuing. Then have students complete this analysis activity; the organizer is included in **Explorer**. At this point, students only complete the first column, identifying imagery in the poem to describe the two abuelos.

C **1.** Now students complete the organizer to make inferences about each *abuelo* based on the information that they found. An example is given on the organizer on page 288 of the student text as well as on the copy in **Explorer**.

2. Since this poem also presents rich imagery to describe the two places, students create or find visual images to represent each and share them with a small group of classmates.

3. This could be a good Exit Slip or homework assignment. Students are using target vocabulary to make connections to the poem. *Yo sé que el narrador es una persona mestiza porque...*

4. Here students connect to their history classes and what they already know about this topic. You could ask for volunteers to present to the class and help direct the discussion. This is important to review as a class since it prepares students for the **¡A tejer!** formative assessment coming up.

¡A tejer!

Students make connections between the poem and history, using textual references. You should be explicit about how you want them to cite examples from the poem. Examples of some possible statements follow:

> **Sample student work:**
> La descripción del abuelo negro es relacionada con la historia del mestizaje en el Caribe porque es un esclavo africano, traído desde África como mucha gente en esa época. Por ejemplo, la descripción "Pie desnudo, torso pétreo los de mi negro" (líneas 9–10) describe al abuelo negro como fuerte y descalzo. Los esclavos trabajaban sin zapatos y a veces sin camisas en el calor del Caribe.

Culture boxes: Luís Palés Matos and Wilfredo Lam are two other artists whose work exemplifies the cultural syncretism of the Caribbean. Have students go to their **Explorer** course to visit the links provided for Luís Palés Matos and complete the additional activity on Wilfredo Lam.

¿Cómo se unen distintas culturas para formar una identidad étnica?

Actividad 4 ¿Cuáles son los diversos aspectos de la identidad étnica de latinoamerica?

Student book page 289
Time estimate: 60 minutes
Grammar in context: relative pronouns

Note: Students can also see a music video of this song in **Explorer**.

 A Use this pre-reading task to activate students' background knowledge about the variety of cultural products, practices and perspectives of Latin America that they have studied thus far. Some examples would be: la ropa de las culturas indígenas, lo que se considera belleza, las comidas, los bailes, la música y las formas de arte.

 B As students read have them complete the chart (in **Explorer**) for these two exercises (1 and 2) to help them identify the metaphors used in the song to describe what it means to be Latin American. A few examples of these metaphors are "**un pueblo** *escondido* en la cima," "**una fábrica** *de humo*," "**el desarrollo** *en carne viva*," "**una canasta** *con frijoles*." You may need to remind students that a metaphor is when an author describes one noun by saying that it is another noun. Like "I am a machine," I am not literally a machine, but machines work really hard and and so do I, therefore "I am a machine" is a metaphor. After the first reading you might encourage them to share what they have found and then add to that list after the second reading. This will also help you to gauge how well students comprehend the lyrics. Also, you will most likely need to provide background information on the lyrics in bold, as these are cultural references that your students may not be able to connect with.

a. *El amor en los tiempo de cólera:* a reference to the book by Gabriel Garcia Marquez, Colombia

b. *la fotografía de un desaparecido:* a reference to the Madres de la Plaza de Mayo in Argentina (Guerra Sucia)

c. *Maradona contra Inglaterra anontándote dos goles:* Diego Maradona is the coach of the Argentine fútbol team and is considered to be the best soccer player of all time

d. *un pueblo sin piernas pero que camina:* a reference to the economical, political and social issues that Latin American countries have faced

e. *un trago de pulque:* a sip of pulque – an alcoholic beverage made from the fermented sap of the agave plant

f. *mascando coca:* a reference to the coca plant and how in certain Andean cultures it is custom to chew on the leaves of the coca plant

g. *todos los santos que cuelgan de mi cuello:* a reference to the Catholic influence on Latin American culture and how it is customary in Catholic culture that some people wear necklaces with their patron saints around their necks

1. After reading give students the opportunity to discuss, with a partner, the information they have collected and answer the guiding questions. There are several answers for each part, so not all are included here but below are example answers for each question.

a. For example: *una fábrica de humo* - a reference to the large industrial plants that exist in Latin America – often associated with foreign companies that build factories in countries with struggling economies so they can keep wages low and save on costs.

b. For example: *el sol que nace y el día que muere/tengo el sol que me seca y la lluvia que me baña* – personification of nature and a reference to the diverse aspects of nature in Latin American cultures.

c. The students should reference how even though Latin American culture encompasses a variety of subcultures, every Latin American can identify with the connection to *la tierra, la patria, y la diversidad que une* – even though these subcultures are unique they come together to form one larger cultural identity.

2. The reflection will be a great time for students to analyze the lyrics and decide the how they believe the song describes what it means to be Latin American.

MANTA 4 Identidades personales y públicas

¡A tejer!

This final activity is a meaningful way to connect the title, Tejidos, to a cultural product that reflects the practices and perspectives of Latin America. In English classes students often make quilts, but now they can work together as a class to create a weaving. Cut long 1.5" to 2" thick pieces of paper (or fabric if you would like to get very creative here) and pass those out to students. Give students time to draw, color or paint a representation of the products, practices and perspectives that form the Latin America identity. Once students have finished, weave them together to create your class weaving and hang it up for students and other classes to see. This is not a right answer wrong answer type of activity. The goal here is to get students to use the images they saw in the video and that were formed in their minds as they read the lyrics along with anything they have learned about cultural practices, products and perspectives at any point (and particularly during their work in this text) to create their pieces of the weaving. The additional activity in **Explorer** gets them thinking about those images and lends itself to preparing them for this activity. Each student could incorporate the geographical features mentioned in the song, the type of work that people do (*campesinos*, etc.), the types of foods and drinks portrayed. Even if you do not do the additional activity, encourage students to watch the music video outside of class or show it to them after reading the lyrics to aid them in developing their visuals that can be used in their weavings.

¿Cómo influye el idioma en la identidad de una persona?

Actividad 5 ¿Cómo se une un idioma a gente de diferentes identidades?

Student book page 294
Time estimate: 2 60-minute classes
Grammar in Context: possessive pronouns and adjectives

Introduction to Activity: Explain the purpose of el *Día E* by having students read the introductory paragraph aloud. What do they think about celebrating the fact that more than 500 million people in all 5 continents speak Spanish?

Before they watch the videos see if they can identify the celebrities in the photos? Where are they from and why are they famous? Students will access the organizer for the celebrities' "palabras favoritas" as well as the embedded videos for this activity in **Explorer**.

Answers for Part A:
1. Gael García Bernal- actor/director from Mexico
2. Eugenia Silva- model from Spain
3. Pau Gasol- basketball player from Barcelona, Spain
4. Shakira- singer from Colombia
5. Isabel Allende- author from Chile who lives in San Francisco
6. Mario Vargas Llosa- author/politician from Peru

B Have students decide their favorite Spanish word, record it on a device (in class, two at a time) then you can play them back for the class. Maybe they could vote on the top 3 or 4 and send them to the e-mail indicated in the student edition.

 C 1. Have students ask each other the 4 questions in the Student Edition to get students comfortable talking about their language learning experiences. Monitor their interpersonal speaking in Spanish.

 2. Have students complete the chart found in **Explorer**. Complete a chart for the class as students share out their ideas.

Sample answers to part C2:

País	Idiomas	Dialectos
España	catalán	
Perú	quechua	
Paraguay	guaraní	
México	náhuatl	
España	castellano	valenciano

 D The Cervantes Institute headquartered in Madrid has offices in 77 cities in 44 countries. Students need to write the phrases in their journals that indicate the purpose and objective for *Día E.* They could do this for homework and then share out the next day. **Note:** Have students study the statistics about the Spanish language; have their thoughts changed since the first discussion from the introduction to this activity?

 E This is an interpersonal writing formative assessment in which students will respond to the e email from the Director of the Cervantes Institute. Begin by having students read this email aloud in class and discuss the request before you have students respond in writing. You may want to suggest something like, have students organize a *Día E* in their school for **Discover Languages** month (February) about the benefits of studying languages and cultures.

 F This video of the Día E celebration in Madrid features all the activities that happened during the day for people of all ages but especially children. It is embedded in **Explorer**.

 G Leave a voice message for a friend, asking him/her to join you at the celebration at the Cervantes Institute in Madrid. **Explorer** has a place for students to record themselves.

 ¡Te toca a ti!

 Students will choose one of the three activity options, prepare it and share with the class. It is intended to get them involved in an activity like the Cervantes Institute celebration. The oral presentation of any option can be a Presentational Speaking grade.

 Culture box: The culture box on page 298 features several indigenous languages of Latin America. There is also a video link in **Explorer** so students can hear the different indigenous languages spoken.

¡Tu opinión cuenta!

A debate on the value of maintaining our mother tongue languages: are you in favor or against of bilingualism? Debate strategies can be found on page 172 of the student book.

¿Cómo influye el idioma en la identidad de una persona?

Actividad 6 ¿Cuál es la situación lingüística actual en España?

Student book page 299
Time estimate: 2 60-minute class periods

  Students will complete the chart found in **Explorer**.

Answers for Part B chart:

Idioma	Dónde se habla	El origen
El catalán	Cataluña, nordeste de la península, Andorra, la Comunidad Valenciana, las Islas Baleares	Del latín vulgar, influencias francesas e italianas
El castellano	Centro de España- Castilla y León, EE.UU., Latinoamérica, Puerto Rico, judíos sefardíes	Castilla y León
El euskera	País Vasco (Vizcaya) Norte de Navarra País Vasco de Francia	Sin raíces latinas, única lengua prerromana peninsular viva; es un enigma Euskal Herría = el país que habla euskera
El gallego	Galicia (noroeste de España), algunas zonas de Asturias, León y Zamora, una colonia en Sudamérica	Previa al castellano, del latín vulgar

    Students will collaborate in pairs on this exercise. Students can work together on the presentational writing based on their organizer. Then, have them peer edit, and both can present orally on the work they did. They can use the comparison organizer found in **Explorer**.

Suggestion for cultural comparisons:

Euskera is one of the official languages in Spain, spoken in el País Vasco. They teach it in schools along with castellano, but they knew that if they didn't maintain the mother tongue that the language would disappear.

Compare it to the Mexicans who emigrated to the United States throughout the 20th century. Children of immigrants were discriminated in schools and in public for using Spanish. Parents wanted their children to learn English so they didn't make them learn Spanish at home.

Culture box: Watch the video and have students complete the comprehension questions either in their notebook or in **Explorer**. Then they can do online research outside of class and share out with the class the following day.

> **Answers to Culture box documentary questions in bold font:**
> 1. Una de las lenguas que está en peligro de extinción antes del final del siglo. **Quechua o aymara**
> 2. Solamente **800,000 o 30% del país vasco** personas hablan el euskera.
> 3. El territorio vasco se extiende desde el noreste de España hasta **Francia**.
> 4. Hace 50 años el **euskera** casi desapareció porque fue prohibido usar el idioma en asuntos estatales y políticos.
> 5. La pérdida de un idioma supone un largo camino para recuperar el idioma; es una decisión personal que empieza con uno mismo y la **identidad**.
> 6. Todas eran herramientas para la recuperación del euskera excepto:
>   a. La unificación por la escritura y literatura
>   b. **Los negocios**
>   c. La educación
>   d. Los medios de comunicación
>   e. La producción cultural
> 7. El motor que ha impulsado el país vasco hacia la recuperación del euskera fue su propia **identidad**.
> 8. Las ikastolas tienen un gran **prestigio** entre la educación académico.
> 9. El modelo de las ikastolas garantiza la enseñanza en **euskera**.
> 10. El eje de la continuidad es el idioma porque es el corazón del pueblo y si pierde la lengua se pierde **el corazón o la identidad de un pueblo**.

This reflection requires use of "si clauses" that combine the past perfect (pluscuamperfecto) subjunctive with conditional perfect, or si clauses with that combine present and future tenses.

Essential questions:
- ¿Cómo se expresan los distintos aspectos de la identidad?
- ¿Cómo se unen distintas culturas para formar una identidad étnica?
- ¿Cómo influye el idioma en la identidad de una persona?

Hilo 10 Evaluación final — ¿Cuál es la diferencia entre la identidad nacional y la identidad étnica?

Student book page 304

Time estimate: 2 60-minute class periods to present promotional message and share one activity with class

Grammar in context: If clauses with imperfect subjunctive and conditional tenses, relative pronouns, imperative: familiar commands

¿Cómo se relaciona el idioma con la identidad de su pueblo y sus orígenes?

Students will need to choose their ethnic group, suggestions on final evaluation checklist, early in the unit to begin research.

Hilo 10 Enlaces in Explorer:

Los idiomas sí que cuentan video on International Day of Mother Tongue (even though the video is in English, you can turn down the sound, and have students read the captions in Spanish) It is a great promotion for the importance of language learning and promoting diversity.

UNESCO estadísticas – an interactive Atlas of all the languages in the world and where they are spoken

Overview: In hilo 7, students learned about the indigenous cultures of Latin America in regards to the ideals of beauty concepts and how those ideals influenced products (fashion), practices (what they do to be beautiful) and perspectives (why). In this summative assessment, they will take it one step further to investigate these indigenous cultures, original peoples or ethnic groups in Spanish-speaking countries that have maintained their original language/mother tongue throughout the years.

What does it mean for a country, where these original people reside, the fact that they maintain the language and culture of their ancestors? Does the language relate to the identity of the group and their origins?

Part I: Students will work in collaborative pairs or at the most a group of 3. Choose one of the original groups to investigate the history, the origin of the language, the current statistics of who speaks the language and where. Include maps of the countries and regions where the ethnic language is spoken. For example, three sources are required; each student is responsible for investigating, summarizing or outlining information for one of the sources.

Part II: Prepare an activity that promotes the maintenance and preservation of the original language of the ethnic group: teach a few words, feature ethnic celebrations that promote their identify and culture, and compare the ethnic language to the language of the nation. For example if they chose *mapuche* or *quechua*, they would compare it to Spanish: are there any words in common?

Part III. Convince your audience to maintain the mother tongue to strengthen the ethnic identity of the original peoples and to also learn the national language to become an integral part of the nation. Use a form of technology for the presentation.

Each student will submit a personal reflection summarizing what he or she learned.

Strategies are included on page 305 of the student edition and there is a detailed checklist in **Explorer**.

MANTA 5 Desafíos mundiales

Hilo 11 Temas del medio ambiente

Essential questions:
- ¿Cuáles son las causas del calentamiento global?
- ¿Cuáles son los efectos del calentamiento global?
- ¿Cómo se puede combatir el calentamiento global?

Student Learning Objectives

Interpersonal Communication: Speaking and Writing
- Exchange information about causes, effects, and victims of global warming.
- Exchange opinions on how individuals contribute to the carbon footprint of the planet.
- Collaborate to develop information for a Hispanic community on environmental threats.
- Exchange messages such as emails, blogs, or social media posts with ideas to combat global warming.
- Engage in discussions and debates about the responsibility of young people to confront climate change.
- Explain and provide examples of environmental threats in Spanish-speaking countries.

Interpretive Communication: Print, Audio, Audiovisual, and/or Visual Sources
- Demonstrate comprehension of content from a variety of authentic sources about climate change and its effects on living things.
- Interpret, analyze, and evaluate a global threat to living things on the planet.
- Interpret and summarize significant details on the environment from audiovisual sources.

Presentational Communication: Spoken and/or Written Presentations to a Variety of Audiences
- Persuade and convince others to be informed and get involved in protecting the environment.
- Collaborate with others to present information on how to protect the environment from global warming.
- Describe actions that young people in Spanish-speaking countries are taking to combat the environmental threats.
- Analyze and debate the global warming controversy.
- Produce reflections and journal entries to demonstrate understanding of global threats to the environment.

Relating Cultural Practices to Perspectives:
- Investigate, explain, and reflect on the relationship between environmental practices and the perspectives (beliefs/values/attitudes) of Hispanic cultures.

Relating Cultural Products to Perspectives:
- Investigate, explain, and reflect on the relationship between products that contribute to global warming and the perspectives (beliefs/values/attitudes) of Hispanic cultures.

Connections: Connect with Other Disciplines
- Make connections to content knowledge about the global environmental threats.

Connections: Acquire New Information
- Acquire and apply new information from authentic sources about environmental threats in Spanish-speaking countries.

Comparisons: Language
- Make linguistic comparisons of cognates, familiar commands with pronouns, *por* and *para*, and conjunctions.

Comparisons: Culture
- Analyze how global warming affects Spanish-speaking countries compared to the U.S.

School and Global Communities:
- Interact with Spanish speakers about global warming threats to the planet.

Lifelong Learning:
- Set goals and reflect on progress in using Spanish for enjoyment, enrichment, and advancement.

Suggested Lesson Plan Sequence/Pacing Guide

Manta 5: Desafíos mundiales
Hilo 11: Temas del medio ambiente

Focus according to Essential Question Pages in SE	Day (based on 60 min class)	Classroom Activities	Homework/ Formative assessment/ Exit pass
Causas del calentamiento global pp. 310–318	1	* Introduce unit with video and viewing activities * Pre-reading: prior knowledge, inferences and vocabulary * Active reading on penguins with note-taking/HW	* ¡Tu opinión cuenta! presentational speaking task * Reading can be assigned in part or in full as homework
	2	* Follow-up discussions to yesterday's reading on penguins * Pre-reading: vocabulary and connections to science * Active reading (two times) with note-taking/HW	* Journal prompt * Five tweets * Assign activity A as HW
	3	* Finish yesterday's activities: debate with a partner * Calculate carbon footprint online * Response to carbon footprint: reflection and conversation * Work on Te toca a ti from Act 1, finish for HW	* ¡Te toca a ti! on causes of global warming (Act 1) * 2–3 paragraph written reflection on carbon footprint activity
Efectos del calentamiento global pp. 319–329	4–5	* Activate prior knowledge on endangered species * Active reading with cause-effect graphic organizer * Discussion of text and map research to then present to class * Comprehension: M-C questions and comparison * Two ¿Qué aprendiste? tasks, begin in class/HW	* ¿Qué aprendiste? journal prompt (comparisons) * ¿Qué aprendiste? formative assessment * HW: Watch PSA video, Journal prompt and questions
	6	* Discussion of video that students saw at home * Collaborative activity on 3 topics from text * Active reading of text with organizer complete for HW	* Graphic organizer
	7 + optional Writer's Workshop	* Group work with placemat organizer and grammar review * ¡Tu opinión cuenta! and Reflexión tasks, (complete for HW) * Writer's Workshop day for in-class support for the Reflexión	* ¡Tu opinión cuenta! connection to local community * Reflexión essay
Maneras de combatir el calentamiento global pp. 330–339	8	* Pre-reading: conversation, journal prompt and cognates * Active reading with organizer to categorize content and grammar; share out organizers * Present C 2 task, to be completed at home * Organize to read second text at home, take notes on voc.	* Presentational speaking task * Reading of second text could be assigned as homework
	9	* Review text on teenagers in Paraguay and vocabulary * Written responses to text: summarize on FB comment * Present ¡A tejer! task and begin in class; students complete outside class to be ready to present on due date	* Written summary of text using target vocabulary * ¡A tejer! formative assessments to be completed at home
	10	* Think-Pair-Share and vocabulary exercises * View video and note-taking * Preview Socratic Seminar details, norms & grading	* Note-taking on video content
	11	* Set-up for Socratic Seminar, including prompts * Socratic Seminar, rotating students from observation to participation posts	* Participation in Socratic Seminar * Reflexión
	12 + one week	* Present parts of summative assessment	* Students develop, edit and present final project

Hilo 11 Temas del medio ambiente

Introducción ¿Qué sabes del calentamiento global?

Student book page 310
Time estimate: 30 to 45 minutes

A To help students activate their background knowledge of global warming, start this unit by having them complete a KWL chart (Tabla S, Q, A) about the theme "medio ambiente" with a focus on the three essential questions of our hilo about global warming. You can access a downloadable version in **Explorer** where you can print it or students can complete it electronically and submit to you. Once students have completed this individually, have students share with the class or add to a large KWL chart on poster paper that you can keep on the wall throughout the unit and update the "learned" column at the end.

B Be sure to show the video twice and have students complete each viewing activity. The first time have students focus on the images in the video and the second time on the text that the creator uses to make his point. Ask students to share out after the second viewing.

C Group students into pairs and have them discuss the questions included in this task. Encourage them to use the vocabulary at the end of this unit to help express their ideas. Once students have had time to discuss in pairs, open the discussion up to the class and allow students to share their ideas to spark their interest in the topics they will discuss in this hilo.

 ¡Tu opinión cuenta!

Have students record their responses in **Explorer** in the space provided. You can use this audio recording to see the level of each student as they begin this unit; you will see which aspects of global warming interest the students.

Antes de empezar ¿Quiénes son las víctimas del calentamiento global?

Student book page 311
Time estimate: 45 minutes

A 1. Before reading, give students a chance to think about any information they already know about penguins using the organizer that is available in **Explorer**. Once students have written what they know, ask them to share out some of the information with the whole class. There are some basic facts that students will know, but there may be a penguin expert in your midst who can help other students have a better understanding of penguins before beginning the reading.

2. Group students into pairs and have them come up with 5 inferences about how global warming impacts penguins and their habitats. You can ask each pair to write down their inferences, and share them with the group. Have students hang onto these inferences and come back to them once they have finished reading the article.

3. Students should recognize or be able to infer the meaning of many of these words from their knowledge of the English language or concepts from science classes.

B As students work on these two reading tasks you can have them record the information they find on sticky notes and post it alongside the text or they can simply make a list. After students have finished reading invite them to share out the information they find in the text.

C 1. After reading, have students either return to their original partners to discuss the inferences they made about penguins and their environments. They should talk about whether or not their inferences were correct and why any of their inferences may not have been included in the article. They should also discuss the environmental effects that the article includes that they did not suggest before reading. Encourage the groups to share out what they discussed.

2. For homework, or as a wrap-up at the end of class, have students complete the Reflexión in their journals. This is an opportunity for them to think about other effects of global warming and what they can be doing to help stop its progress, which are two themes that will be discussed later in the hilo.

MANTA 5 Desafíos mundiales

¿Cuáles son las causas del calentamiento global?

Actividad 1 ¿Cuáles son las cinco causas principales del calentamiento global?

Student book page 314
Time estimate: 60 minutes with homework (reading with note-taking) plus 20 minutes

 A

1. Before reading the text, give students an opportunity to be creative with some of the technical vocabulary that they will encounter and use in this activity. Assign this as homework before beginning the activity or a warm-up in class to prepare them for the reading.

2. This pair activity is a way to make connections with other content areas. Encouraging students to work together to think about what they know about global warming will give them confidence to tackle the text. Once students have had a chance to discuss in pairs, ask the class to predict the 5 causes of global warming that they think the article will address. Students can also do this activity online in **Explorer**.

 B

1. As students read through the text the first time encourage them to look up the vocabulary they don't understand rather than just skim over it. Have them use dictionaries to look up words or phrases they don't know so that they can better understand the text. If your school allows the use of cell phones or tablets, have students look up the words/phrases using www.wordreference.com instead of paper dictionaries.

2. For the second reading, have students make note of the human actions or habits that contribute to global warming. For example with the first cause, burning fossil fuels for energy, they can say that humans have multiple electronic devices on at the same time burning electricity.

 C

1. After students have finished reading have them create 5 tweets (140 characters or less) and submit these either in an **Explorer** forum (Hilo 11, Vocabulario), on paper or another web-based resource you have access to (Todaysmeet.com or Polleverywhere.com). The goal here is to have students summarize what they have read in their own words.

2. Pair students up and have them discuss the topics mentioned. One person defends why we as humans need to continue using fossil fuels for energy and gas, etc. and the other person will counter with why those habits are causing global warming and how dangerous that is for our environment. Encourage students to argue for both sides during this exercise to help them explore the pros and cons of the issues related to global warming. You can also make this a whole class debate and give them more time to do research so that they can form meaningful and articulate responses to share in the debate.

¡Te toca a ti!

This last task also serves as a formative assessment. Students can complete a variety of presentations to demonstrate their mastery of the causes of global warming. This can be an in-class or at-home activity. Students can create pamphlets, posters, Power Points, Prezis, videos or podcasts. The goal here is for students to communicate these ideas in the target language so encourage them to add in images, videos or other resources, but remind them that their presentations should clearly communicate in complete sentences the causes of global warming.

¿Cuáles son las causas del calentamiento global?

Actividad 2 ¿Cuál es tu huella de carbono personal?

Student book page 317
Time estimate: 1 class period with homework the night before and after
Grammar in context: Present subjunctive and/or informal commands to give advice in final conversation

Before students start researching and working on their carbon footprint calculations, have them read what a carbon footprint is and how it is calculated. You can also ask students to share if they have ever heard of the calculator and in what context.

A For homework have students do some research about how they and their families use different forms of energy that negatively impact the environment. An alternative to having students share their family information, would be for them to gather information about the school's use of energy. Before students go home with this list, go over a few of the key terms to ensure that they will be able to complete the research.

B We have embedded the calculator into our *Tejidos* **Explorer**. There are several other calculators out there in Spanish but they are specific to different countries and would yield skewed results. What might be interesting is to find a friend or family member of yours or a student in the class who lives in Spain or Chile (see links in **Explorer** for this activity) and collect that information to complete the respective carbon footprint calculations and see how they compare to the students in your class. You might even Skype those people during class one day to talk about the results your class discovered about their global footprint.

C 1. As students finish the calculator activity, have them write a reflection about how they think their results turned out, how they compare to the averages mentioned on the results page and what areas of their lives have the greatest negative impact on the environment.

2. To finish this activity, have students get into pairs. Each student should share with his/her partner the results of their carbon footprint and the ways they most negatively impact the environment. Their partner should then offer them advice on how to reduce their carbon foot print using the subjunctive to make suggestions or informal commands. Then they should switch roles.

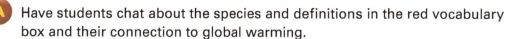
¿Cuáles son las causas del calentamiento global?

Actividad 3 ¿Cuáles son los efectos del cambio climatico en España?

Student book page 319
Time estimate: 2 60-minute classes with homework and 1 day (not consecutive) to present the collaborative assignment. The reading in this activity can be assigned as homework prior to beginning the activity in class.

 A Have students chat about the species and definitions in the red vocabulary box and their connection to global warming.

 B Have students access the flow chart organizer in **Explorer** to indicate effects and their consequences on the environment.

> **Answers to Part B:**
>
> 1. **La aparición de especies invasoras** – proliferación del mejillón cebra – modifica las características del agua, lo cual afecta la flora y fauna y obstruye construcciones hidráulicas
>
> 2. **La aparición de especies invasoras** – proliferación de la medusa - perjudica las playas y la pesca
>
> 3. **La alteración del vitivíncola** – producción reducida en el sur de España – afecta la economía
>
> 4. **La alteración del turismo** – temporadas más cortas de esquí --el calor extremo para el turismo estival (del verano)
>
> 5. **La subida del nivel del mar** – inundaciones en la costa de Vizcaya – arriesgan industrial y residencias
>
> 6. **Menos precipitaciones** – ideal para los incendios forestales – Grandes Incendios Forestales difíciles de combatir
>
> 7. **Riesgos para la salud** – olas de frío y calor causan muertes humanas – proliferación de mosquitos transmiten enfermedades infecciosas y reaparecerán enfermedades ya erradicadas

 C Students will compare organizers and decide which 3 are the greatest threats to Spain and which regions of Spain will be most effected.

Answers to Part D:
1. a. (not mentioned in text as a specific threat to humans)
2. b. (Disappearance of the cork tree will not affect tourism)

 Culture box: The text and documentary refer to the scarcity of drinking water that affects many areas world-wide. There are interviews of indigenous women in an area northeast of Peru, "El agua más preciada de las mujeres Wayuu de Colombia". Go to your **Explorer** course to access this activity.

 This formative assessment can be assigned as homework in their journal or can be collected. Students will complete an organizer to compare environmental threats in Spain to threats in the U.S.

 There are 3 options for students to show what they have learned about environmental threats to regions of Spain or Latin America. This formative assessment can be on the same topic that they are researching for the summative assessment so students can use the same information twice! You may have them work in collaborative pairs and present to other Spanish classes or have a Skype session with a Spanish class at another school. There are links, additional activities, and scaffolding in **Explorer** that will guide them.

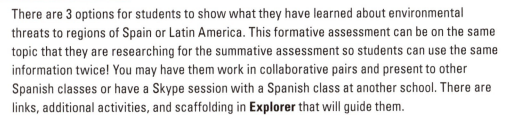

¿Cuáles son los efectos del calentamiento global?

Actividad 4 ¿Te puedes enfermar debido al calentamiento global?

Student book page 323
Time estimate: 2 60-minute classes with optional Writer's Workshop day for Reflexión essay; have students finish reading and the graphic organizer at home after the first day in class
Grammar in context: por and para

    The day before beginning this activity, assign students to watch the PSA video on *¿Qué haces con las pilas que botas?* with accompanying questions and journal assignment. This activity introduces health effects to humans caused by human activity and climate change.

Answers for Culture box questions:
1. personal answer
2. B

A Pre-assessment: what do students already know about…? Hang 3 sheets of chart paper in 3 sections of the classroom with the titles of each of the topics (which are listed again below for your reference). Form 3 groups of students, one group starting at each chart. Give them a time limit to record what they know (2-3 minutes), then they will circulate to the next chart until they have recorded what they know at all three charts. Review as a class. Advise them not to repeat the same ideas as another group.

1. las enfermedades o las condiciones médicas que sufre la gente debido al aumento de las temperaturas

2. las enfermedades o las condiciones médicas provocadas por la contaminación del aire y el agua

3. las enfermedades o las condiciones médicas provocadas por los desastres naturales

 B Let students begin to read the article and start the organizer available in **Explorer**, in class with a classmate; they can finish it for homework. An option would be for each student to chart 6 of the diseases but they need to decide who is doing which ones so they are all covered.

 C **1.** The next day, form groups of 4 for this activity. Using their organizers, have students make inferences regarding the following categories on the placemat organizer. It is a good idea to enlarge the organizer found in **Explorer** to an 11 x 17 size, one per group. They each start with one category and write as much as they can, after 2–3 minutes, have them rotate the organizer and begin adding to the next category. Students may make corrections to the prior student's work, with their permission but may not record the same information. They can also use the information in the culture box about *Efectos de cambios climáticos a la salud.*

 2. Compare the organizers with the other groups in the class in order to add more ideas and reference them when they are writing their reflections.

 ¡Tu opinión cuenta!

Students connect and personalize what they have learned by identifying and analyzing how climate change could cause an illness in your community or in a community in your region or country. For example, what are some illnesses that can result from natural disasters?

Reflexión

 This cultural comparison can be a formative assessment, written and submitted to you, or synthesized in their journals. Students are provided with strategies on page 329 in the Student Edition to support the writing of the cultural comparisons.

¿Cómo se puede combatir el calentamiento global?

Actividad 5 *¿Qué pueden hacer los jóvenes para combatir el calentamiento global?*

Student book page 330
Time estimate: 2 60-minute class periods with homework (assign second text as homework for the second lesson)
Grammar in context: Informal commands with pronouns

 A   **3.** This is a linguistic activity that could help students practice their pronunciation in Spanish to make sure that they are saying the words correctly.

 B   **1.** Students organize their answers according to their own experience on this organizer, which is available in **Explorer**, meaning that there will not be one "correct" way to complete it. There is space in the organizer for students to fill in other suggestions that they have heard. Grammar points that can be drawn out of this text include:

- "si" clause: *se podría crear si los polos se derritieran*
- use of "lo que"
- informal commands – positive and negative
- the use of "dejar de" + infinitive

 C   **2.** In **Explorer** students can hear the recording for this activity, and then record themselves speaking to leave a message for their friend in response.

> **« | » Audio script**
>
> Hola, parece que no te encuentras en este momento. Oye, acabo de leer algo en línea que me preocupó, no me había dado cuenta del alcance del calentamiento global y parece que ya nos está afectando a todos de manera muy grave. Yo sé que has estudiado más sobre el tema y quisiera que me dijeras qué podría hacer yo para ayudar. ¿Qué puede hacer una persona para no contribuir tanto a la destrucción del medio ambiente? Me siento con muchas ganas de hacer algo ya que supongo que también soy responsable de tanta contaminación y explotación de recursos. Avísame si puedes. ¡Gracias!

 D   Students should be able to infer the meaning of at least some/most of these words in context; you could have them work together to share answers afterward. Definitions are included in the list at the end of the hilo for reference.

 E   **1.** Here students work with their list of words from Part D and share the list of cognates with the same classmate. At this point they have a significant amount of vocabulary to use in their written summary. This is a nice presentational writing formative assessment, both as a comprehension check and to see students' ability to paraphrase textual information using target vocabulary.

2. Students can complete this activity on the Facebook message template available in **Explorer**, Recursos, Organizadores gráficos.

¡A tejer!

This can be individual or pair work. Just like the final project for hilo 4, when students proposed and defended their travel plan, this asks students to use persuasive language when presenting their ideas. See if you can find ways to really use this material in your school! In **Explorer**, in the Enlaces section for this hilo there are other sites that students can use for ideas. This is also another place where students can use the research that they have found for the summative assessment or build on what they have done in this activity for the summative assessment. The persuasive message will serve as practice for the public service announcement that they will do for the summative.

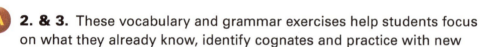

¿Cómo se puede combatir el calentamiento global?

Actividad 6 *Juntos, ¿cómo podemos mejorar el medio ambiente?*

Student book page 334
Time estimate: 2 60-minute class periods

A **2. & 3.** These vocabulary and grammar exercises help students focus on what they already know, identify cognates and practice with new vocabulary. You may consider having students switch partners for Part A Steps 1, 2, and 3 to get them up and moving around the classroom a bit during this time.

Culture box: This context will help students understand the international importance of protecting the environment as a goal and priority that crosses borders, as the United Nations' work in this area demonstrates.

B You might want to consider having the students watch the video once without sound, or watch a part of it as time allows. This activates students' vocabulary and background knowledge and will have them making predictions about what the video will be about. Have them turn and talk to a partner and share a few ideas with the class. Then they are primed and ready to watch with sound – this time fully tuned in to listen! The note-taking strategies give suggestions how students can be responsible for the information in the video for the follow-up tasks – everyone accomplishes this differently depending on their learning style so be open to students' different approaches. Consider having the class watch the video twice, or allow them to watch it at home to prepare for the Socratic Seminar-style conversation the following class. This will help all students feel prepared and more confident.

C **1.** Be sure to thoroughly review the expectations for participation in a Socratic Seminar (pages 336–337 including strategy box) especially if you have not done this with your class before. You might put the sentence starters from the blue strategy box on the board or on a poster for students to easily see. If the class is large you may consider doing this in a "fishbowl" style where half the class sits in an inner circle and takes part in the conversation where the other half sits on the outside and observes, making tally marks and written comments on another student's participation. (A guide is provided in **Explorer** under Apoyo adicional for this purpose). In either case, be sure to keep a running checklist of each student's participation and following of norms. Showing all students the observation sheet can help motivate them to follow the norms and participate.

 Reflexión

Asking students to reflect on their participation in the Socratic Seminar is an important piece to the process; this can help them see how their participation affected the overall conversation and how each student's respectful listening and thoughtful participation counts!

Culture box: In addition to checking out this group's Facebook page (link available in **Explorer**) you might have students look for other such groups and share them with the class.

Essential questions:
- ¿Cuáles son las causas del calentamiento global?
- ¿Cuáles son los efectos del calentamiento global?
- ¿Cómo se puede combatir el calentamiento global?

Hilo 11 Evaluación final — *Juntos cuidemos nuestro planeta ¡Haz tu parte!*

Student book page 338
Time estimate: 1 60-minute class to present the 2-minute public service announcements and showcase the brochures plus class time over a one week period to collaborate and plan the evaluation
Grammar in context: Subjunctive and indicative after conjunctions; infinitives after prepositions

This is a collaborative summative assessment that involves researching an international threat to the environment. The purpose is to prepare a brochure/flyer to inform and involve the Hispanic community in your region in solving the problem and support sustainable development.

Announce the summative assessment at the beginning of the hilo so students can think about what they want to do. If they work in pairs, they will need some class time to research, decide a layout, compose the brochure, and prepare a script for a public service announcement. The summative assessment rubric outlines all the criteria and their performance level.

Part I: Students will choose a topic from those listed on the Final Evaluation link in **Explorer**. Encourage them to sign up for a topic of interest but not more than one pair per topic. If they have another idea, they will need your approval. They will research how the problem affects living things on the planet and what can be done to protect the planet from these changes. There are many links in **Explorer** and sources in the hilo that they can access. Encourage them to do the research outside of class, possibly as homework.

Part II. They will produce the brochure/flyer in a digital format (Microsoft Publisher, Pages) or a newsletter type flyer. Other formats are acceptable depending on their access to technology. The four sections to be included are on the checklist. Encourage them to peer edit brochures of other teams for feedback.

Parte III: Students will prepare a script to include the most pertinent information from the brochure including tips to remedy the problem. There are some very brief sample PSA announcements on the Final Evaluation. Find more links in **Explorer**. Ideally, they will video record their PSA and show it to the class. Students may even post them to their social media sites!

MANTA 5 **Desafíos mundiales**

Hilo digital **Población y demografía**

Essential questions:
- ¿Cuáles son las razones por las que la gente decide emigrar de su país?
- ¿Cuáles son los desafíos a los que se enfrentan en el proceso de emigrar a otro país?
- ¿Cuáles son los desafíos a los que se enfrentan los emigrantes en un nuevo país?

Student Learning Objectives

Interpersonal Communication: Speaking and Writing
- Exchange information about reasons people emigrate.
- Exchange opinions about immigration reform in the U.S.
- Explain and evaluate the process of citizenship for immigrants to the U.S.
- Explain and analyze the acculturation process an immigrant faces in a new culture.
- Exchange phone calls, letters, emails, blogs, or social media posts about emigration experiences in the new culture.
- Explain and provide examples of the challenges emigrants face in the process of migration.

Interpretive Communication: Print, Audio, Audiovisual, and/or Visual Sources
- Demonstrate comprehension from a variety of authentic sources about migration, emigration, and immigration.
- Interpret and evaluate the acculturation process an immigrant faces in a new culture.
- Interpret and analyze challenges and opportunities for Spanish-speaking immigrants in a new country.
- Interpret and summarize significant details about the process of citizenship in the U.S. for immigrants.
- Interpret and analyze testimonies about emigration experiences from authentic sources.

Presentational Communication: Spoken and/or Written Presentations to a Variety of Audiences
- Present information about migration and cultural perspectives.
- Summarize and reflect on the acculturation process an emigrant faces in a new culture.
- Research, analyze, compare, and present information about emigrant motives and experiences before, during and after emigration to a new culture.
- Develop a persuasive argument about advantages and disadvantages of emigration.
- Produce reflections on forums to demonstrate understanding of cultural perspectives on migration, emigration, and immigration.

Relating Cultural Practices to Perspectives:
- Investigate, explain, and reflect on the relationship between migration practices and the perspectives (motivation/attitudes) of Hispanic cultures.

Relating Cultural Products to Perspectives:
- Investigate, explain, and reflect on the relationship between migration policies/laws and the perspectives (beliefs/values/attitudes) of Hispanic cultures.

Connections: Connect with Other Disciplines
- Make connections to content knowledge about the history and social impact of immigration in the U.S.

Connections: Acquire New Information
- Acquire and apply new information from authentic sources about migration, emigration, and immigration.

Comparisons: Language
- Make linguistic comparisons of cognates, progressive tenses, past participles as adjectives, and uses of *por/para* in Spanish to English.

Comparisons: Culture
- Compare and contrast challenges immigrants face when adapting to new cultures.

School and Global Communities:
- Interact with Spanish speakers about immigration from the perspective of a Hispanic culture.

Lifelong Learning:
- Set goals and reflect on progress in using Spanish for enjoyment, enrichment, and advancement.

Suggested Lesson Plan Sequence/Pacing Guide
Manta 5: Desafíos mundiales
Hilo digital: Población y demografía

Focus according to Essential Question Actividades	Day (based on 60 min class)	Classroom Activities	Homework/ Formative assessment/ Exit pass
Las razones por las que la gente decide emigrar de su país Introducción, Antes de empezar, Actividades 1, 2	1	* Introduce unit as a digital hilo: all activities will be accessible and completed online * Unit hook, vocabulary review and conversation * Graph interpretation * Forum with initial opinions (follow-up in activity 4)	* Graph interpretation questions 1-4 * ¡Tu opinión cuenta! response * Antes de empezar Te toca a ti
	2	* Anticipation Guide * Active viewings of video with graphic organizer * Vocabulary exercise * Present ¡Te toca a ti! homework	* Graphic organizers for comprehension and vocabulary
	3–4	* Activator: readings and forum * Pre-viewing predictions with graphic organizer * Active viewings of documentary with organizer, discussion and comprehension check * Pre-reading vocabulary inferences * Active reading with Venn diagram and forum * ¡A tejer! Synthesis essay	* Graphic organizer * Venn diagram * Synthesis essay
	5–7	* Pre-reading conversation * Active reading with pro's/con's and rating of countries; share out answers * Comprehension check: short answer questions * Active listening to podcasts with note-taking * Second time listening and comprehension check * ¡Te toca a ti! interpersonal oral task * Guatemala documentary and questions	* Text and audio comprehension checks * ¡Te toca a ti! simulated conversation * Short answer questions to Guatemala documentary
Los desafíos a los que se enfrentan en el proceso de emigrar a otro país Actividades 3, 4	8	* Citizenship exam practice * Active reading with statistics graphic organizer * Comprehension checks: questions, quiz * ¡Tu opinión cuenta! presentational oral task	* Short answer * Recording and multiple-choice quiz * ¡Tu opinión cuenta! task
	9–10	* Pre-reading: video, forums and vocabulary * Active reading twice through with graphic organizer * Post-reading conversation and vocabulary * Reflection and optional debate	* Graphic organizer * Vocabulary exercises * Reflexión
Los desafíos para emigrantes en un nuevo país Actividad 5, Evaluación final	11–12	* Think-Pair-Share and preview of reading * Active reading with graphic organizer * Sharing out and discussion * ¡Te toca a ti! Listening and speaking task * Grammar review	* Graphic organizer * ¡Te toca a ti! listening and speaking task
	13–14	* Present summative assessment requirements * Students prepare and present projects	* Students develop, edit and present final projects

Hilo digital Población y demografía

This is an hilo digital, meaning that all of the material can be found online in *Tejidos* **Explorer**. Students can work together on some tasks, meaning not every student needs individual access to a computer or other device at all times. Use your best judgment of your students and the available technology; many of the online forum activities can be modified to be completed as journal prompts, for example. In **Explorer**, PDFs are provided of different activities so that you could print these out if needed, and use them as a paper version for students.

Introducción ¿Qué sabes de la emigración?

Time estimate: 1 60-minute class period

A Have students observe the sign and write what they think about it in the forum, then exchange ideas with a partner.

B In a small group students will talk about how to remember the differences between the three words and then design a symbol, image or graphic that symbolizes what the words mean. It can be a simple sketch or computer generated; if possible, students can share it on the digital forum.

> **Vocabulary answers to Part B 1:**
> 1. B   2. C   3. A

C Students will interpret the 4 graphs on the country facts regarding immigrants, those who emigrate and those who send remittances to their home countries. Have students answer the questions in their notebooks and then share out their answers for numbers 5 and 6 in the online forum.

> **Answers to Part C: Answers may vary.**
> 1. México, India, Rusia, China, Ucrania: Los de India y China vienen para estudiar y/o trabajar en profesiones; los de México y Ucrania- vienen para una mejor vida y/o trabajos
> 2. EE.UU., Rusia, Alemania tienen las tasas más altas. Será por las oportunidades de trabajar y la mejor vida
> 3. EE.UU.,Arabia Saudita, Suiza, Rusia, Alemania: los inmigrantes trabajan y mandan remesas (dinero) a sus familias en sus países de origen.
> 4. India, China, México, Francia, Filipinas: reciben el dinero de los países en # 3.

Note to teachers: As a homework assignment for day 2 you may want to assign **¡Te toca a ti!** from the Antes de empezar activity coming up next.

> **Antes de empezar** ¿Qué sabes de las experiencias de los inmigrantes hispanos?

Time estimate: 1 60-minute class plus homework
Grammar in context: progressive tenses and uses

  Anticipation guide: There is no right or wrong answer; this activity is designed to gauge what students think at this point and to see if their opinions or attitudes change by the end of the hilo, Actividad 4 Reflexión.

  As they watch the video for the first and second times, students note information in the forum about voluntary and involuntary reasons for migration.

> **Answers to Part B:**
> **Razones involuntarias:**
> 1) los refugiados se consideran forzados por razones políticas o por las condiciones de vida
> 2) también por la persecución o falta de seguridad
> 3) son trabajadores calificados pero sin oportunidades de empleo en su país de origen
>
> **Razones voluntarias:**
> 1) emigran para reunirse con su pareja, después siguen los hijos y los padres
> 2) por curiosidad de cómo es al otro lado
> 3) no le gusta la forma de vida en su país de origen y prefieren vivir de otra manera

  Students will indicate advantages and disadvantages of immigration, based on the video and/or their background knowledge. **Answers may vary** as long as they can justify their answers. If they are unfamiliar with the vocabulary, they can refer to the *hilo* vocabulary list available online. Have them think of other words they can include in these two categories.

> **Suggested answers for C:**
> 1st column: V, D, D, V, V, D, V, D
> 2nd column: D, D, D, V, V, V, D
> 3rd column: D, V, D, D, V, D, D, D

 ¡Te toca a ti!

As a homework assignment, have students write about an immigrant experience; if they or their family/friends have no personal experience, they can write about one of the young men in the video. You may want to assign this as a homework/journal assignment day 1 of this unit so that students can share info with the class or on the forum.

 Optional: The next day, have students share what they wrote, in their journal or on the online forum, about an immigrant experience. Post three charts around the room; each chart will reflect an aspect of immigrant experiences that students will share based on their homework reflection. Each chart will note one of the following: a) reasons for leaving, b) reasons for coming and c) how their life changed. After all the information is on the chart paper; have each group compile the three most frequent reasons for each category. Find out if everyone agrees and if this truly reflects the reality of immigration.

¿Cuáles son las razones por las que la gente decide emigrar de su país?

Actividad 1 ¿Qué motiva a la gente a tomar la decisión de emigrar de su país de origen?

Time estimate: 2 60-minute classes with readings for homework
Grammar in context: uses of progressive tenses, review and exercises in **Explorer**

A As a homework assignment or to start out this activity in class, have students read this text and explain in the forum the three fundamental factors that push people to leave their home countries. The links provided can help provide additional information. Students should read the **Culture box** text from MeQuieroIr.com at this point as well.

B **1.** Before watching the documentary "Los peligros de la migración", students will predict what dangers the Central American immigrants will face when crossing through Mexico to get to the U.S. Have students activate prior knowledge and indicate their predictions in column one of the graphic organizer.

Description of documentary:
En "Los peligros de la migración", las historias siguen a migrantes centroamericanos que viajan a través de México abordo de trenes de carga. Migrantes en este viaje enfrentan innumerables riesgos incluyendo asaltos, secuestros, violaciones, y hasta la muerte mientras intentan llegar a los Estados Unidos en búsqueda de una mejor vida.

2. Have students verify what they predicted and add additional information heard on the video: *robos, asaltos, secuestros, violaciones y hasta la muerte* to columns two and three of the organizer.

C After sharing their information from the organizer with the class in step 1, here students discuss in small groups. They can also share their answers on the digital forum. Afterwards make sure the class mentions the following points:

Answers to Part C 2:
- Condiciones que los empuja: aumento de violencia, precios más altos de la comida y tasas de empleo cada vez más altas, siguen intentando el viaje,
- asaltos, secuestros, violaciones, y hasta la muerte
- quiere mejorar la vida, no quiere aguantar hambre
- Answers will vary

D While students are watching the documentary a second time, have them notice the differences between those who emigrate with "papers" and those who are undocumented. This will be discussed in more detail in forthcoming activities. Have students listen more specifically for comprehension of facts and opinions offered in the documentary to complete the statements for this activity.

Answers to Part D completion:

1. leyes
2. albergue
3. gente local
4. las amenazas
5. secuestrados
6. Las condiciones
7. derechos
8. ranchos
9. un rescate
10. seres humanos

E As they watch the documentary, have students keep adding information to their Venn Diagram organizers on reasons for emigrating from their countries with or without documentation. They can hand in this organizer during part G at the end of the exercise.

F Before students read the articles, have them make three inferences/predictions from the vocabulary about the emigrant population they will be reading about.

G What do people emigrating from Colombia, Spain and Venezuela have in common? While reading, have students add this information to their organizers for the documented emigrants and can also share it in the online forum if you wish. Ex: The desire of young professionals to have a better life due to unstable economical and political conditions in their countries.

¡A tejer!

To synthesize all the information they have read and seen about the two groups of emigrants, using the comparisons organizer in **Explorer**, students will write an analysis of the similarities and differences of what pushes the two groups of emigrants to leave their countries: one group is educated and may have the appropriate papers for legal immigration, visa, green card, blue card, etc. and the other group is arriving without documentation. After describing their experiences, students conclude by noting what these groups have in common. Follow steps 1, 2 and 3.

¡Tu opinión cuenta!

In this digital forum, students have the opportunity to read about one particular case study and decide what they think this young man should do. It is important that students justify their answers!

¿Cuáles son las razones por las que la gente decide emigrar de su país?

Actividad 2 ¿Cuáles son algunos países que atraen a los emigrantes y por qué?

Time estimate: 3 60-minute classes
Grammar in context: uses of por/para, review and exercises in **Explorer**

A Before students start reading, this is a good time to provide provocations for students to predict the content of this activity. Post images of other countries or create a slide show on your computer of different countries where Spanish-speakers emigrate other than the United States and Canada; have them give reasons why they would choose these countries. The link given in **Explorer** can provide further food for thought.

  While reading, students indicate the pros and cons of each country mentioned in the text that follows, then decide which country they would choose and why. After reading, students share their lists. What country did the majority of students choose? Students can create their own graph and upload them to the digital forum or you can create one as a class.

  ¿Qué aprendiste?

Students can answer the questions in small groups or take the online quiz.

Possible answers to ¿Qué aprendiste?

1. La política de inmigración que aporta la fuerza laboral, el ingenio y la diversidad cultural.
2. Los Estados Unidos, los latinos son la primera minoría étnica del país.
3. Prefieren España por las raíces históricas, políticas y culturas compartidas, ya saben el idioma y quizás sea mas fácil conseguir los papeles para emigrar.
4. Los peninsulares prefieren destinos tales como las naciones de la Unión Europea, por ello son Alemania, Francia y el Reino Unido, Los españoles identifican las naciones europeas desarrolladas con la oportunidad de conseguir trabajo. también apuestan por una mejor vida en otros continentes: Estados Unidos, Argentina, Ecuador y Venezuela en las Américas o en Marruecos.
5. Answers may vary

   Students answer the questions about the two Bolivians' experiences while listening to the podcasts. Give them time to look over and understand the information that they will need to participate in the online forum before starting the audio. The introduction is very fast but the actual testimonies are reasonable for most students to understand, especially if they listen more than once.

Answers to Part C:

1. Es neutral por la mayor parte, todavía hay diferencias culturales entre los dos países- la forma de hablar, el clima, la comida, etc.
2. Por lo general, para mejorar sus condiciones, oportunidades laborales.
3. El clima, la comida, el transporte público, la tecnología, el orden de los servicios públicos como la cuestión sanitaria
4. La manera de hablar es más fuerte, la gente menos cariñosa según los bolivianos.
5. Answers may vary: no están con sus familias, no era tan fácil buscar empleo como pensaban, etc.

  Students listen a second time and complete the True/False activity (answers on following page).

Answers to Part D:
1. Falsa - Es el segundo país.
2. Cierta
3. Falsa - Tiene dos hijos en Bolivia.
4. Falsa - Su manera es más fuerte, parece ser de insulto.
5. Falsa - El clima en España hace más frío en el invierno y más calor en el verano (en Madrid).
6. Cierta
7. Cierta
8. Cierta
9. Cierta
10. Falsa - España tiene mucho más orden sanitario.

¡Te toca a ti!

This formative assessment is an example of the Advanced Placement Language & Culture exam interpersonal speaking task. This is a telephone call between an undocumented immigrant and his/her family in Central America. Instructions to the students on the recording are in Spanish.

Here are the English instructions: You will participate in a conversation. You will have 90 seconds to read the preview of the conversation and an outline of each speaker in the conversation. Each time it is your turn to speak, you will have 30 seconds to record each response so that you get used to the recording process.

We suggest that you model the process with the whole class so they understand the format. They are encouraged to say one or two complete thoughts but they do not have to speak for the entire 30 seconds.

« | » | Audio script

Llamada telefónica entre Roberto y su familia

Vas a participar en una conversación. Primero vas a tener 90 segundos para leer la introducción y el esquema de la conversación. Después, comenzará la conversación, siguiendo el esquema. Cada vez que te corresponda participar en la conversación, vas a tener 30 segundos para grabar tu respuesta. Debes participar de la manera más completa y apropiada posible pero no hay que llenar el tiempo completo en la grabación.

Tienes 90 segundos para leer la introducción y el esquema de la conversación.

For teacher only: This provides the actual script that students will hear but they do not see this script. The script that they see in order to follow the conversation is below.

Tu familia	Hola
Tú	Salúdalos y diles quién eres.
Tu familia	Ay Dios mío Roberto, cuánto te extrañamos, ¿cómo te va allá en el norte?
Tú	Contéstenles con unos detalles
Tu familia	Cuanto me alegro, cuéntame de tu vida allá ¿qué tipo de trabajo tienes? Te agradecemos por la plata que nos manda de vez en cuando, hemos podido comprar unas cosas para los niños para que asistan a la escuela.
Tú	Contéstenles con detalles.
Tu familia	¿Cómo es la gente, te trata bien?
Tú	Responde con algunos detalles de tus circunstancias.
Tu familia	Esperamos que estés seguro/a. Te mandamos muchos besos y abrazos de toda la familia, qué estés bien Roberto.
Tú	Asegúrales que estás bien y después despídete.

This is the outline of the conversation that students will be able to view while they record their conversation:

Eres un/a inmigrante latino/a indocumentado/a de Centroamérica en Washington D.C. por nueve meses. Vas a hacer una llamada telefónica para comunicar con tu familia en tu país de origen contándole cómo te va en tu nuevo "hogar". Cuéntales de tus dificultades que enfrentas al no poder hablar inglés y la situación de los ilegales que conoces. Afortunadamente tienes un empleo y la oportunidad de tomar unas clases gratis para aprender inglés.

Antes de hacer la llamada, piensa en lo que vas a decir cuando contesten el teléfono.

El esquema de la conversación entre tú y tu familia:

Tu familia:	Te saludan.
Tú	Salúdalos y diles quién eres.
Tu familia:	Te responden y te hacen una pregunta.
Tú	Contéstenles con unos detalles.
Tu familia:	Te hacen una pregunta y te agradecen por algo.
Tú	Contéstenles con detalles.
Tu familia:	Te hacen una pregunta.
Tú	Responde con algunos detalles de tus circunstancias.
Tu familia:	Se despiden de ti.
Tú:	Asegúrales que estás bien y después despídete.

Reflexión

The link to the video is available when you first click to enter the quiz. Students will view "La realidad de niños en Guatemala: Viajan solos para ir a los EE.UU.", an 18-minute documentary produced by UNICEF Guatemala. Students will then complete the short-answer questions online.

Answers to Reflexión assessment (answers may vary somewhat):

1. *¿Cuál es el motivo por el cual los niños toman el riesgo de ser violados o asaltados?*
   - Mejorar sus condiciones económicas
   - Conseguir un empleo
   - Reunificación familiar
2. *¿Cuáles son los factores que los empujan hacia la migración?*
   - La pobreza
   - La falta de oportunidades
   - La violencia en la sociedad, intrafamiliar o el abuso sexual
   - La desintegración familiar
3. *¿Por qué piensas que ignoran los peligros de la migración?* Como jóvenes, piensan que el éxito de llegar a los EE.UU. vale más que el riesgo y los peligros.
4. *¿De qué trabajan en camino a los EE.UU.?* Venden artículos o dulces en la calle.
5. *¿Qué les pasa en la mayoría de los casos si las autoridades los detienen?* Se quedan un rato en un albergue juvenil pero por lo general los deportan a su país de origen lo más pronto posible. El problema es que no siempre hay familiares que los reciban.

¿Cuáles son los desafíos a los que se enfrentan en el proceso de emigrar a otro país?

Actividad 3 ¿Cómo es el proceso de emigrar legalmente y conseguir ciudadanía en los EE.UU?

Time estimate: 1 60-minute class with homework (presentational oral tasks and multiple choice quiz)

Grammar in context: Passive voice with *ser* and *se*, exercises are included in Activity 5 Uso del lenguaje

1. For this first pre-reading activity engage students in this portion of the Naturalization Exam to help them empathize with the population of US residents and citizens they will be reading about in the article.

The first link at the bottom of the activity allows students to access the Citizenship Test in Spanish that provides more questions, answers, and audio recordings of each question. You can have students ask each other the questions, or you can play the questions using the audio links on the site and then have students to take turns responding. Review some of the vocabulary that they might not know, like *enmienda*.

Answers for Citizenship Test A & B:

Exam A
1. la constitución
2. declaró la independencia de los Estado Unidos (de Gran Bretaña)
3. Congreso (Poder legislative, Presidente, Poder ejecutivo, los tribunales, Poder judicial)
4. el Senado y la Cámara (de Representantes)
5. el Vicepresidente
6. Republicano y Demócrata
7. 18 años
8. Indios americanos y Nativos americanos
9. Virginia, Massachusetts, …
10. La Guerra Civil

Examen B
1. expresión y religión
2. la vida, la libertad, la búsqueda de la felicidad
3. el Presidente
4. (answers will vary state to state and election results)
5. Secretario de Agricultura, Secretario de Comercio, Secretario de Defensa, Secretario de Educación, Secretario de Energía, Secretario de Salud y Servicios Humanos
6. Demócrata
7. libertad de expression, libertad de la palabra, libertad de reunion…
8. Thomas Jefferson
9. 1787
10. Franklin Roosevelt

As students read have them complete the table to help them organize the statistics into a format that will help them understand what those numbers mean. Answers are provided on the next page. Then have students read the article again and take note of any information or statistics in the text that surprise them (for example that some people who have requested residency for family reasons can wait between 1 and 18 years to receive their permanent resident visa).

Answers to Part B:

La población de las personas que viven en los EE.UU. que nacieron en el extranjero

% de ciudadanos estadounidenses naturalizados	37
% de inmigrantes legales permanentes	31
% de portadores de una visa legal temporal	4
% de no autorizados	28

De los 1.1 millones de residentes permanentes legales…

% de los que fueron patrocinados por parientes inmediatos con ciudadanía	47
% de los que fueron admitidos por preferencias familiares	29
% de los que fueron admitidos como refugiados	16
% de los que fueron admitidos por preferencias de empleo	13
% de los que fueron admitidos como parte de la lotería de diversidad	4

De los residentes permanentes legales …

% de recién llegados	33
% que han vivido en los EEUU antes de forma legal	15
% que viven en los EEUU que no son autorizados	52

C Each student will choose two of the questions to record their answers in **Explorer**. Then the answers can be exchanged in a forum where they can hear all the answers. This can be given as an assignment to complete outside of class, along with the following two tasks, as needed.

¿Qué aprendiste?

Have students complete the 5 multiple-choice questions online and then review the answers as a class.

Answers to ¿Qué aprendiste?
1) C
2) B
3) A
4) B
5) B

¡Tu opinión cuenta!

Give students time to analyze the information in the article and make their own decision about how the data listed impacts their opinion on immigration reform. Students will record and submit their message in **Explorer**.

> ¿Cuáles son los desafíos a los que se enfrentan en el proceso de emigrar a otro país?

Actividad 4 ¿Cómo es la experiencia al cruzar la frontera?

Time estimate: 2 60-minute classes (reading can be finished outside of class as homework)

 A As a provocation for this activity, have students watch and respond to the video clip "Un viaje al lomo de la bestia".

  B This reflection will help students begin to connect to individuals who choose to risk everything to move to another country.

  C This vocabulary is not glossed in the reading as it is easily inferred from the context. This activity gives students a chance to determine the meaning of these words and phrases within the context of immigration before approaching the text.

> **Part C answers:**
> - mojado – otro nombre para el que cruza la frontera sin papeles
> - casa de seguridad – lugar de refugio para protegerse al llegar al otro lado
> - etiquetas – categorías sociales, legales o étnicas que se dan a los que cruzan la frontera
> - coyote – el que pagas para ayudarles a cruzar la frontera
> - pruebas – los desafíos con los que se enfrentan al emigrar
> - la frontera – límite/línea entre dos países
> - indocumentado – sin papeles
> - otro lado – después de cruzar la frontera/los Estados Unidos
> - rito de pasaje – la experiencia de cruzar la frontera y convertirse en migrante
> - el norte – después de cruzar la frontera/los Estados Unidos

  D As students read, these two tasks will guide them to better understand the text. Have students access the T-chart and label the headings 1) Desafíos en camino and 2) Desafíos al llegar. As students read the first time through, they should be looking for challenges that individuals face in the journey to cross the border. As they read the second time, they are to look for the challenges that individuals face once they have crossed the border and arrived in the US. Once students have finished reading and have completed these two tasks, you might want to make a list as a class so that students can have an opportunity to vocalize and share out what they learned in the reading.

   E You can assign these questions as homework, or give students time in class to individually write out or think about their responses to each question. You might encourage students to write words or short phrases they would like to use in their responses without writing out their complete answers. If you finish class with the Piensa task, it would be good to start the next day with the Conversa task so that students can recall what they learned the day before. Before moving on, be sure to give students time to share out their responses in a class discussion. You can go question by question, or you can choose the three or four questions you think will be most important to address in a class discussion.

  The vocabulary task can be completed as homework or as students finish reading. You can either go over this immediately after the reading or the next day, once students have completed it for homework.

Answers to Part F:
- la migra
- jornaleros agrícolas
- pollero
- cansancio
- arroyito
- atravesar

 Reflexión

The reflection is a follow up to students' original opinion, in Antes de empezar, about immigration. This will be a time for students to reflect on what they learned in the article and to determine if what they read has changed how they think about undocumented immigration.

Optional:
Debate: The issue of immigration is a topic that your students may want to debate as a class. It is important to plan some time for additional research on the topic before the debate. You can give students a series of points that will be addressed in the debate so that they can research both sides of those specific topics. Remind students how important it is to understand how each side views the issues, in order to form a strong argument to support their own ideas and opinions.

¿Cuáles son los desafíos que enfrentan los emigrantes en un nuevo país?

Actividad 5 ¿Cómo se adapta un emigrante a un nuevo país?

Time estimate: 2 60-minute classes
Grammar in context: Use of past participle as an adjective, review and exercises in **Explorer**

Acculturation is an assimilation process that people undergo to assume the culture traits of the new country/culture. There are several stages of the adjustment cycle that emigrants experience until they adapt and feel more "en casa".

     As a provocation for this activity, you might want to put up some images of different places in the U.S. and Latin America. Have students brainstorm what it would be like to move to that place and use it as a context for answering the questions. After sharing the answers to the questions, students will decide the emotions that a new emigrant might feel and share them on the online forum.

2. Have students read this as a follow up to their discussion in part A and verify if they considered all the factors mentioned here: *ambiente, costumbres, relaciones,* and *el aspecto psicológico*. The questions scaffold the brief reading and ask them what an emigrant can do to prepare for a move.

 Students will take notes on the graphic organizer for this activity, including the visual representations of the five stages of acculturation that immigrants experience when moving to a new culture. They will need the organizer in order to answer the open-ended follow-up questions in part D in a small group or in the online forum.

 After reading about the five stages of acculturation in Part C *Al leer*, 1) have students sit with two or three classmates to present their summaries and visuals using their graphic organizer. 2) Next, they will take turns answering the three questions in the forum or in a classroom discussion.

 ¡Te toca a ti!

 As a formative assessment, students will listen to a voicemail from a friend who is studying abroad for the semester. Each student will leave a message for the friend sharing the information learned in this activity about the acculturation process. A one-minute message should be sufficient. Students will record and submit the message online. It can be scored with the presentational speaking rubric.

There is a grammar practice for the use of the past participle on the **Uso del lenguaje** link for this *hilo*.

Essential questions:
- ¿Cuáles son las razones por las que la gente decide emigrar de su país?
- ¿Cuáles son los desafíos a los que se enfrentan en el proceso de emigrar a otro país?
- ¿Cuáles son los desafíos a los que se enfrentan los emigrantes en un nuevo país?

Hilo Digital Evaluación final — *Caras de la migración*

Time estimate: 1 60-minute class period to present in small groups + 60 minutes throughout the preceding week to prepare in class in addition to time outside of class.

Grammar in context: past tenses (imperfect/preterit, past progressive tense), por/para, uses of past participle as adjectives to express feelings with *ser/estar*

This summative assessment has students reflecting on the emigrant/immigrant experiences that they viewed, read, and heard in this *hilo* along with additional information that they will research for this assessment. The three essential questions will guide and organize their research as they dig into the motives, challenges, opportunities, and acculturation that emigrants face upon emigration to another country. Students need to reflect, compare, and analyze the cultural practices and perspectives that influence the emigrants' adjustment process.

Part I. Research: Students will research (outside of class) a minimum of two appropriate sources about emigrants and their reasons, challenges, and opportunities for leaving their country. They should also consider information about the acculturation process. If possible, one of the sources should be a primary source, such as an immigrant in your community who can be interviewed; there are also audio and video links in **Explorer**. The three essential questions will guide and organize research as students dig into the motives, challenges, opportunities, and acculturation that they face upon emigration to another country.

Part II. Compare and Analyze: Students will analyze the information from the research by breaking it into parts and interpreting the information in order to reach conclusions. Students will apply the information about the emigrant experiences by comparing it to an emigrant from a source in this *hilo*. What are the cultural practices and perspectives that influence how they adjust to a new country? How are they similar and different? Are they documented or undocumented? Did they bring the whole family with them? Refer to the checklists and criteria for the Hilo Digital Summative Assessment in **Explorer**. Students' final product for this part of the project will be a two-paragraph written presentation.

Part III. Persuasive conversation: Each student will prepare a persuasive argument to convince friends to emigrate, or not, to a new country. Include:

- *Reasons for emigrating from your country (EQ #1)*
- *Advantages and disadvantages of emigration (EQ #2)*
  - *Opportunities for employment, education and a better life for your family*
  - *Challenges of getting the documents needed to emigrate legally*
- *The acculturation process: culture and language barriers (EQ #3)*

This interpersonal presentation can be done in small groups with students taking turns presenting to groups of 4 to 6 students. They can use the summative assessment rubric to provide input to the teacher on their peers' presentations.

MANTA 6 Ciencia y tecnología

Hilo 12 Cuidado de la salud y la medicina

Essential questions:
- ¿Cómo coexisten las prácticas de la medicina tradicional y la moderna?
- ¿Cómo varía el cuidado de la salud en distintas regiones del mundo hispano?
- ¿Cómo influye la comunidad en la salud del individuo?

Student Learning Objectives

Interpersonal Communication: Speaking and Writing
- Exchange information about health practices and perspectives in Hispanic cultures.
- Exchange opinions about the characteristics of a healthy community.
- Engage in discussions about the community influence on healthy lifestyles.
- Exchange letters, emails, blogs, or social media posts with suggestions to improve healthcare practices in Hispanic cultures.
- Engage in discussions about the access to health care in Spanish-speaking countries.
- Explain and provide examples of a Hispanic culture that practices traditional medicine.

Interpretive Communication: Print, Audio, Audiovisual, and/or Visual Sources
- Demonstrate comprehension of content from a variety of authentic sources about healthcare practices in Spanish-speaking countries.
- Interpret and evaluate the organ donation process in a Spanish-speaking country.
- Interpret and analyze the role of healthcare workers in rural areas of a Spanish-speaking country.
- Interpret and summarize significant details about the characteristics of a healthy community.
- Interpret and analyze disease prevention and support from authentic educational materials.

Presentational Communication: Spoken and/or Written Presentations to a Variety of Audiences
- Present information about the connection between traditional and modern medical practices and the influence of cultural perspectives.
- Collaborate with others to present information on access to healthcare in rural regions of Latin America.
- Research, present, and distribute information on a healthcare problem and prevention.
- Evaluate community healthcare practices and their influence on individuals in a Spanish-speaking country.
- Produce reflections and journal entries to demonstrate understanding of cultural perspectives on healthcare practices and products.

Relating Cultural Practices to Perspectives:
- Investigate, explain, and reflect on the relationship between healthcare practices (modern/traditional) and the perspectives (beliefs/values/attitudes) of Hispanic cultures.

Relating Cultural Products to Perspectives:
- Investigate, explain, and reflect on the relationship between healthcare products and the perspectives (beliefs/values/attitudes) of Hispanic cultures.

Connections: Connect with Other Disciplines
- Make connections to content knowledge about healthcare practices and prevention.

Connections: Acquire New Information
- Acquire and apply new information from authentic sources about healthcare and medicine in Spanish-speaking countries.

Comparisons: Language
- Make linguistic comparisons of cognates and the concept of negation in Spanish.

Comparisons: Culture
- Analyze and compare healthcare practices and perspectives in a Spanish-speaking community with a community in the U.S.

School and Global Communities:
- Interact with Spanish speakers about healthcare practices in Spanish-speaking countries.

Lifelong Learning:
- Set goals and reflect on progress in using Spanish for enjoyment, enrichment, and advancement.

Suggested Lesson Plan Sequence/Pacing Guide
Manta 6: Ciencia y tecnología
Hilo 12: Cuidado de la salud y medicina

Focus Pages in SE	Day	Classroom Activities	Homework/ Formative assessment/ Exit pass
La coexistencia de las prácticas tradicionales y modernas de la medicina pp. 346–358	1	* Introduce unit with video and vocabulary review * Think-Pair-Share on healthy communities * Two active readings of text (HW)	* ¡Tu opinión cuenta! response to video * Annotated text & organizer
	2	* Follow-up discussions to yesterday's reading: conversation, journal prompt, comparison to video * Present ¡Te toca a ti! task and time to start working on it; to be completed outside of class * Pre-reading: conversation and categorization * Active reading while annotating text	* Journal prompt using the present subjunctive * ¡Te toca a ti! project * Annotated text (can be completed for homework)
	3	* Post-reading: comprehension comparison * Debate	* Journal questions * Venn diagram
	4–5	* Think-Pair-Share * Active reading with cultural analysis/comprehension check * 2nd active reading with cultural analysis & investigation/HW * Pre-listening prediction exercise * Active listening with comprehension activities * ¡Tu opinión cuenta! forum	* Cultural analysis graphic organizers * Audio comprehension checks * ¡Tu opinión cuenta! forum participation
El cuidado de la salud en distintas regiones del mundo hispanohablante pp. 358–364	6	* Pre-listening vocabulary and conversation * Active listening with conversation and comprehension checks * Pre-reading journal prompt, conversation and research of Millennium Development Goals (HW)	* Comprehension checks: fill ins, multiple choice * ¡Tu opinión cuenta! formative assessment (can be completed outside of class)
	7	* Active reading with graphic organizer * 2nd reading: answer journal questions; share with classmates * Present ¡Tu opinión cuenta! formal letter	* Graphic organizer * ¡Tu opinión cuenta! formal letter (to complete outside of class)
La influencia de la comunidad en la salud del individuo pp. 364–373	8	* Think-Pair-Share survey, preview of fotonovela & characters * Active reading of fotonovela with grammar foci	* Grammar notes * Reading assigned as homework for two nights
	9	* Review grammar notes with classmate * Inferences and vocabulary exercises * Present ¡A tejer! formative assessments as homework	* Written summary of text using target vocabulary * ¡A tejer! formative assessments
	10	* Post-reading exercises and voice message * ¡Tu opinión cuenta! forum discussion * Presentation of ¡Te toca a ti!/summative evaluation * Deductive process about role of promotoras * Homework: online research on Anesvad	* Formative assessments (can be homework): presentational oral task, paragraph for forum discussion, ¡Te toca a ti!
	11	* Active viewing of video: web and vocabulary * Post-viewing conversation and journaling * ¡Te toca a ti! community analysis task * Cultural comparison presentational oral task: HW or during class	* Graphic organizer * ¡Te toca a ti! and ¿Qué aprendiste? formative assessments
	12–14	* Present summative assessment requirements * Students prepare project, using previous work * Day to participate in class Health Fair	* Students develop, edit and present final projects

Hilo 12 Cuidado de la salud y medicina

Introducción ¿Cómo es vivir sano?

Student book page 346
Time estimate: 20 minutes

A Activate students' prior knowledge of vocabulary relating to the topic about what it means to be "healthy." The chart for this activity is in **Explorer**.

B Now students can check and add to their ideas as they watch the video.

C Students discuss what the differences are between their thoughts and what they saw in the video. What does this tell us about what kind of healthy living the government of Chile is trying to promote with this Public Service Announcement?

¡Tu opinión cuenta!

If you have students do this as a homework assignment, they can share their opinions in **Explorer**; the forum provided gives them a way to record themselves speaking.

Antes de empezar ¿Qué necesita una comunidad para que la gente tenga una vida saludable?

Student book page 347
Time estimate: 1 class period with homework (¡Te toca a ti! project)
Grammar in context: Negation and pero/sino; Present subjunctive to describe something ideal

A When the whole class shares out, push students to think outside the box if needed: Beyond hospitals and doctor's offices, how do parks affect a community's wellbeing? Health food stores, farmer's markets?

B 1. This text is available in **Explorer** for students to annotate. You could assign this reading for homework.

2. This organizer is available in **Explorer** and tries to help students break it down: what does the text say about what people need to be healthy, and what a community needs to provide toward that end?

3. This is an open-ended question since students may already have a similar answer to the question of what a healthy community is, or they might find significant differences. You could have students do a quick Turn and Talk to share with a partner. The diagram in the culture box at the top of pg. 350 is another attempt to answer this same question. Now what do students think?

 ¡Te toca a ti!

 This task is designed to have students think like urban designers as they imagine then describe an ideal community where people have everything they need to be healthy. Their design should be completed entirely in Spanish and be accompanied by a written paragraph as explained in the template in **Explorer**. Additionally, students should be prepared to explain and defend their designs to others. This could be on the forum provided in **Explorer**, where students can post their documents and record themselves speaking about it. You could also do this on a class wiki or blog, or have a showing of the presentations, including "judges" (Spanish speakers from your school or community) who visit and choose what they consider the best and most well defended design. An audience always raises the stakes!

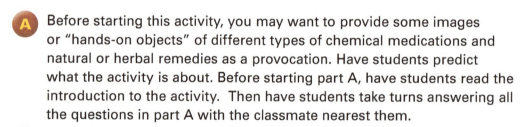

¿Cómo coexisten las prácticas de la medicina tradicional y la moderna?

Actividad 1 *Medicina Tradicional versus Medicina Científica ¿En verdad somos tan diferentes en lo esencial?*

Student book page 350
Time estimate: 1 or 2 60-minute classes; reading can be assigned for homework for second day

A Before starting this activity, you may want to provide some images or "hands-on objects" of different types of chemical medications and natural or herbal remedies as a provocation. Have students predict what the activity is about. Before starting part A, have students read the introduction to the activity. Then have students take turns answering all the questions in part A with the classmate nearest them.

   B The chart in part B 2 is in **Explorer** for students to complete. They can work on this in pairs or small groups as most medical terms are cognates and the rest are defined in the vocabulary at the end of the hilo.

Answers to La medicina tradicional y la medicina científica, note that some could be considered both.

masajes	T	remedios florales	T	reflexología	T	quimioterapia	C
hidroterapia	T	traumatología	C	psiquiatría	C	antioxidantes	T
cirugía	C	radioterapia	C	acupuntura	T	farmacología	C
aceites esenciales	T	dieta	C/T	aromaterapia	T	terapéutica física	T/C
reiki	T	hemoterapia	C				

 C The article is in **Explorer** for students to mark accordingly. This is a good text to discuss if they agree or disagree with the tenets of one type of medicine or the other in preparation for the debate in **Tu opinión cuenta**.

¿Cómo coexisten las prácticas de la medicina tradicional y la moderna?

Actividad 2 ¿En qué se basa la medicina mapuche?

Student book page 354
Time estimate: 2 60-minute classes

 A Before reading, activate students background knowledge about 1) the Mapuche Indians in South America (featured in hilo 4 pg 102) and 2) use of natural medicines in general. After this discussion, show the 4 minute video clip from the Spanish university students' (expedicionarios) trip when they visited Temuco, Chile. They provide background information about the Mapuche and their cultural perspectives of medicine. It includes an interview with Ana Isabel, a Mapuche nurse, who is the same nurse interviewed on the audio clip for part F of this activity. The video is in **Explorer** as a fuente for this activity.

 B While reading students will jot down any products the Mapuche use for medicinal purposes. For homework, have students research how the products are used medicinally and what they think the Mapuche perspective might be. Answers follow on the next page.

Answers to Part B organizer:

Productos	Prácticas médicas: lo que hacen	Perspectivas: sus creencias
Las medicinas vienen de las plantas- el pino y el eucalipto	Se basan en la naturaleza y las energías positivas del mundo natural	Si violan la naturaleza, las plantaciones se desaparecerán
Las plantaciones son sus farmacias naturales	Conservación de las plantaciones es lo fundamental	Si no tienen las medicinas naturales, se pueden enfermar
Los machi cumplen la función de médicos	Sus estudios son con otro machi por 3 meses experimentando y desarrollando	Cada familia tiene alguien con el don de ser machi, es genético. Como adolescente tiene sueños que le hace saber que está destinado a ser machi
		La naturaleza es su vida

C After reading, have students complete true/false statements to verify comprehension of the article on Mapuche philosophy.

Answers to Part C:

1. Los hospitales interculturales representan un respeto entre la medicina tradicional y la medicina científica.
2. Las enfermedades son los efectos de violaciones (transgresiones) de la naturaleza y la única manera de curarlas es por medio de las medicinas naturales según los mapuche.
3. Los machi controlan los poderes de las energías de la naturaleza.

Answers to Part D.

Productos	Prácticas: Investigar	Perspectivas en común: Inferir
el pino	1) El aroma es descongestionante 2) La corteza (cáscara) se mezcla con agua para curar la fiebre	• Existe en la naturaleza como un recurso natural para aprovechar y no destruir. • Los mapuche tienen una fuerte conexión con la naturaleza y respetan lo que la naturaleza ofrece al humano.
El canelo – árbol con hojas como el laurel	Para la caída del pelo	
El boldo – arbusto de Chile	Una infusión para malestares del hígado	
El sauce – planta que crece a las orillas del río	Para resfríos, dolores y estados gripales	

E Before listening to the interview about Mapuche medicinal practices, have students work in pairs to study the vocabulary list to make inferences about the interview, then write a brief summary. Have them join another pair of students to share their inferences and summaries in order to come up with a joint summary to share with the class.

F This activity can be done in **Explorer** and sent to you for a grade. In the interview you will hear "medicina alopática" with Ana Isabel, the Mapuche nurse. This is not a term that students will hear or see on the IB or AP exams but they may be curious to know what the Mapuche say about it. "La medicina alopática es la ciencia que busca prevenir, tratar y curar las enfermedades mediante el uso de fármacos, ataca las consecuencias, casi nunca las causas". (Extraído de http://planocreativo.wordpress.com)

> **Answers to Part F 1 & 2:**
> 1. ¿En qué se basa la medicina mapuche?
>   **a** científico   **b.** La enfermedad   **c.** Me enfermo   **d** El prevenir   **e.** Una patología
> 2. ¿Cuáles son para las dolencias más comunes?
>   **a.** Una yerba (hierba)   **b.** Acostar   **c.** Largo   **d.** Cambio de vida   **e.** El remedio

¿Cómo varía el cuidado de la salud en distintas regiones del mundo hispano?

Actividad 3 ¿Cómo está liderando España en el campo médico?

Student book page 358
Time estimate: 45 minutes

A Before listening to the audio, have your students (1) complete the vocabulary practice activity and go over this as a class, and (2) pair them up to complete the interpersonal task. The interpersonal task requires them to think about what they already know about organ donation and to ponder briefly their own opinion on who the decision makers are in those situations.

> **Answers to A 1:**
> a) esperanza   d) calidad
> b) donantes   e) trasplantes
> c) salvar   f) órganos

1. Allow your students to listen to the audio one time through without completing any sort of written task. We want to give students the opportunity to listen and try to make meaning from what they hear.

« | » Audio script

Muchos norteamericanos piensan esta semana cómo les afectará personalmente el nuevo **sistema sanitario**.[1] En Europa, también se habla de salud estos días, más específicamente de **trasplantes**.[2] Muchos enfermos que esperan la donación de un **órgano**[3] han recibido estos días buenas noticias desde Madrid. Aquí se celebra la Conferencia Europea sobre Donación y Trasplante de Órganos. No es casualidad. España lidera en este momento la Presidencia de la Unión Europea. Este honor no tiene mérito, pues la Presidencia política **es rotativa**[4] entre los 27 países miembros. Pero España lidera también la tasa de donación de órganos en el mundo, y esta posición, sin duda, tiene mucho mérito. Desde hace casi 20 años España tiene un 34,5 de **donantes**[5] por millón de habitantes. Son 8 puntos más que la **media**[6] en Estados Unidos y el doble de la media en Europa. En la Conferencia de Madrid, los países europeos **han acordado**[7] copiar el sistema español y coordinar su funcionamiento. Los especialistas esperan **salvar**[8] 20.000 vidas al año con este nuevo modelo.

En el pasado, muchas de las donaciones **procedían**[9] de personas jóvenes **muertas**[10] en accidentes de tráfico. La **calidad**[11] de estos órganos jóvenes y **sanos**[12], y la rapidez y **eficacia**[13] del sistema español garantizaban el éxito de muchos trasplantes. Afortunadamente, el número de accidentes se ha reducido en España de manera espectacular en los últimos años. El futuro está ahora, según los médicos especialistas, en los **donantes vivos**.[14] La **esperanza**[15] de vida aumenta cada día. Los órganos de personas mayores tienen peor calidad, pero pueden ser **útiles**[16] durante 10 o 20 años a otras personas mayores. Además las donaciones de **riñón**[17] o de **hígado**[18] de personas jóvenes y sanas también aumentan. España **tiene** hoy **el doble de**[19] estos trasplantes que hace un año, pero aún está lejos de Noruega, Reino Unido, Suecia o Dinamarca. En estos países la tasa de **donantes familiares vivos**[20] es del 30% o 40%.

60.000 enfermos esperan un trasplante en Europa. Los **especialistas**[21] y representantes de la sanidad reunidos en Madrid no pueden perder el tiempo.

2. As students listen for the second time, have them focus on marking down the statistics mentioned in the audio as these are important for comprehension. This and the following multiple-choice activity are available to take online in **Explorer**. Be sure to go over these as a class after reading, or have students turn these in for a grade.

Answers to B 2:
- **a)** 20; 34,5; millón
- **b)** 8; doble
- **c)** 20.000
- **d)** 10 a 20
- **e)** 30 a 40 %
- **f)** 60.000

After reading, students should complete the comprehension task with the multiple choice questions. You can have them turn these in for a grade or you can go over them quickly as a whole class.

Answers to Part C:
- **1)** C
- **2)** B
- **3)** A
- **4)** C
- **5)** B

¡Tu opinión cuenta!

Some of your students may already have or may soon be getting a drivers license. In many states you can choose to indicate if you would like to be an organ donor. Have students record their opinions on whether or not a teenager should make this decision for themselves or if they should wait and let their parents/family make the decision for them. This connects to the discussion students had earlier in this activity. You can have students record their opinions on the space provided in **Explorer**.

¿Cómo varía el cuidado de la salud en distintas regiones del mundo hispano?

Actividad 4 ¿Cómo varía el cuidado de la salud en áreas rurales vs. urbanas?

Student book page 360
Time estimate: 1 60-minute class plus 20 minutes, with homework
(**¡Tu opinion cuenta!** task)

A 1. The vocabulary provided at the end of this set of questions is to determine what students already know about this topic – including cognates with English. In your defining and discussing these terms only in Spanish, you are immediately increasing students' vocabulary and comfort level on the topic.

Culture box: First ask students what they remember about the U.N. Millennium Goals, then refer back to hilo 11 and/or have students research online to learn more. These goals are worth knowing and it helps to put this activity in context.

B Use an image search tool or Google Earth to show students what the regions of Peru look like: coast, sierra (highlands), jungle. This will be helpful to understand going forward.

1. This organizer is available in **Explorer** and should help students focus on the main ideas of the text.

C 2. To answer these questions students will need to refer to the map and graph and think beyond what the text says, in order to analyze and interpret the situation. Give them time to work independently – this could be a homework or bellwork (Do Now) assignment – then collaborate with a classmate to share their answers, or work together in a group of three or four, before asking them to share their answers with the class.

¡Tu opinión cuenta!

In this formative assessment, a formal interpersonal writing task, students are asked to present the problem and propose a solution. It does not have to be a long letter to accomplish those objectives! You may want to model for students how to correctly refer to information they have read or viewed on the graph without copying directly from the text; paraphrasing and citing information correctly is a very important skill that hopefully they have been developing in their other classes. An email template is available in **Explorer**.

¿Cómo influye la comunidad en la salud del individuo?

Actividad 5 ¿Cómo se puede concientizar a una comunidad sobre su salud?

Student book page 364
Time estimate: 2 60-minute classes plus 30 min, with reading and grammar/inference work and formative assessments assigned outside of class
Grammar in context: Formal Usted commands, uses of the present and past subjunctive

1. To reach the average ratings for each type of program, have students vote and have a student volunteer to tally their votes.

2. After students journal you may want to have a few students give examples: What kinds of ads, PSAs, etc have they seen on health issues recently?

3. This initial step is just to get students familiar with what a fotonovela looks like and to guess at the purpose of this one. Students shouldn't worry about reading and understanding every single word at this point.

4. Here students have a chance to get to know the characters in the fotonovela before they begin to read. The text and questions also help them understand the basic plot. After students have conversed in pairs, you might take answers from the class and ask students to defend their answers: Where does it say that in the text? Show me how you know.

Teacher and students can access the full fotonovela PDF in **Explorer**. Originally it was published in both English and Spanish, alternating pages, but we were given a Spanish-only version for use in this learning program. In class, you could have students volunteer to be actors and play one of the characters! This could be done as a whole-class activity or in groups. You could assign part or all of this reading for homework, and completion of Part B 1 and/or B 2. Note that you could choose to do Part B 1 and/or B 2 depending on the needs of your students and as time allows; both offer a different lens while students are reading.

1. This **enfoque gramatical** asks students to pay attention to certain salient features that appear in the fotonovela and explain their use. *Why does that character speak in that way and use that structure?* This is an excellent test of students' foundational understanding of grammar.

2. In this organizer, available in **Explorer**, students infer relationships between characters based on what they read and see in the fotonovela. Encourage them to write something in the second column more specific than "bien" or "mal"; you may want to model the first one together. The most important part is the last column: How do you know? Here students cite evidence from the text to support their inferences which is a very important and transferable literacy skill.

3. This could be a quick Do-Now or Exit Slip assignment: How can you use these words to accurately talk about a character in the fotonovela? Here again is a chance to practice paraphrasing and not copying directly from the text!

2. Now students are evaluating the effectiveness of the fotonovela to serve its stated purpose. Besides if a student liked or disliked the fotonovela's design, story, etc, what does it teach someone about diabetes and their health? The last question asks students to evaluate the validity of the information presented – another very important skill that we often forget to teach! Have students defend their answers to the class: Why do you think that way? This activity prepares students for the individual writing assignment below in ¡**Tu opinion cuenta**!

3. This is a real-world task that asks students to record themselves; students can use the space provided to record themselves in **Explorer**. Students' completion of this task demonstrates their comprehension of the information included in the fotonovela (which they reviewed with a classmate in step 2) and requires that they use the relevant target vocabulary.

¡Tu opinión cuenta!

Students share their paragraphs on the forum provided in **Explorer** so that they can then respond to one another's evaluations.

¡Te toca a ti!

Students begin to prepare for the **evaluación final** by choosing a healthcare topic that is important to them and, using the worksheet in **Explorer**, noting initial ideas about why they think it is important to increase community awareness on this issue. Students may choose the same topic which is fine. In order to get students sharing their ideas so far, you could ask students to do a 1-minute presentation to the class as a check-in on their thoughts so far or present to a small group of classmates.

¿Cómo influye la comunidad en la salud del individuo?

Actividad 6 ¿Qué hacen promotoras para influir en la salud de su comunidad?

Student book page 369
Time estimate: 1 60-minute class with two formative assessments for homework or as an additional workshop day

A **2.** Students create their own definition by making an inference based on the vocabulary (information) provided. There is no one right answer here, but ask students to Turn and Talk and explain to a classmate how they came up with their definition.

3. It is important to read aloud the definition given in the brochure produced by *Iniciativa Latina de Salud*. See the Enlaces section for this hilo in **Explorer**. Students add to their definition based on what they have heard, or put a check next to something in their original definition affirmed by the auditory information.

4. Now students have a third source of information: a written text. This is more specific about a certain group of promotoras. What do they do in their work?

B Watch the video once without sound so students focus solely on the visual content and all they can understand just from that! The organizer is available in **Explorer** or students could quickly make their own in their notebook.

3. Students might not get all of these words while watching the video again, but hopefully a pair of students working together can share their ideas to infer the meaning of the words. Students can refer to the vocabulary list at the back of the hilo for what they are missing. Go over these words as a class together at the end, stressing the use of the words *in context*.

C **1.** These questions help students "map out" the resources in their own community and think critically about healthcare in their local context. These ideas could prove useful for the development of their final project, so make sure they do step 2 and write them down!

¡Te toca a ti!

Students are once again working toward their final project by completing this task. Regarding the health concern that they identified at the end of the last activity, also **¡Te toca a ti!**, the next step is how this information could be disseminated to the community and whom to target. There is a worksheet in **Explorer** with some guiding questions.

¿Qué aprendiste?

This is a formative assessment that asks students to think about what they have learned throughout the hilo and choose what they would like to speak about. This presentational speaking task mirrors the cultural analysis speaking task that students have to do on the revised Advanced Placement Spanish Language & Culture exam.

Essential questions:
- ¿Cómo coexisten las prácticas de la medicina tradicional y la moderna?
- ¿Cómo varía el cuidado de la salud en distintas regiones del mundo hispano?
- ¿Cómo influye la comunidad a la salud del individuo?

Hilo 12 Evaluación Final — *Una feria de la salud*

Student book page 372

Time estimate: 2–3 60-minute classes for preparation and presentation (with work on the project being completed outside of class)

Grammar in context: negation, a variety of tenses: This really can encompass so many different grammar concepts depending on the topic that students wish to discuss. There should be some preterit/imperfect and preterit perfect to talk about this health issue in the past. Students should use the conditional y future to talk about what could or will be done in the future. Also, the subjunctive would be a good tie in here as students offer suggestions to the audience.

The links for this activity are included on the Summative Assessment checklist in **Explorer**.

Depending on the order in which you teach the units in this book, this may be the last final assessment your students complete for the year. This is a great time to have them demonstrate their abilities and the skills they have mastered during their year of study.

The context for this final evaluation is that students have been asked to participate in a local health fair for the Spanish-speaking community in their city. Students can pick a health topic of their choice (although it would be best to give them suggestions and require that they approve their idea with you before proceeding) about which they will prepare a written and spoken presentation. A few topics you might want to share

with students are:
- Salud pública gratuita
- Protección contra el gripe
- Acceso a los beneficios de salud
- Ejercicio y buenos hábitos de alimentación
- La obesidad
- Diabetes
- Alergias temporales
- Alergias (de gluten o leche)
- Prevención de cardiopatía
- La importancia de no fumar

If possible, have students do the research in class so that you can see the resources they have found and give them feedback about how effective/appropriate these resources are in supporting their research topic.

Once students have completed their research they can work on the written portion either in class or at home, depending on your timeframe and your preference. Set a date for when a rough draft is due and then another later date for the final draft. By collecting a rough draft you can help students clarify their ideas and improve their presentation before they begin creating their support materials. Along with their written essay, students should also submit a written resource they would like to distribute to people who visit their booth at the health fair. This can be a brochure, poster or a digital presentation (like a PowerPoint or a Prezi). Once students have received your feedback on the rough draft, they can begin working on the resource materials.

The speaking presentation should be something that students practice in advance. You can allow them to use their resource materials or flashcards or you can require that they have no written support during their presentation whatsoever.

The Health Fair itself can be presented in a variety of ways:

1) You can find out if a community fair like this exists in your city and actually take your students there to present and distribute information.

2) Students can present to the class in a traditional presentation format.

3) You can set up a fair in your classroom or another space in the school where you will host an actual health fair. You can have students decorate tables or desks, dress up, bring in food, do demonstrations, etc. You can either divide your class into two groups and let one half present while the other half walks around and visits the different booths, or you can invite another class to visit your fair and your students can present to them (like an AP class).

Use your creativity to determine what will work best with your students and make this a memorable experience for them!

As always in projects like this encourage students to be creative and to make their presentations meaningful by creating something that engages the other students.

APPENDICES

A. Rubrics

Analytic
Interpersonal Speaking 210
Interpersonal Writing 211
Interpretive 212
Presentational Speaking 213
Presentational Writing 214
Cooperative Group Work with
    Presentational Speaking 215

Holistic
Interpersonal Speaking 216
Interpersonal Writing 217
Interpretive 218
Presentational Speaking 219
Presentational Writing 220

"Can do" Rubrics for Students
Interpersonal Speaking 221
Interpersonal Writing 222
Interpretive 223
Presentational Speaking 224
Presentational Writing 225

Summative Assessments
Hilo 1 Estructura de la familia 226
Hilo 2 Redes sociales 227
Hilo 3 Ciudadanía global 228
Hilo 4 Viajes y ocio 230
Hilo 5 Educación y carreras profesionales . . . 232
Hilo 6 Relaciones personales 234
Hilo 7 Belleza y moda 236
Hilo 8 Artes visuals y escénicas 238
Hilo 9 Héroes y personajes históricos 240
Hilo 10 Identidad nacional e identidad étnica . 242
Hilo 11 Temas del medio ambiente 244
Hilo Digital Población y demografía 246
Hilo 12 Cuidado de la salud y medicina 248

B. Grammar Guide 250

Interpersonal Speaking Analytic Rubric

Individual — Mid–High Intermediate

ANALYTIC Interpersonal Speaking

Domain	7 Exceeds Expectations	6 Meets Expectations	5 Almost Meets Expectations	4 Needs Improvement
Content and Completion of Task	• *Consistently* addresses the task and stays on topic • *Effectively* uses examples to support topic • Completes all requirements	• *Adequately* addresses the task and stays on topic • *Adequately* uses examples to support topic • Completes most requirements	• *Somewhat* addresses the task and stays on topic • *Sometimes* uses examples to support topic • Completes some requirements	• *Rarely* addresses the task or may be off topic • *Rarely* uses examples to support topic • Completes few requirements
Communication Strategies *Strategies used to negotiate meaning, understand text/messages, and to express oneself.*	• *Consistently* initiates and maintains conversation by asking questions using strategies to get team members to respond • Asks for clarification using strategies such as, repeating words, rephrasing questions or providing examples • Uses words, circumlocution, self-correction, phrases and some complex sentences to express ideas	• *Adequately* initiates and maintains conversation by asking questions using strategies to get team members to respond • Asks for clarification using strategies such as, repeating words, rephrasing questions or providing examples • Uses words, circumlocution, self-correction, phrases and some complex sentences to express ideas	• *Sometimes* attempts to maintain the conversation by asking questions • Reacts to questions when asked • Uses limited strategies when requesting clarification (e.g., what?) • Uses memorized words and phrases, may resort to English if lacking vocabulary	• *Rarely* attempts to maintain the conversation by asking questions • *Sometimes* responds to questions when asked • *Rarely* uses strategies when requesting clarification • *Rarely* uses memorized words and phrases but rather uses English to fill in the gaps
Comprehensibility to others	• *Consistently* communicates message by understanding and creating personal meaning with confidence and little hesitation • Is comprehensible to a native speaker • Uses mostly accurate pronunciation • Communicates without assistance	• *Adequately* communicates message by understanding and creating personal meaning with some hesitation • Is mostly comprehensible to a native speaker • Uses mostly accurate pronunciation • Requires some teacher assistance	• *Sometimes* communicates message by understanding and creating personal meaning but with frequent hesitation • May not be comprehensible to a native speaker • Uses somewhat poor pronunciation • Requires extensive teacher assistance	• *Rarely* communicates message without extensive hesitation • Is barely comprehensible to a native speaker • Uses poor pronunciation • Cannot proceed without teacher assistance
Cultural Awareness	• *Consistently* recognizes and uses culturally appropriate vocabulary, expressions, and gestures in interactions • *Consistently* recognizes that differences exist in cultural behaviors and perspectives and can mostly adjust in familiar situations	• *Adequately* recognizes and uses culturally appropriate vocabulary, expressions, and gestures in interactions. • *Sometimes* recognizes that differences exist in cultural behaviors and perspectives and sometimes can adjust in familiar situations	• *Occasionally* recognizes and uses culturally appropriate vocabulary, expressions, and gestures in interactions. • *Occasionally* recognizes that differences exist in cultural behaviors and perspectives but cannot adjust in familiar situations	• *Rarely* recognizes and uses culturally appropriate vocabulary, expressions, and gestures in interactions. • May recognize that differences exist in cultural behaviors and perspectives but cannot adjust in familiar situations
Language Control	• *Consistently* understands and produces language that contains mostly familiar structures • *Appropriate* use of language with minimal errors that do not interfere with the message	• *Mostly* understands and produces language that contains mostly familiar structures • *Adequate* use of language with some errors that may interfere with the message	• *Sometimes* understands and produces language that contains mostly familiar structures • *Fair* use of language with frequent errors that interfere with the message	• *Rarely* understands or produces language that contains mostly familiar structures • *Poor* use of language with many errors that interfere with the message
Vocabulary	• Comprehends and uses a broad range of high frequency and personalized vocabulary within familiar themes or topics	• *Mostly* comprehends and uses high frequency and personalized vocabulary within familiar themes or topics	• *Sometimes* comprehends and uses high frequency and personalized vocabulary within familiar themes or topics	• *Rarely* comprehends or uses high frequency and personalized vocabulary within familiar themes or topics

Adapted from ACTFL Performance Descriptors for Language Learners, 2012

© 2013 Wayside Publishing (This document is editable with permission from publisher)

Interpersonal Writing Analytic Rubric
for E-mails, blogs, social media

Individual
Mid–High Intermediate

Domain	7 Exceeds Expectations	6 Meets Expectations	5 Almost Meets Expectations	4 Needs Improvement
Content and Completion of Task	• *Consistently* addresses the task and stays on topic • Completes all requirements	• *Adequately* addresses the task and stays on topic • Completes most requirements	• *Sometimes* addresses the task and stays on topic • Completes some requirements	• Does not address the task or may be off topic • Task is incomplete
Communication Strategies	• *Consistently* uses words, circumlocution, phrases and may use some complex sentences to express ideas • *Consistently* self-corrects	• *Adequately* uses words, circumlocution, phrases and mostly simple sentences to express ideas • May self-correct	• *Sometimes* uses memorized words and phrases, may resort to English if lacking vocabulary • May not self-correct	• *Rarely* uses memorized words and phrases and uses English to fill in the gaps • Does not self-correct
Comprehensibility of Message to Others	• *Consistently* communicates message • *Consistently* produces language that native speakers can understand if they are accustomed to language learners	• *Adequately* communicates message • Mostly produces language that native speakers can understand if they are accustomed to language learners	• Shows some difficulty communicating the message • *Sometimes* produces language that native speakers can understand if they are accustomed to language learners	• Struggles to communicate message • *Rarely* produces language that native speakers can understand even if they are accustomed to language learners
Cultural Awareness	• *Consistently* uses culturally appropriate vocabulary and expressions	• *Adequately* uses culturally appropriate vocabulary and expressions	• *Sometimes* uses culturally appropriate vocabulary and expressions	• *Rarely* uses culturally appropriate vocabulary and expressions
Language Control	• *Consistently* uses expressions appropriate to the situation, mostly familiar structures in different time frames and some complex structures • Appropriate use of language with minimal errors that do not interfere with the message	• *Adequately* uses expressions appropriate to the situation, mostly familiar structures in different time frames and occasional complex structures • Adequate use of language with some errors that interfere with the message	• *Sometimes* uses expressions appropriate to the situation, familiar structures only • Fair use of language with frequent errors that may interfere with the message	• Struggles with expressions and familiar structures • Poor use of language with many errors that interfere with the message
Vocabulary	• *Consistently* uses a broad range of high frequency and personalized vocabulary within familiar themes or topics of study	• *Adequately* uses a range of high frequency and personalized vocabulary within familiar themes or topics of study	• *Sometimes* uses high frequency and personalized vocabulary within familiar themes or topics of study	• *Rarely* uses high frequency and personalized vocabulary within familiar themes or topics of study

Adapted from ACTFL Performance Descriptors for Language Learners, 2012

© 2013 Wayside Publishing (This document is editable with permission from publisher)

Interpretive Analytic Rubric
for Printed Text, Audio, or Visual Sources

Individual
Mid-High Intermediate to Pre-Advanced

Domain	7 Exceeds Expectations	6 Meets Expectations	5 Almost Meets Expectations	4 Needs Improvement
Functions	• Identifies main ideas and many supporting details on familiar topics, and *limited* details from more complex texts	• Identifies most main ideas and some supporting details on familiar topics, and *limited* details from more complex texts	• Identifies some main ideas and obvious supporting details on familiar topics, and *minimal* details from more complex texts	• Identifies some obvious main ideas but *minimal* or no supporting details on familiar topics
Text type	• Shows *consistent* evidence to comprehend paragraph discourse found in short stories, descriptive texts, news articles and concrete topics with some scaffolding • Comprehends most authentic audio and audiovisual sources with some scaffolding	• Shows *adequate* evidence to comprehend most paragraph discourse in short stories, descriptive texts, news articles and concrete topics with scaffolding • Comprehends authentic audio and audiovisual sources with scaffolding	• Shows evidence to comprehend some paragraph-like discourse in short stories, descriptive texts, news articles and concrete topics with extensive scaffolding • Comprehends limited authentic audio and audiovisual sources with extensive scaffolding	• Shows some evidence to comprehend connected sentences or paragraph discourse in simple and short descriptive texts • *Limited* comprehension of authentic audio and audiovisual sources even with extensive scaffolding
Communication strategies	*Effectively* uses the following strategies: • Skim and scan • Visual support and background knowledge • Predict and determine meaning based on prior knowledge or experiences and context clues • Recognition of word family roots, prefixes, suffixes and cognates	*Adequately* uses the following strategies: • Skim and scan • Visual support and background knowledge • Predict and determine meaning based on prior knowledge or experiences and context clues • Recognition of word family roots, prefixes, suffixes and cognates	*Sometimes* uses the following strategies: • Skim and scan • Visual support and background knowledge • Predict and determine meaning based on prior knowledge or experiences and context clues • Recognition of word family roots, prefixes, suffixes and cognates	*Rarely* uses the following strategies: • Skim and scan • Visual support and background knowledge • Predict and determine meaning based on prior knowledge or experiences and context clues • Recognition of word family roots, prefixes, suffixes and cognates
Language Control	• *Sufficient* control of oral and written language to fully understand simple texts, and *adequate* control on complex texts	• *Adequate* control of oral and written language to fully understand simple texts, and some control on complex texts	• *Some* control of oral and written language to understand simple texts, and limited control on complex texts	• *Limited* control of oral and written language to fully understand simple texts, and no control on complex texts
Vocabulary	• *Consistently* comprehends high frequency vocabulary and idiomatic expressions related to everyday topics and those related to study	• *Mostly* comprehends high frequency vocabulary and idiomatic expressions related to everyday topics and those related to study	• *Sometimes* comprehends high frequency vocabulary and idiomatic expressions related to everyday topics and those related to study	• *Occasionally* comprehends high frequency vocabulary and idiomatic expressions related to everyday topics and those related to study
Cultural awareness	• *Mostly* uses knowledge of own culture and Hispanic culture to interpret texts that are heard, read or viewed	• *Sometimes* uses knowledge of own culture and Hispanic culture to interpret texts that are heard, read or viewed	• *Occasionally* uses knowledge of own culture and Hispanic culture to interpret texts that are heard, read or viewed	• *Rarely* uses knowledge of own culture and Hispanic culture to interpret texts that are heard, read or viewed

© 2013 Wayside Publishing (This document is editable with permission from publisher)

Adapted from *ACTFL Keys to Assessing Language Performance* by Paul Sandrock and ACTFL Performance Descriptors for Language Learners, 2012

Presentational Speaking Analytic Rubric
Individual — Mid–High Intermediate

ANALYTIC Presentational Speaking

Domain	7 Exceeds Expectations	6 Meets Expectations	5 Almost Meets Expectations	4 Needs Improvement
Content and Topic Development	• *Clear* focus on topic: relevant, organized, and thorough with supporting details • *Consistently* offers own opinion, examples, and suggestions • *Consistent* use of cohesive devices and transitions • Information is accurate	• *Adequate* focus on topic: relevant and well developed with supporting details • *Sometimes* offers own opinion, examples, and suggestions • *Some* use of cohesive devices and transitions • Information is generally accurate	• *Partially* on topic: may be irrelevant and not well organized with few supporting details • May not offer own opinion, examples, and suggestions • *Limited* use of cohesive devices and transitions • Information may be inaccurate	• May be off topic: irrelevant and disorganized with minimal supporting details • Does not offer own opinion, examples, and suggestions • *Minimal* or no use of cohesive devices and transitions • Information is inaccurate
Communication Strategies	• *Consistently* uses words, circumlocution, phrases and some complex sentences to express ideas • *Consistently* self-corrects	• Uses words, circumlocution, phrases and mostly simple sentences to express ideas • *Sometimes* self-corrects	• Uses memorized words and phrases, may resort to English if lacking vocabulary • Attempts to self correct	• Uses some memorized words and phrases and uses English to fill in the gaps • Does not attempt to self-correct
Delivery of Message and Comprehensibility to Others	• *Consistently* communicates message with confidence in a clear voice • Well-rehearsed with minimal hesitation • Is comprehensible to a native speaker accustomed to language learners • Errors do not interfere with the message • Maintains audience attention with visuals, dramatic language or creative presentation that support the message	• *Adequately* communicates message with some confidence in a generally clear voice • Rehearsed but with some hesitation • Is comprehensible to a native speaker accustomed to language learners • Errors may interfere with the message • Maintains audience attention with visuals that support the message	• Shows some difficulty communicating the message • Some rehearsal is evident with frequent hesitation • May not be comprehensible to a native speaker • Errors frequently interfere with the message • May not maintain audience attention and visuals may not support the message	• Struggles to communicate message • *Minimal* rehearsal with frequent hesitation • Is barely comprehensible to a native speaker • Errors make the message incomprehensible • Does not maintain audience's attention and poor visuals do not support message
Cultural Awareness	• Uses mostly culturally appropriate vocabulary and expressions	• Uses some culturally appropriate vocabulary and expressions	• Uses limited cultural vocabulary and expressions	• Uses minimal cultural vocabulary and expressions
Language Control	• *Consistent* control of basic structures with some errors in complex structures	• *Adequate* control of basic structures and frequent errors in complex structures	• *Limited* control of basic structures and minimal attempts at complex structures	• *Minimal* control of basic structures, mostly memorized language
Vocabulary	• *Accurate* use of new and familiar vocabulary and idioms within themes or topics of study	• *Mostly accurate* use of new and familiar vocabulary and idioms within themes or topics of study	• *Limited* use of new and familiar vocabulary and idioms within themes or topics of study	• *Minimal* use of new and familiar vocabulary and idioms within themes or topics of study

Adapted from *ACTFL Keys to Assessing Language Performance* by Paul Sandrock and ACTFL Performance Descriptors for Language Learners, 2012

© 2013 Wayside Publishing (This document is editable with permission from publisher)

Presentational Writing Analytic Rubric
Individual — Mid–High Intermediate

Domain	7 Exceeds Expectations	6 Meets Expectations	5 Almost Meets Expectations	4 Needs Improvement
Content and Topic Development	• Clear focus on topic with supporting details and examples • Treatment of topic is relevant, well-organized, and thorough • Effective use of cohesive devices and transitions to guide reader • Information is *accurate*	• *Adequate* focus on topic with supporting details and examples • Treatment of topic is relevant, organized, and well developed • Some use of cohesive devices and transitions to guide reader • Information is generally accurate	• *Partially* on topic with some supporting details and examples • Treatment of topic may be irrelevant and not well organized • *Limited* use of cohesive devices and transitions • Information may be inaccurate	• May be off topic with *minimal* supporting details and examples • Treatment of topic is irrelevant and disorganized • *Minimal* or no use of cohesive devices and transitions • Information is in*accurate*
Functions	• *Consistently* produces and presents thoughts and descriptions using *mostly* basic structures accurately and some complex structures • Uses simple and some complex sentences to express ideas	• *Adequately* produces and presents thoughts and descriptions using mostly basic structures with some accuracy • Uses simple sentences and occasional complex sentences to express ideas	• *Partially* produces and presents thoughts and descriptions using basic structures with limited accuracy • Only uses simple sentences to express ideas	• *Rarely* produces and presents thoughts and descriptions using basic structures accurately • May use some simple sentences to express ideas
Cultural Awareness	• Uses mostly culturally appropriate vocabulary and expressions	• Uses some culturally appropriate vocabulary and expressions	• Uses limited cultural vocabulary and expressions	• Uses minimal cultural vocabulary and expressions
Language Control	• *Consistent* control of basic structures with some errors in complex structures • *Minimal* errors in spelling and punctuation do not interfere with message	• *Adequate* control of basic structures and frequent errors in complex structures • Some errors in spelling and punctuation do not interfere with message	• *Limited* control of basic structures and minimal attempts at complex structures • *Frequent* errors in spelling and punctuation may interfere with message	• *Minimal* control of basic structures, *mostly* memorized language • *Frequent* errors in spelling and punctuation that interfere with the message
Vocabulary	• *Accurate* use of new and familiar vocabulary and idioms within themes or topics of study.	• *Mostly accurate* use of new and familiar vocabulary and idioms within themes or topics of study.	• *Limited* use of new and familiar vocabulary and idioms within themes or topics of study. • May resort to English if lacking vocabulary	• *Minimal* use of new and familiar vocabulary and idioms within themes or topics of study. • Uses English to fill in the gaps

Adapted from *ACTFL Keys to Assessing Language Performance* by Paul Sandrock and ACTFL Performance Descriptors for Language Learners, 2012

© 2013 Wayside Publishing (This document is editable with permission from publisher)

Cooperative Group Work And Speaking Presentation Analytic Rubric

Criteria	Indicators	7 Exceeds Expectations	6 Meets Expectations	5 Almost Meets Expectations	4 Needs Improvement
Process	**Cooperation**	• The student contributes fully to the group effort	• The student contributes frequently to the group effort	• The student contributes minimally to the group effort	• The student does not contribute to the group effort
	Preparation	• The presentation is well-rehearsed with smooth transitions	• The presentation is rehearsed but may have inconsistent transitions	• The presentation needed more rehearsal	• No evidence that presentation has been rehearsed
Oral Presentation	**Structures**	• *Accurate* use of targeted structures	• *Mostly accurate* use of targeted structures	• Some errors in targeted structures that interfere with communication	• Many errors in structures that interfere with communication
	Verbal Variety and Vocabulary	• Rich variety of vocabulary and verbs	• Variety of vocabulary and verbs	• Some variety of vocabulary and verbs	• *Limited* variety of vocabulary and verbs
	Delivery	• Presenter speaks clearly, with good eye contact and poise. • *Mostly accurate* pronunciation. Comprehensible to a native speaker.	• Presenter generally speaks clearly with some poise and eye contact. *Mostly accurate* pronunciation. Comprehensible to a native speaker.	• Presenter lacks clarity, with minimal eye contact and poise. May not be comprehensible to a native speaker due to poor pronunciation.	• Presentation is difficult to follow. Hesitation and poor pronunciation impeded communication. Incomprehensible to a native speaker.
Visual Product Power Point, Brochure, Catalog, or Advertisement	**Creativity and Visual Appeal**	• Visual leaves a lasting impression due to its neatness, originality, mechanics and organization	• Visual is well done, neat, original and organized, with good mechanics	• Visual lacks neatness, originality, mechanics or organization	• Visual lacks neatness, originality, mechanics and organization
	Accuracy of Content	• Visual represents well-researched and accurate information	• Visual contains some accurate information	• Visual contains limited *accurate* information	• Visual contains inaccurate information

© 2013 Wayside Publishing (This document is editable with permission from publisher)

Interpersonal Speaking Holistic Rubric
(Daily class work, participation, class discussion, pair work, group work)
Mid-High Intermediate

4 Exceeds Expectations	• *Consistently* makes appropriate contributions to class discussions • *Consistently* initiates and maintains conversation by asking questions to get team members to respond • *Consistently* comprehends and answers questions with extensive responses, easily understood • Appropriate use of language with *minimal* errors that do not interfere with message • Uses a broad range of high frequency and specialized vocabulary from hilos
3 Meets Expectations	• *Generally* makes appropriate contributions to class discussions • *Generally* initiates and maintains conversation by asking questions to get team members to respond • *Generally* comprehends and answers questions with mostly appropriate responses, mostly understood • *Adequate* use of language with some errors that may interfere with message • Uses *mostly* high frequency and some specialized vocabulary from hilos
2 Almost Meets Expectations	• *Sometimes* makes appropriate contributions to class discussions • May not initiate and maintain conversation by asking questions to get team members to respond • *Sometimes* comprehends and may answer some questions with appropriate responses, may be difficult to understand • Fair use of language with frequent errors that interfere with message • Uses some high frequency vocabulary and limited specialized vocabulary from hilos
1 Needs Improvement	• Has difficulty making appropriate contributions to class discussions • Does not initiate or maintain conversation • *Occasionally* comprehends and barely answers questions, difficult to understand • Poor use of language with many errors that interfere with message • Uses *limited* high frequency vocabulary and *minimal* specialized vocabulary from hilos

© 2013 Wayside Publishing (This document is editable with permission from publisher)

Adapted from ACTFL Performance Descriptors for Language Learners, 2012

Interpersonal Writing Holistic Rubric

(Daily class work, participation, journal, email, blog, social media comment, answers to questions, in Explorer)

Mid-High Intermediate

4 **Exceeds Expectations**	• *Effectively* completes the task and stays on topic • *Effectively* expresses, organizes, and connects ideas • Provides details and examples as needed • Uses a broad range of high frequency and specialized vocabulary from hilos • Appropriate use of language with minimal errors that do not interfere with message
3 **Meets Expectations**	• *Generally* completes the task and stays on topic • *Generally* expresses, organizes, and connects ideas • Provides some details and examples as needed • Uses mostly high frequency and some specialized vocabulary from hilos • *Adequate* use of language with some errors that may interfere with message
2 **Almost Meets Expectations**	• *Sometimes* completes the task and stays on topic • *Sometimes* expresses, organizes, and connects ideas • Provides limited details and examples as needed • Uses some high frequency vocabulary and limited specialized vocabulary from hilos • Fair use of language with frequent errors that interfere with message
1 **Needs Improvement**	• *Rarely* completes the task and stays on topic • *Rarely* expresses ideas using simple tenses appropriately • Provides minimal details and examples • Uses limited high frequency vocabulary and minimal specialized vocabulary from hilos • Poor use of language with many errors that interfere with message

© 2013 Wayside Publishing (This document is editable with permission from publisher)

Adapted from ACTFL Performance Descriptors for Language Learners, 2012

HOLISTIC Interpersonal Writing

Interpretive Holistic Rubric
for Printed Text, Audio, Audiovisual Sources
Mid-High Intermediate to Pre-Advanced

4 **Exceeds Expectations**	• Identifies main ideas and many supporting details on familiar topics, and limited details from more complex texts • Shows evidence of the ability to comprehend paragraph discourse in short stories, descriptive texts, news articles, and concrete topics with some scaffolding • Comprehends most authentic audio and audiovisual sources with some scaffolding • *Effectively* uses interpretive strategies such as skim and scan, visual support and background knowledge to predict and determine meaning based on prior knowledge or experiences, and context clues • *Consistently* and *effectively* comprehends high frequency vocabulary and idiomatic expressions related to everyday topics and those related to study • *Mostly* uses of own culture and Hispanic culture to interpret texts that are heard, read, or viewed
3 **Meets Expectations**	• Identifies most main ideas and some supporting details on familiar topics, and *limited* details from more complex texts • Shows evidence of the ability to comprehend most paragraph discourse in short stories, descriptive texts, news articles, and concrete topics with some scaffolding • Comprehends some authentic audio and audiovisual sources with some scaffolding • *Adequately* uses interpretive strategies such as skim and scan, visual support and background knowledge to predict and determine meaning based prior knowledge or experiences, and context clues but may need help implementing these strategies • *Mostly* comprehends high frequency vocabulary and idiomatic expressions related to everyday topics and those related to study • *Sometimes* uses knowledge of own culture and Hispanic culture to interpret texts that are heard, read or viewed
2 **Almost Meets Expectations**	• Identifies some main ideas and obvious supporting details on familiar topics, and *minimal* details from more complex texts • Shows evidence of the ability to comprehend some paragraph-like discourse in short stories, descriptive texts, news articles and concrete topics with extensive scaffolding • *Limited* comprehension of authentic audio and audiovisual sources with extensive scaffolding • *Sometimes* uses interpretive strategies such as skim and scan, visual support and background knowledge to predict and determine meaning based on prior knowledge or experiences, and context clues but needs some help implementing these strategies • *Sometimes* comprehends high frequency vocabulary and idiomatic expressions related to everyday topics and those related to study • *Occasionally* uses knowledge of own culture and Hispanic culture to interpret texts that are heard, read or viewed
1 **Needs Improvement**	• Identifies some obvious main ideas but has difficulty identifying supporting details on familiar topics • Shows limited evidence of the ability to comprehend connected sentences or paragraph discourse in simple and short descriptive texts • *Minimal* comprehension of authentic audio and audiovisual sources even with extensive scaffolding • *Rarely* uses interpretive strategies such as skim and scan, visual support and background knowledge to predict and determine meaning based on prior knowledge or experiences, and context clues • *Occasionally* comprehends high frequency vocabulary and idiomatic expressions related to everyday topics and those related to study • *Rarely* uses knowledge of own culture and Hispanic culture to interpret texts that are heard, read or viewed unless provided extensive scaffolding and support

© 2013 Wayside Publishing (This document is editable with permission from publisher)

Adapted from ACTFL Performance Descriptors for Language Learners, 2012

Presentational Speaking Holistic Rubric
(Daily class work, participation, report or present to class, present in a group, Te toca a ti oral, Reflexión oral, Tu opinión cuenta oral)

Mid-High Intermediate

4 **Exceeds Expectations**	• *Consistently* offers own opinion, examples, and supporting details • *Effectively* expresses and connects ideas using a variety of tenses appropriately • Effective use of some cohesive devices and transitions • Easily understood, *minimal* errors do not interfere with message • Uses a broad range of high frequency and specialized vocabulary from topics of study • *Consistently* self-corrects and uses circumlocution as needed
3 **Meets Expectations**	• *Generally* offers own opinion, examples, and supporting details • *Generally* expresses and connects ideas using some tenses appropriately • *Adequate* use of some cohesive devices and transitions • Easily understood, most errors do not interfere with message • Uses mostly high frequency and some specialized vocabulary from topics of study • Generally self-corrects and uses circumlocution as needed
2 **Almost Meets Expectations**	• *Occasionally* offers own opinion, examples, and supporting details • *Sometimes* expresses ideas using simple tenses tenses appropriately • *Limited* use of cohesive devices and transitions • May be difficult to understand, frequent errors may interfere with message • Uses some high frequency vocabulary and limited specialized vocabulary from topics of study • *Occasionally* self corrects or uses circumlocution
1 **Needs Improvement**	• Does not offer own opinion, examples, or supporting details • *Rarely* expresses ideas using simple tenses appropriately • *Minimal* or no use of cohesive devices and transitions • Difficult to understand, many errors make the message incomprehensible • Uses limited high frequency vocabulary and minimal specialized vocabulary from topics of study • Does not attempt to self-correct and uses English to fill in the gaps

© 2013 Wayside Publishing (This document is editable with permission from publisher)

Adapted from ACTFL Performance Descriptors for Language Learners, 2012

Presentational Writing Holistic Rubric

(Reflexión, Te toca a ti, Tu opinión cuenta, Qué aprendiste,
A tejer, paragraphs, short essays, compositions)

Mid-High Intermediate

4 Exceeds Expectations	• *Effectively* addresses the task and stays on topic • *Effectively* expresses, organizes and connects ideas using a variety of tenses appropriately • Provides details and examples as needed • Uses a broad range of high frequency and specialized vocabulary from topics of study • *Minimal* errors that do not interfere with message
3 Meets Expectations	• *Generally* completes the task and stays on topic • *Generally* expresses and connects ideas using some tenses appropriately • Provides some details and examples as needed • Uses mostly high frequency and some specialized vocabulary from topics of study • Most errors do not interfere with message
2 Almost Meets Expectations	• *Somewhat* completes the task and stays on topic • *Sometimes* expresses ideas using simple tenses appropriately • Provides limited details and examples • Uses some high frequency vocabulary and limited specialized vocabulary from topics of study • Errors may interfere with message
1 Needs Improvement	• *Rarely* completes the task and stays on topic • *Rarely* expresses ideas using simple tenses appropriately • Provides minimal details and examples • Uses limited high frequency vocabulary and minimal specialized vocabulary from topics of study • Errors interfere with message

© 2013 Wayside Publishing (This document is editable with permission from publisher)

Adapted from ACTFL Performance Descriptors for Language Learners, 2012

Interpersonal Speaking Holistic Rubric
(Daily class work, participation, class discussion, pair work, group work)
Mid-High Intermediate

Superé mi gol **4**	• I can make appropriate contributions to class discussions and enjoy doing so consistently • I can initiate and maintain conversation by asking questions to get team members to respond • I can comprehend and answer questions with well-developed responses, and am easily understood • I can use Spanish with *minimal* errors that do not interfere with my message • I can use a broad range of high frequency and specialized vocabulary from hilos
Llegué a mi gol **3**	• I can make appropriate contributions to class discussions and do so often • I can generally initiate and maintain conversation by asking questions to get team members to respond • I can comprehend and answer questions with mostly appropriate responses and can be mostly understood • I can use Spanish adequately, but I make some errors that may interfere with my message • I can use mostly high frequency and some specialized vocabulary from hilos
Estoy progresando hacia mi gol **2**	• I can follow a model when contributing to class discussions and can occasionally share my own thoughts and ideas • I can initiate conversation by asking questions to get team members to respond, but may need help maintaining the conversation • I can comprehend and may answer some questions with appropriate responses, but my answers may be difficult to understand • I can use Spanish in conversation, but may often make errors that interfere with my message • I can use some high frequency vocabulary and *limited* specialized vocabulary from hilos
Necesito más práctica para llegar a mi gol **1**	• I can imitate a model, but have difficulty making unique contributions to class discussions • I can answer simple questions about topics I am familiar with, but have difficulty initiating and maintaining a conversation • I can comprehend simple questions and can answer with simple phrases from memory, but I may be difficult to understand • I can use basic Spanish grammar structures and vocabulary to communicate, but my errors make it difficult to understand my message • I can use limited high frequency vocabulary and minimal specialized vocabulary from hilos

© 2013 Wayside Publishing (This document is editable with permission from publisher)   Adapted from ACTFL Performance Descriptors for Language Learners, 2012

Interpersonal Writing Holistic Rubric

(Daily class work, participation, journal, email, blog, social media comment, answers to questions, in Explorer)

Mid-High Intermediate

Superé mi gol **4**	• I can effectively complete the task and stay on topic • I can clearly express, organize, and connect ideas • I can provide details and examples as needed • I can use a broad range of high frequency and specialized vocabulary from hilos • I can use Spanish appropriately with minimal errors that do not interfere with my message
Llegué a mi gol **3**	• I can complete the task and stay on topic • I can express, organize, and connect ideas • I can provides some details and examples as needed • I use mostly high frequency and some specialized vocabulary from hilos • I can use Spanish adequately with some errors that may interfere with my message
Estoy progresando hacia mi gol **2**	• I can complete simple tasks, but may go off topic • I can express, organize, and connect ideas on familiar topics, but may need a model or examples to do so for unfamiliar topics • I can provide a few details and examples as needed • I can use some high frequency vocabulary and limited specialized vocabulary from hilos • I can use more basic Spanish skills, but may make frequent errors that interfere with my message when trying to incorporate more advanced language
Necesito más practica para llegar a mi gol **1**	• I can complete simple tasks using a model, but I may have difficulty staying on topic • I can express familiar ideas using simple tenses appropriately • I can provide minimal details and examples • I can use limited high frequency vocabulary and minimal specialized vocabulary from hilos • I can use familiar Spanish skills, but make many errors that interfere with my message

© 2013 Wayside Publishing (This document is editable with permission from publisher)

Adapted from ACTFL Performance Descriptors for Language Learners, 2012

STUDENT "I CAN DO" Interpersonal Writing

Interpretive Holistic Rubric
for Printed Text, Audio, Audiovisual Sources
Mid-High Intermediate to Pre-Advanced

Superé mi gol **4**	• I can identify main ideas and many supporting details on familiar topics, and limited details from more complex texts • I can comprehend paragraph discourse in short stories, descriptive texts, news articles, and concrete topics with some assistance • I can comprehend most authentic audio and audiovisual sources with limited assistance • I can use strategies such as skim and scan, context clues, visual support and background knowledge to predict and determine meaning based on prior knowledge or experiences • I can comprehend high frequency vocabulary and idiomatic expressions related to our themes and topics • I can mostly use knowledge of my own culture and Hispanic culture to interpret texts that are heard, read, or viewed
Llegué a mi gol **3**	• I can identify most main ideas and some supporting details on familiar topics, and limited details from more complex texts • I can comprehend most paragraph discourse in short stories, descriptive texts, news articles, and concrete topics with assistance • I can comprehend some authentic audio and audiovisual sources with some assistance • I can use strategies such as skim and scan, context clues, visual support and background knowledge to predict and determine meaning based on prior knowledge or experiences but may need help implementing these strategies • I can mostly comprehend high frequency vocabulary and idiomatic expressions related to our themes and topics • I can sometimes use knowledge of my own culture and Hispanic culture to interpret texts that are heard, read or viewed
Estoy progresando hacia mi gol **2**	• I can identify some main ideas and obvious supporting details on familiar topics, and minimal details from more complex texts • I can comprehend some paragraph-like discourse in short stories, descriptive texts, news articles and concrete topics with extensive assistance • I can comprehend limited authentic audio and audiovisual sources with extensive assistance • I can use strategies such as skim and scan, context clues, visual support and background knowledge to predict and determine meaning based on prior knowledge or experiences, and context clues, but need some help implementing these strategies • I can sometimes comprehend high frequency vocabulary and idiomatic expressions related to our themes and topics with some support • I can occasionally use knowledge of my own culture and Hispanic culture to interpret texts that are heard, read or viewed
Necesito más práctica para llegar a mi gol **1**	• I can identify limited main ideas, but have difficulty identifying supporting details on familiar topics • I can comprehend very simple texts, but have difficulty with connected sentences or paragraph discourse in simple and short descriptive texts • I can comprehend a few familiar words and phrases from authentic audio and audiovisual sources with extensive assistance • I can use strategies such as skim and scan, context clues, visual support and background knowledge to predict and determine meaning based on prior knowledge or experiences if I am given extensive assistance, but have difficulty doing this on my own • I can occasionally comprehend high frequency vocabulary and idiomatic expressions related to our themes and topics if I am given support • I can rarely use knowledge of my own culture and Hispanic culture to interpret texts that are heard, read or viewed, unless I am given extensive assistance

© 2013 Wayside Publishing (This document is editable with permission from publisher)

Adapted from ACTFL Performance Descriptors for Language Learners, 2012

Presentational Speaking Holistic Rubric

(Daily class work, participation, report or present to class, present in a group, Te toca a ti oral, Reflexión oral, Tu opinión cuenta oral)   Mid-High Intermediate

Superé mi gol **4**	• I can offer my own opinion, examples, and supporting details • I can express and connect my own unique ideas using a variety of tenses appropriately • I can use some connecting words and transitions • I can be easily understood, and any minimal errors do not interfere with message • I can use a broad range of high frequency and specialized vocabulary from topics of study • I can self-correct and use circumlocution as needed
Llegué a mi gol **3**	• I can generally offer my own opinion, examples, and supporting details • I can express and connect ideas using some tenses appropriately • I can use some connecting words and transitions, but may need to follow a model • I can be easily understood, and although I make may some errors, most do not interfere with my message • I can mostly use high frequency and some specialized vocabulary from topics of study • I can generally self-correct and use circumlocution as needed
Estoy progresando hacia mi gol **2**	• I can occasionally offer my own opinion, examples, and supporting details • I can express ideas using simple tenses appropriately • I can use connecting words and transitions if given a model and examples • I can be difficult to understand, and may make frequent errors that interfere with my message • I can use some high frequency vocabulary and limited specialized vocabulary from topics of study • I can occasionally self-correct or use circumlocution
Necesito más practica para llegar a mi gol **1**	• I can follow a model to offer my own opinion, but have difficulty giving examples or supporting details • I can expresses ideas if given a model, using simple tenses appropriately • I can use simple connecting words and transitions if given a model or several examples • I can be difficult to understand, and may make many errors that make my message incomprehensible • I can use limited high frequency vocabulary and minimal specialized vocabulary from topics of study • I can rarely self-correct or use circumlocution but may use English to fill in the gaps

© 2013 Wayside Publishing (This document is editable with permission from publisher)   Adapted from ACTFL Performance Descriptors for Language Learners, 2012

Presentational Writing Holistic Rubric

(Reflexión, Te toca a ti, Tu opinión cuenta, Qué aprendiste,
A tejer, paragraphs, short essays, compositions)

Mid-High Intermediate

Superé mi gol **4**	• I can effectively address the task and stay on topic • I can effectively express, organize and connect ideas using a variety of tenses appropriately • I can provide details and examples as needed • I can use a broad range of high frequency and specialized vocabulary from topics of study • I can use familiar language but may make minimal errors that interfere with my message
Llegué a mi gol **3**	• I can generally complete the task and stay on topic • I can generally express and connect ideas using some tenses appropriately • I can provide some details and examples as needed • I can use mostly high frequency and some specialized vocabulary from topics of study • I can use familiar language but may make several errors that interfere with my message
Estoy progresando hacia mi gol **2**	• I can somewhat complete the task and stay on topic • I can sometimes express ideas using simple tenses appropriately • I can provide limited details and examples • I can use some high frequency vocabulary and limited specialized vocabulary from topics of study • I can use familiar language but may make some errors that interfere with my message
Necesito más práctica para llegar a mi gol **1**	• I can complete simple tasks, but may have difficulty staying on topic • I can express familiar ideas using simple tenses appropriately • I can provide minimal details and examples • I can use limited high frequency vocabulary and minimal specialized vocabulary from topics of study • I can use familiar language, but may make many errors that interfere with my message

© 2013 Wayside Publishing (This document is editable with permission from publisher)

Adapted from ACTFL Performance Descriptors for Language Learners, 2012

Hilo 1 Summative Assessment/Evaluación final
Participa en un concurso/Podcast contest

Mid-High Intermediate

Communication Mode/Domain	7 Exceeds Expectations	6 Meets Expectations	5 Almost Meets Expectations	4 Does Not Meet Expectations
Interpretive	• *Consistently* and accurately interprets textual information on the structure of the family from a minimum of two sources	• *Adequately* interprets textual information on the structure of the family from two sources	• *Sometimes* interprets textual information on the structure of the family from one source	• *Minimally* interprets textual information on the structure of the family
Presentational Writing	• *Effectively* develops a podcast script in a detailed **two paragraph** narrative addressing all criteria on the checklist • *Effectively* uses cohesive devices and transitions to guide reader	• *Adequately* develops a podcast script in some detail in a **two paragraph** narrative addressing most criteria on the checklist • *Adequately* uses of cohesive devices and transitions to guide reader	• *Sometimes* develops a podcast script with limited detail in a one **paragraph** narrative addressing some criteria on the checklist • *Sometimes* uses cohesive devices and transitions to guide reader	• *Minimally* develops a podcast script as addressing few criteria on the checklist • *Rarely* uses cohesive devices and transitions to guide reader
Presentational Speaking	• *Effectively* addresses the task in detail and stays on topic • Communicates the message with little hesitation and minimal teacher assistance • Is comprehensible to a native speaker with mostly accurate pronunciation • Few errors in targeted structures interfere with communication • Completes all requirements	• *Adequately* addresses the task with some detail and stays on topic • Communicates the message with some hesitation and some teacher assistance • Is comprehensible to a native speaker with mostly accurate pronunciation • Several errors in targeted structures interfere with communication • Completes most requirements	• Addresses the task with limited detail and may not stay on topic. • Has difficulty communicating the message and needs extensive teacher assistance. • May not be comprehensible to a native speaker and pronunciation is poor. • Some errors in targeted structures interfere with communication. • Completes some requirements	• Does not address the task or may be off topic • Hesitation and pronunciation impede communication • Cannot proceed without teacher assistance. • Many errors in targeted structures interfere with communication • Completes few requirements
Language Control	*Consistently and effectively* uses the following grammatical structures appropriately. • Present and present subjunctive tenses • Comparatives and superlatives	*Adequately* uses the following grammatical structures appropriately. • Present and present subjunctive tenses • Comparatives and superlatives	*Sometimes* uses the following grammatical structures appropriately. • Present and present subjunctive tenses • Comparatives and superlatives	*Rarely* uses the following grammatical structures appropriately. • Present and present subjunctive tenses • Comparatives and superlatives
Vocabulary	• Uses at least 12 vocabulary words and expressions from the hilo appropriately • *Effectively* uses conjunctions, transition words and idiomatic expressions appropriately	• Uses 10–12 vocabulary words and expressions from the hilo appropriately • *Adequately* uses conjunctions, transition words and idiomatic expressions appropriately	• May use 7–9 vocabulary words and expressions from the hilo appropriately • *Sometimes* uses conjunctions, transition words and idiomatic expressions appropriately	• May use 5–6 vocabulary words and expressions from the hilo appropriately • *Rarely* uses conjunctions, transition words and idiomatic expressions appropriately
Cultural awareness	• Indicates awareness of differences in cultural behaviors and perspectives	• May indicate some awareness of differences in cultural behaviors and perspectives	• May not indicate awareness of differences in cultural behaviors and perspectives	• Does not indicate awareness of differences in cultural behaviors and perspectives

© 2013 Wayside Publishing (This document is editable with permission from publisher)

Hilo 2 Summative Assessment/Evaluación final
Entrada en un blog/Blog entry

Mid-High Intermediate

Communication Mode/Domain	7 Exceeds Expectations	6 Meets Expectations	5 Almost Meets Expectations	4 Does Not Meet Expectations
Interpretive	• *Consistently and accurately* interprets textual or audio information on the role of social media from a minimum of two sources	• *Adequately* interprets textual or audio information on the role of social media from two sources	• *Sometimes* interprets textual or audio information on the role of social media from one source	• *Minimally* interprets textual or audio information on the role of social media
Presentational Writing	• *Effectively* summarizes the information gained from the interviews • *Effectively* develops a blog entry in a detailed **three paragraph** description, comparison, and evaluation addressing all questions on the checklist • *Effectively* uses of cohesive devices and transitions to guide reader	• *Adequately* summarizes the information gained from the interviews • *Adequately* develops a blog entry in some detail in a **three paragraph** description, comparison, and evaluation addressing almost all of the questions on the checklist • *Adequately* uses cohesive devices and transitions to guide reader	• *Sometimes* summarizes the information gained from the interviews • Develops a blog entry with limited detail in a **one to two paragraph** description, comparison, and evaluation addressing some of the questions on the checklist • *Limited* use of cohesive devices and transitions to guide reader	• *Minimally* summarizes the information gained from the interviews • Does not develop a blog entry as indicated on the checklist • *Rarely* uses cohesive devices and transitions to guide reader
Control	• *Effectively* addresses the content in detail and stays on topic • Interviews a minimum of two sources • *Effectively* integrates a personal reflection, interview information, and authentic sources • *Effectively* compares social and cultural life before and after social networks • Completes all requirements	• *Adequately* addresses the task with some detail and stays on topic • Interviews two sources • *Adequately* integrates a personal reflection, interview information, and authentic sources • *Adequately* compares social and cultural life before and after social networks • Completes most requirements	• Addresses the task with limited detail and may not stay on topic. • May Interview one or two sources • *Sometimes* integrates a personal reflection, interview information, and authentic sources • *Sometimes* compares social and cultural life before and after social networks • Completes some requirements	• Does not address the task or may be off topic • Completes few requirements
Language Control	*Consistently and effectively* uses the following grammatical structures appropriately. • Present and present subjunctive tenses • Preterit and imperfect • Comparatives	*Adequately* uses the following grammatical structures appropriately. • Present and present subjunctive tenses • Preterit and imperfect • Comparatives	*Sometimes* uses the following grammatical structures appropriately. • Present and present subjunctive tenses • Preterit and imperfect • Comparatives	*Rarely* uses the following grammatical structures appropriately. • Present and present subjunctive tenses • Preterit and imperfect • Comparatives
Vocabulary	• Uses at least 12 vocabulary words and expressions from the hilo appropriately • *Effectively* uses conjunctions, transition words and idiomatic expressions appropriately	• Uses 10–12 vocabulary words and expressions from the hilo appropriately • *Adequately* uses conjunctions, transition words and idiomatic expressions appropriately	• May use 7–9 vocabulary words and expressions from the hilo • *Sometimes* uses conjunctions, transition words and idiomatic expressions appropriately	• May use 5–6 vocabulary words and expressions from the hilo appropriately • *Rarely* uses conjunctions, transition words and idiomatic expressions appropriately
Cultural awareness	• Indicates awareness of differences in cultural behaviors and perspectives	• May indicate some awareness of differences in cultural behaviors and perspectives	• May not indicate awareness of differences in cultural behaviors and perspectives	• Does not indicate awareness of differences in cultural behaviors and perspectives

© 2013 Wayside Publishing (This document is editable with permission from publisher)

Hilo 3 Summative Assessment/Evaluación final
Súenalo, hazlo/Dream It, Do It

Mid-High Intermediate

Communication Mode/Domain	7 Exceeds Expectations	6 Meets Expectations	5 Almost Meets Expectations	4 Does Not Meet Expectations
Interpersonal *Individual collaborative work on proposal and action plan, speaking Spanish*	• *Consistently* initiates and maintains discussion by asking questions to get team members to respond • *Consistently* asks for clarification, such as repeating words, rephrasing questions or providing examples • Uses words, circumlocution, self-correction, phrases and occasional complex sentences to express ideas • *Effectively* collaborates with team to complete all requirements	• *Adequately* initiates and maintains discussion by asking questions to get team members to respond • *Sometimes* asks for clarification, such as repeating words, rephrasing questions or providing examples • Uses words, circumlocution, self-correction, phrases and simple sentences to express ideas • *Mostly* collaborates with team to complete all requirements	• *Sometimes* participates in the discussion by asking or answering questions • *Sometimes* asks for clarification, such as repeating words • Uses words, circumlocution, self-correction, phrases and simple sentences to express ideas • *Sometimes* collaborates with team to complete all requirements	• *Minimally* participates in the discussion • *Minimally* asks for clarification • May use words and memorized phrases or simple sentences to express ideas • *Minimally* collaborates with team to complete all requirements
Interpretive *Individual contribution to research*	• *Consistently* and *effectively* interprets research on community needs from a variety of written, visual and audio sources	• *Adequately* interprets research on community needs from a variety of written, visual and audio sources	• *Sometimes* interprets research on community needs from a variety of written, visual and audio sources	• *Minimally* interprets research on community needs
Presentational Writing *Team product: Proposal/Action Plan*	• *Effectively* describes the proposal in a detailed **one paragraph** narrative addressing all criteria on the checklist • Describes the Action Plan in a detailed **five paragraph** narrative addressing all criteria on the checklist	• *Adequately* describes the proposal in some detail in a **one paragraph** narrative addressing most of the criteria on the checklist • Describes the Action Plan in some detail in a **five paragraph** narrative addressing most of the criteria on the checklist	• Describes the proposal with *limited* detail in a **one paragraph** narrative addressing some of the criteria on the checklist • Describes the Action Plan in less than a **five paragraph** narrative addressing some of the criteria on the checklist	• *Minimally* describes the proposal with few criteria on the checklist • *Minimally* describes the Action Plan with few criteria on the checklist
Presentational Speaking *Individual presentation of Proposal/Action Plan*	• *Effectively* addresses the task in detail and stays on topic • Communicates the message with little hesitation and *minimal* teacher assistance • Is comprehensible to a native speaker with mostly accurate pronunciation • Occasional errors in targeted structures may interfere with communication • Uses a variety of vocabulary from hilo • Completes all requirements	• *Adequately* addresses the task with some detail and stays on topic • Communicates the message with some hesitation and some teacher assistance • Is comprehensible to a native speaker with adequate pronunciation • Several errors in targeted structures may interfere with communication • Uses appropriate vocabulary from hilo • Completes most requirements	• Addresses the task with *limited* detail and may not stay on topic. • Has difficulty communicating the message and needs extensive teacher assistance. • May not be comprehensible to a native speaker and pronunciation is poor. • Some errors in targeted structures interfere with communication • Uses limited vocabulary from hilo • Completes some requirements	• *Minimally* addresses the task or may be off topic • Hesitation and pronunciation impede communication • Cannot proceed without teacher assistance. • Errors in targeted structures interfere with communication • Uses minimal vocabulary from hilo • Completes few requirements

continued on next page

HILO 3 Summative assessment

Communication Mode/Domain	7 Exceeds Expectations	6 Meets Expectations	5 Almost Meets Expectations	4 Does Not Meet Expectations
Presentational Writing Individual reflection	• *Effectively* writes a minimum 200 word well developed evaluation of the team project and his/her role in project • Clear focus on topic with supporting details and examples • *Effective* use of cohesive devices and transitions to guide reader • Completes all requirements	• *Adequately* writes a minimum 200 word evaluation of project and his/her role in project • *Adequate* focus on topic with some supporting details and examples • *Adequate* use of cohesive devices and transitions to guide reader • Completes most requirements	• Writes less than a 200 word evaluation of project and his/her role in project • *Limited* focus on topic with few supporting details and examples • *Limited* use of cohesive devices and transitions to guide reader • Completes some requirements	• Writes less than a 100 word evaluation of project and his/her role in project • May be off topic with minimal supporting details and examples • *Minimal* or no use of cohesive devices and transitions to guide reader • Completes few requirements
Language Control	*Consistently and effectively* uses the following grammatical structures appropriately: • Present and future tenses • Imperfect subjunctive and conditional tenses	*Adequately* uses the following grammatical structures appropriately: • Present and future tenses • Imperfect subjunctive and conditional tenses	*Sometimes* uses the following grammatical structures appropriately: • Present and future tenses • Imperfect subjunctive and conditional tenses	*Rarely* uses the following grammatical structures appropriately: • Present and future tenses • Imperfect subjunctive and conditional tenses
Vocabulary	• Uses at least 12 vocabulary words and expressions from the hilo appropriately • *Effectively* uses conjunctions, transition words and idiomatic expressions appropriately	• Uses 10–12 vocabulary words and expressions from the hilo appropriately • *Adequately* uses conjunctions, transition words and idiomatic expressions appropriately	• May use 7–9 vocabulary words and expressions from the hilo appropriately • *Sometimes* uses conjunctions, transition words and idiomatic expressions appropriately	• May use 5–6 vocabulary words and expressions from the hilo appropriately • *Rarely* uses conjunctions, transition words and idiomatic expressions appropriately
Cultural awareness	• Uses mostly culturally appropriate vocabulary and expressions • Indicates awareness of differences in cultural behaviors and perspectives	• Uses *some* culturally appropriate vocabulary and expressions • May indicate some awareness of differences in cultural behaviors and perspectives	• May use culturally appropriate vocabulary and/or expressions • May not indicate awareness of differences in cultural behaviors and perspectives	• *Rarely* uses culturally appropriate vocabulary or expressions • Does not indicate awareness of differences in cultural behaviors and perspectives

© 2013 Wayside Publishing (This document is editable with permission from publisher)

Hilo 4 Summative Assessment/Evaluación final
Un viaje virtual/A Virtual Trip

Mid-High Intermediate

Communication Mode/Domain	7 Exceeds Expectations	6 Meets Expectations	5 Almost Meets Expectations	4 Does Not Meet Expectations
Interpersonal *Individual team member: Collaborative process*	• *Consistently* initiates and maintains discussion by asking questions to get team members to respond • *Consistently* asks for clarification, such as repeating words, rephrasing questions or providing examples • Uses words, circumlocution, self-correction, phrases and occasional complex sentences to express ideas • *Effectively* collaborates with team to complete all requirements	• *Adequately* initiates and maintains discussion by asking questions to get team members to respond • *Mostly* asks for clarification, such as repeating words, rephrasing questions or providing examples • Uses words, circumlocution, self-correction, phrases and simple sentences to express ideas • *Mostly* collaborates with team to complete requirements	• *Sometimes* participates in the discussion by asking or answering questions • *Sometimes* asks for clarification, such as repeating words • Uses words, circumlocution, self-correction, phrases and simple sentences to express ideas • *Sometimes* collaborates with team to complete all requirements	• *Minimally* participates in the discussion • *Minimally* asks for clarification • May use words and memorized phrases or simple sentences to express ideas • *Minimally* collaborates with team to complete requirements
Interpretive *Individual contribution to research*	• *Consistently and effectively* interprets research on travel and leisure from a variety of texts, visual and audio sources	• *Adequately* interprets research on travel and leisure from a variety of texts, visual and audio sources	• *Sometimes* interprets research on travel and leisure from a variety of texts, visual and audio sources	• *Minimally* interprets research on travel and leisure
Presentational Writing *Team product: Proposal/Action Plan*	• *Effectively* describes and analyzes the travel and leisure itinerary in a detailed persuasive format addressing all questions on the checklist	• *Adequately* describes and analyzes the travel and leisure itinerary in a persuasive format addressing most of the questions on the checklist	• Describes with limited detail, and may not analyze, the travel and leisure itinerary in a persuasive format detail only addressing some of the questions on the checklist	• *Minimally* describes the travel and leisure itinerary in a persuasive format as indicated on the checklist
Team/Individual Visual Product	• *Effectively* develops a persuasive written and visual product with a clear focus on travel and leisure using supporting details and examples • Visual leaves a lasting impression due to neatness, originality, mechanics, and organization • *Effective* use of cohesive devices and transitions to guide audience • Completes all requirements	• *Adequately* develops a persuasive written and visual product with a *mostly* clear focus on travel and leisure using some supporting details and examples • Visual is mostly neat, original, mechanically correct, and organized • *Adequate* use of cohesive devices and transitions to guide reader • Completes most requirements	• *Somewhat* develops a persuasive written and visual product with a *limited* focus on travel and leisure using few supporting details and examples • Visual is somewhat neat and organized but lacks originality and correct use of mechanics. • *Limited* use of cohesive devices and transitions to guide reader • Completes some requirements	• *Minimal* focus on a persuasive written and visual product on travel and leisure • Visual product demonstrates *minimal* organization with minimal supporting details and examples • *Minimal* or no use of cohesive devices and transitions to guide reader • Completes few requirements

continued on next page

HILO 4 Summative assessment

Communication Mode/Domain	7 Exceeds Expectations	6 Meets Expectations	5 Almost Meets Expectations	4 Does Not Meet Expectations
Presentational Speaking Delivery Individual persuasive presentation	• *Effectively* addresses the task in detail and stays on topic • Communicates the message clearly with good eye contact and poise; minimal hesitation or teacher assistance • Is comprehensible to a native speaker with mostly accurate pronunciation • Occasional errors interfere with communication • Uses a variety of vocabulary from hilo • Completes all requirements	• *Adequately* addresses the task with some detail and stays on topic • Communicates the message adequately with some eye contact and poise; some hesitation and/or teacher assistance • Is comprehensible to a native speaker with adequate pronunciation • Several errors in targeted structures may interfere with communication • Uses appropriate vocabulary from hilo • Completes most requirements	• Addresses the task with limited detail and may not stay on topic. • Communicates without clarity and minimal eye contact and poise; needs significant hesitation or teacher assistance • May not be comprehensible to a native speaker and pronunciation is poor. • Some errors in targeted structures may interfere with communication. • Uses limited vocabulary from hilo • Completes some requirements	• Does not address the task or may be off topic • Hesitation and pronunciation impede communication • Cannot proceed without teacher assistance. • Errors in targeted structures interfere with communication • Uses minimal vocabulary from hilo • Completes few requirements
Language Control	*Consistently and effectively* uses the following grammatical structures appropriately: • Present and future tenses • Imperfect subjunctive and conditional tenses	*Adequately* uses the following grammatical structures appropriately. • Present and future tenses • Imperfect subjunctive and conditional tenses	*Sometimes* uses the following grammatical structures appropriately. • Present and future tenses • Imperfect subjunctive and conditional tenses	*Rarely* uses the following grammatical structures appropriately. • Present and future tenses • Imperfect subjunctive and conditional tenses
Vocabulary	• Uses at least 12 vocabulary words and expressions from the hilo appropriately • *Effectively* uses conjunctions, transition words and idiomatic expressions appropriately	• Uses 10–12 vocabulary words and expressions from the hilo appropriately • *Adequately* uses conjunctions, transition words and idiomatic expressions appropriately	• May use 7–9 vocabulary words and expressions from the hilo appropriately • *Sometimes* uses conjunctions, transition words and idiomatic expressions appropriately	• May use 5–6 vocabulary words and expressions from the hilo appropriately • *Rarely* uses conjunctions, transition words and idiomatic expressions appropriately
Cultural awareness	• Uses mostly culturally appropriate vocabulary and/or expressions • Indicates awareness of differences in cultural behaviors and perspectives	• Uses some culturally appropriate vocabulary and expressions • May indicate some awareness of differences in cultural behaviors and perspectives	• *Occasionally* uses culturally appropriate vocabulary and/or expressions • May not indicate awareness of differences in cultural behaviors and perspectives	• *Rarely* uses culturally appropriate vocabulary or expressions • Does not indicate awareness of differences in cultural behaviors and perspectives

© 2013 Wayside Publishing (This document is editable with permission from publisher)

Hilo 5 Summative Assessment/Evaluación final
Exposición de carreras profesionales/Career Fair — Mid-High Intermediate

Communication Mode/Domain	7 Exceeds Expectations	6 Meets Expectations	5 Almost Meets Expectations	4 Does Not Meet Expectations
Interpretive Research	• *Consistently* and *effectively* interprets research on professionals in careers of interest from a variety of authentic written, audio, and audiovisual resources	• *Adequately* interprets research on professionals in careers of interest from a variety of authentic written, audio, and audiovisual resources	• *Sometimes* interprets research on professionals in careers of interest from a variety of authentic written, audio, and audiovisual resources	• *Minimally* interprets research on professionals in careers of interest from a variety of authentic written, audio, and audiovisual resources
Presentational Writing — Personal narrative — Part I	• *Effectively* produces a personal narrative about past experiences related to a current career/profession • *Effectively* describes past experiences in a detailed **two paragraph** narrative addressing all criteria on the checklist	• *Adequately* produces a personal narrative about past experiences related to a current career/profession • *Adequately* describes past experiences in a **two paragraph** narrative addressing most criteria on the checklist	• Produces a limited personal narrative about past experiences related to a current career/profession • *Sometimes* describes past experiences in a narrative addressing some criteria on the checklist	• *Minimally* produces a personal narrative about past experiences related to a current career/profession • *Minimally* describes past experiences in a narrative addressing few criteria on the checklist
Presentational Writing — Professional resume — Part II	• *Effectively* develops a detailed professional resume with all required components • *Clear* focus on educational background, professional preparation, and work experiences	• *Adequately* develops a somewhat detailed professional resume with most required components • *Adequate* focus on educational background, professional preparation, and work experiences	• *Sometimes* develops a professional resume with some required components • *Limited* focus on educational background, professional preparation, and work experiences	• *Minimally* develops a professional resume with few required components • *Minimal* focus on educational background, professional preparation, and work experiences
Presentational Speaking — Part III	• *Effectively* presents a detailed history of a professional career in first person • Communicates the history of a professional career with little hesitation and minimal teacher assistance • Is comprehensible to a native speaker with mostly accurate pronunciation • Occasional errors in targeted structures may interfere with communication • Uses a variety of vocabulary from hilo • Completes all requirements	• *Adequately* presents a history of a professional career in some detail in first person • Communicates the history of a professional career with some hesitation and some teacher assistance • Is comprehensible to a native speaker with adequate pronunciation • Several errors in targeted structures interfere with communication • Uses appropriate vocabulary from hilo • Completes most requirements	• *Sometimes* presents a history of a professional career with limited detail in first person • Has difficulty communicating the history of a professional career and needs teacher assistance • *Somewhat* comprehensible to a native speaker with fair pronunciation • Some errors in targeted structures interfere with communication • Uses limited vocabulary from hilo • Completes some of the requirements	• *Minimally* presents a history of a professional career, only with minimal detail • Hesitation and pronunciation impede communication • Cannot proceed without teacher assistance. • Errors in targeted structures interfere with communication • Uses minimal vocabulary from hilo • Completes few requirements
Interpersonal Speaking — Role Plays — Part III	• *Consistently* Initiates and maintains discussion in role plays by preparing and asking questions to get others to respond • *Consistently* asks for clarification, such as repeating words, rephrasing questions or providing examples • Uses words, circumlocution, self-correction, phrases and occasional complex sentences to express ideas • *Effectively* collaborates with others to ask and answer questions about professions	• *Adequately* Initiates and maintains discussion in role plays by preparing and asking questions to get others to respond • *Sometimes* asks for clarification, such as repeating words, rephrasing questions or providing examples • Uses words, circumlocution, self-correction, phrases and simple sentences to express ideas • *Mostly* collaborates with others to ask and answer questions about professions	• *Sometimes* participates in the discussion in role plays by preparing and asking questions to get others to respond • *Sometimes* asks for clarification, such as repeating words • Uses words, circumlocution, self-correction, phrases and simple sentences to express ideas • *Sometimes* collaborates with others to ask and answer questions about professions	• *Minimally* participates in the discussion in role plays • *Minimally* asks for clarification • May use words and memorized phrases or simple sentences to express ideas • *Minimally* collaborates with others to ask and answer questions about professions

continued on next page

Communication Mode/Domain	7 Exceeds Expectations	6 Meets Expectations	5 Almost Meets Expectations	4 Does Not Meet Expectations
Language Control	*Consistently and effectively* uses the following grammatical structures appropriately: • Past tenses: imperfect and preterit • Present and imperfect subjunctive tenses	*Adequately* uses the following grammatical structures appropriately: • Past tenses: imperfect and preterit • Present and imperfect subjunctive tenses	*Sometimes* uses the following grammatical structures appropriately: • Past tenses: imperfect and preterit • Present and imperfect subjunctive tenses	*Rarely* uses the following grammatical structures appropriately: • Past tenses: imperfect and preterit • Present and imperfect subjunctive tenses
Vocabulary	• Uses at least 12 vocabulary words and expressions from the hilo appropriately • *Effectively* uses conjunctions, transition words and idiomatic expressions appropriately	• Uses 10–12 vocabulary words and expressions from the hilo appropriately • *Adequately* uses conjunctions, transition words and idiomatic expressions appropriately	• May use 7–9 vocabulary words and expressions from the hilo appropriately • *Sometimes* uses conjunctions, transition words and idiomatic expressions appropriately	• May use 5–6 vocabulary words and expressions from the hilo appropriately • *Rarely* uses conjunctions, transition words and idiomatic expressions appropriately
Cultural awareness	• Uses mostly culturally appropriate vocabulary and expressions • Indicates awareness of differences in cultural behaviors and perspectives regarding careers and professions in Spanish-speaking cultures and countries	• Uses some culturally appropriate vocabulary and expressions • May indicate some awareness of differences in cultural behaviors and perspectives regarding careers and professions in Spanish-speaking cultures and countries	• Uses limited culturally appropriate vocabulary and/or expressions • May not indicate awareness of differences in cultural behaviors and perspectives regarding careers and professions in Spanish-speaking cultures and countries	• *Rarely* uses culturally appropriate vocabulary or expressions • Does not indicate awareness of differences in cultural behaviors and perspectives regarding careers and professions in Spanish-speaking cultures and countries

© 2013 Wayside Publishing (This document is editable with permission from publisher)

Hilo 6 Summative Assessment/Evaluación final
Jóvenes de hoy/Today's Youth

Mid-High Intermediate

Communication Mode/Domain	7 Exceeds Expectations	6 Meets Expectations	5 Almost Meets Expectations	4 Does Not Meet Expectations
Interpersonal Individual: Collaborative work on script during writing process	• *Consistently* initiates and maintains discussion by asking questions to collaborate with team members • *Consistently* asks for clarification, such as repeating words, rephrasing questions or providing examples • Uses words, circumlocution, self-correction, phrases and occasional complex sentences to express ideas • *Effectively* collaborates with team to complete all requirements	• *Adequately* Initiates and maintains discussion by asking questions to collaborate with team members • *Sometimes* asks for clarification, such as repeating words, rephrasing questions or providing examples • Uses words, circumlocution, self-correction, phrases and simple sentences to express ideas • *Mostly* collaborates with team to complete all requirements	• *Occasionally* participates in the discussion by asking or answering questions to collaborate with team members • *Occasionally* asks for clarification, such as repeating words • Uses words, circumlocution, self-correction, phrases and simple sentences to express ideas • *Sometimes* collaborates with team to complete all requirements	• *Minimally* participates in the discussion to collaborate with team members • *Minimally* asks for clarification • May use words and memorized phrases or simple sentences to express ideas • *Minimally* collaborates with team to complete all requirements
Interpretive Individual: Alternative advice to "character" in presentation	• *Effectively* interprets situation in a minimum of three presentations to provide alternative recommendations to a character, using a minimum of two appropriate commands, one affirmative and one negative	• *Adequately* interprets situation in a minimum of two presentations to provide alternative recommendations to a character, using two appropriate commands, one affirmative and one negative	• *Sometimes* interprets situation in a minimum of one presentation to provide alternative recommendations to a character, using at least one appropriate command	• *Minimally* interprets situation in a presentation to provide recommendations to a character, may not use appropriate commands
Presentational Writing Collaborative: script	• *Effectively and consistently* collaborates with team members to develop a detailed script for all team members • Addresses all criteria on the checklist • Meets all deadlines	• *Adequately* collaborates with team members to develop a *somewhat* detailed script for all team members • Addresses most criteria on the checklist • Meets most deadlines	• *Sometimes* collaborates with team members to develop a script for all team members, • Addresses some criteria on the checklist • *Sometimes* meets deadlines	• *Minimally* collaborates with team members to develop a script for all team members • Addresses few criteria on the checklist
Presentational Speaking Delivery Collaborative presentation of script	• *Effectively* presents speaking role in the scenario without notes • Communicates the message clearly with good eye contact and poise; *minimal* hesitation or teacher assistance • Is comprehensible to a native speaker with mostly accurate pronunciation • Occasional errors in targeted structures may interfere with communication	• *Adequately* presents speaking role in the scenario with minimal notes • Communicates the message *adequately* with some eye contact and poise; some hesitation and/or teacher assistance • Is comprehensible to a native speaker with adequate pronunciation • Several errors in targeted structures interferes with communication	• Presents speaking role in the scenario with some notes • Communicates without clarity and *minimal* eye contact and poise; needs significant hesitation or teacher assistance • May not be comprehensible to a native speaker, pronunciation is poor. • Some errors in targeted structures interfere with communication.	• Struggles to present speaking role in the scenario with some notes • Hesitation and pronunciation impede communication • Cannot proceed without teacher assistance. • Errors in targeted structures interfere with communication
Presentational Writing Reflection Individual: alternative scenario for a character in script	• *Effectively* writes a minimum 100 word well developed alternative scenario for a character in the script • *Clear* focus on topic with supporting details and examples • *Effectively* uses cohesive devices and transitions to guide reader • Completes all requirements	• *Adequately* writes a 100 word alternative scenario for a character in the script • *Adequate* focus on topic with some supporting details and examples • *Adequately* uses cohesive devices and transitions to guide reader • Completes most of the requirements	• Writes less than a 100 word alternative scenario for a character in the script • *Limited* focus on topic with few supporting details and examples • *Limited* use of cohesive devices and transitions to guide reader • Completes some of the requirements	• Writes less than a 50 word alternative scenario for a character in the script • May be off topic with minimal supporting details and examples • *Minimal* or no use of cohesive devices and transitions to guide reader • Completes few requirements

continued on next page

© 2013 Wayside Publishing (This document is editable with permission from publisher)

Communication Mode/Domain	7 Exceeds Expectations	6 Meets Expectations	5 Almost Meets Expectations	4 Does Not Meet Expectations
Language Control	*Consistently and effectively* uses the following grammatical structures appropriately: • Present subjunctive for giving advice • Si clauses with imperfect subjunctive and conditional tenses • Familiar and plural commands	*Adequately* uses the following grammatical structures appropriately: • Present subjunctive for giving advice • Si clauses with imperfect subjunctive and conditional tenses • Familiar and plural commands	*Sometimes* uses the following grammatical structures appropriately: • Present subjunctive for giving advice • Si clauses with imperfect subjunctive and conditional tenses • Familiar and plural commands	*Rarely* uses the following grammatical structures appropriately: • Present subjunctive for giving advice • Si clauses with imperfect subjunctive and conditional tenses • Familiar and plural commands
Vocabulary	• Uses at least 12 vocabulary words and expressions from the hilo appropriately • *Effectively* uses conjunctions, transition words and idiomatic expressions appropriately	• Uses 10–12 vocabulary words and expressions from the hilo appropriately • *Adequately* uses conjunctions, transition words and idiomatic expressions appropriately	• May use 7–9 vocabulary words and expressions from the hilo appropriately • *Sometimes* uses conjunctions, transition words and idiomatic expressions appropriately	• May use 5-6 vocabulary words and expressions from the hilo appropriately • *Rarely* uses conjunctions, transition words and idiomatic expressions appropriately
Cultural awareness	• Uses mostly culturally appropriate vocabulary and expressions • Indicates awareness of differences in cultural behaviors and perspectives	• Uses some culturally appropriate vocabulary and expressions • May indicate some awareness of differences in cultural behaviors and perspectives	• Uses limited culturally appropriate vocabulary and/or expressions • May not indicate awareness of differences in cultural behaviors and perspectives	• *Rarely* or may not use culturally appropriate vocabulary or expressions • Does not indicate awareness of differences in cultural behaviors and perspectives

© 2013 Wayside Publishing (This document is editable with permission from publisher)

Hilo 7 Summative Assessment/Evaluación final
El "look" indígena para los jóvenes

Mid-High Intermediate

Communication Mode/Domain	7 Exceeds Expectations	6 Meets Expectations	5 Almost Meets Expectations	4 Does Not Meet Expectations
		Team/individual evaluation for process		
Interpersonal Individual collaborative contributions during process	• *Consistently* initiates and maintains discussion by asking questions to get team members to respond • *Consistently* asks for clarification, such as repeating words, rephrasing questions or providing examples • Uses words, circumlocution, self-correction, phrases and occasional complex sentences to express ideas • *Effectively* collaborates with team to complete all requirements	• *Adequately* initiates and maintains discussion by asking questions to get team members to respond • *Mostly* asks for clarification, such as repeating words, rephrasing questions or providing examples • Uses words, circumlocution, self-correction, phrases and simple sentences to express ideas • *Mostly* collaborates with team to complete most requirements	• *Sometimes* participates in the discussion by asking or answering questions • *Sometimes* asks for clarification, such as repeating words • Uses words, circumlocution, self-correction, phrases and simple sentences to express ideas • *Sometimes* collaborates with team to complete some requirements	• *Minimally* participates in the discussion • *Minimally* asks for clarification • May use words and memorized phrases or simple sentences to express ideas • *Minimally* collaborates with team to complete requirements
Interpretive Individual: each team member summarizes a different source	• *Effectively* interprets a minimum of three sources selected from a variety of texts, visual and audio sources • *Effectively* summarizes each source in one paragraph indicating what was used to inspire the "look" from each source	• *Adequately* interprets three sources selected from a variety of texts, visual and audio sources • *Adequately* summarizes each source in one paragraph indicating what was used to inspire the "look" from each source	• *Sometimes* interprets two or more sources selected from a variety of texts, visual and audio sources • *Sometimes* summarizes each source in one paragraph indicating what was used to inspire the "look" from each source	• *Minimally* interprets sources selected from a variety of texts, visual and audio sources • *Minimally* summarizes a source in one paragraph indicating what was used to inspire the "look" from each source
Individual Presentational Writing Product	• *Effectively* describes a minimum of two (of four) articles of clothing in a detailed two paragraph format addressing all criteria on the checklist • *Effectively* indicates the sustainable materials used and the advantages to the environment	• *Adequately* describes two (of four) articles of clothing in a two paragraph format addressing most criteria on the checklist • *Adequately* indicates the sustainable materials used and the advantages to the environment	• Describes with limited detail, less than two (of four) articles of clothing in a one paragraph format addressing some criteria on the checklist • *Sometimes* indicates the sustainable materials used and the advantages to the environment	• Does not describe articles of clothing in a paragraph format and addresses few criteria on the checklist • *Minimally* indicates the sustainable materials used and the advantages to the environment
Team Visual Product	• *Effectively* develops a visual product illustrating a minimum of 4 articles of clothing or personal items, using technology or other tools • Visual leaves a lasting impression due to neatness, originality, mechanics, and organization • Completes all requirements	• *Adequately* develops a visual product illustrating 4 articles of clothing or personal items, using technology or other tools • Visual is mostly neat, original, mechanically correct, and organized • Completes most requirements	• *Somewhat* develops a visual product illustrating 4 articles of clothing or personal items, using technology or other tools • Visual is somewhat neat and organized but lacks originality and correct use of mechanics. • Completes some requirements	• *Minimally* develops a visual product illustrating a minimum of 4 articles of clothing or personal items, using technology or other tools • Visual product demonstrates *minimal* organization with *minimal* supporting details and examples • Completes few requirements
Cultural awareness	• Uses mostly culturally appropriate vocabulary and expressions • Indicates awareness of differences in cultural behaviors and perspectives	• Uses some culturally appropriate vocabulary and expressions • May indicate some awareness of differences in cultural behaviors and perspectives	• *Occasionally* uses culturally appropriate vocabulary and/or expressions • May not indicate awareness of differences in cultural behaviors and perspectives	• *Rarely* or may not use culturally appropriate vocabulary or expressions • Does not indicate awareness of differences in cultural behaviors and perspectives

continued on next page

© 2013 Wayside Publishing (This document is editable with permission from publisher)

HL0 7 Summative assessment

Communication Mode/Domain	7 Exceeds Expectations	6 Meets Expectations	5 Almost Meets Expectations	4 Does Not Meet Expectations
Presentational Speaking Delivery Part 1 Individual persuasive message	• *Effectively* persuades young people to wear the articles of clothing • Communicates the message clearly with good eye contact and poise; minimal hesitation or teacher assistance • Is comprehensible to a native speaker with *mostly accurate* pronunciation • Occasional errors in targeted structures may interfere with communication	• *Adequately* persuades young people to wear the articles of clothing • Communicates the message *adequately* with some eye contact and poise; some hesitation and/or teacher assistance • Is comprehensible to a native speaker with *adequate* pronunciation • Several errors in targeted structures may interfere with communication	• *Sometimes* persuades young people to wear the articles of clothing • Communicates without clarity and *limited* eye contact and poise; *frequent* hesitation, teacher assistance needed • May not be comprehensible to a native speaker and pronunciation is fair. • Some errors in targeted structures interfere with communication.	• *Minimally* persuades young people to wear the articles of clothing • Hesitation and pronunciation impede communication • Cannot proceed without teacher assistance. • Errors in targeted structures interfere with communication
Presentational Speaking Delivery Part 2 Individual presentation to design team	• *Effectively* presents a minimum of two (of four) articles of clothing to designers and why they chose the indigenous culture • *Effectively* indicates the sustainable materials used and its advantages • Communicates the message clearly with good eye contact and poise; minimal hesitation or teacher assistance • Is comprehensible to a native speaker with *mostly accurate* pronunciation • Occasional errors interfere with communication	• *Adequately* presents a minimum of two (of four) articles of clothing to designers and why they chose the indigenous culture • *Adequately* indicates the sustainable materials used and its advantages • Communicates the message with good eye contact and poise; some hesitation or teacher assistance • Is comprehensible to a native speaker with *adequate* pronunciation • Several errors in targeted structures may interfere with communication	• *Occasionally* presents two (of four) articles of clothing to designers and why they chose the indigenous culture • *Occasionally* indicates the sustainable materials used and its advantages • Has difficulty communicating the message without hesitation and needs teacher assistance • Is comprehensible to a native speaker with fair pronunciation • Some errors may interfere with communication	• *Minimally* presents two (of four) articles of clothing to designers and why they chose the indigenous culture • *Minimally* indicates the sustainable materials used and its advantages • Hesitation and pronunciation impede communication • Cannot proceed without extensive teacher assistance • Errors interfere with communication
Language Control	*Consistently and effectively* uses the following grammatical structures appropriately: • If clauses with imperfect subjunctive and conditional tenses • Relative pronouns • Familiar commands	*Adequately* uses the following grammatical structures appropriately: • If clauses with imperfect subjunctive and conditional tenses • Relative pronouns • Familiar commands	*Sometimes* uses the following grammatical structures appropriately: • Imperfect subjunctive and conditional tenses • Relative pronouns • Familiar commands	*Rarely* uses the following grammatical structures appropriately: • Imperfect subjunctive and conditional tenses • Relative pronouns • Familiar commands
Vocabulary	• Uses at least 12 vocabulary words and expressions from the hilo appropriately • *Effectively* uses conjunctions, transition words and idiomatic expressions appropriately	• Uses 10–12 vocabulary words and expressions from the hilo appropriately • *Adequately* uses conjunctions, transition words and idiomatic expressions appropriately	• May use 7–9 vocabulary words and expressions from the hilo appropriately • *Sometimes* uses conjunctions, transition words and idiomatic expressions appropriately	• May use 5–6 vocabulary words and expressions from the hilo appropriately • *Rarely* uses conjunctions, transition words and idiomatic expressions appropriately

© 2013 Wayside Publishing (This document is editable with permission from publisher)

Hilo 8 Summative Assessment/Evaluación final
Museo Tejidos/Tejidos museum

Mid-High Intermediate

Communication Mode/Domain	7 Exceeds Expectations	6 Meets Expectations	5 Almost Meets Expectations	4 Does Not Meet Expectations
Interpretive Artist and work of art	• *Effectively* researches a work of art and the artist from a minimum of two sources selected from a variety of texts and visual materials • *Effectively* interprets the artist's message about the work of art and states point of view about the artwork; one paragraph minimum	• *Adequately* researches a work of art and the artist from two sources selected from a variety of texts and visual materials • *Adequately* interprets the artist's message about the work of art and states point of view about the artwork; one paragraph	• *Limited* research on a work of art and the artist from one or two sources selected from a variety of texts and visual materials • *Limited* interpretation of the artist's message about the work of art and point of view about the artwork; less than one paragraph	• *Minimally* researches a work of art and the artist, possibly one source • *Minimally* interprets the artist's message about the work of art or states point of view about the artwork; two or three sentences
Presentational Writing 1 Museum wall plaque	• *Effectively* provides detailed and organized information on artist and artwork addressing all criteria	• *Adequately* provides some detail and organized information on artist and artwork addressing most criteria	• Provides limited information on artist and artwork addressing some criteria	• *Minimally* provides information on artist and artwork addressing few criteria
Presentational Writing 2 Art analysis of artist	• *Effectively* analyzes the selected artist's work, the message it communicates, and expressing own point of view	• *Adequately* analyzes the selected artist's work, the message it communicates, and expressing own point of view	• *Limited* analysis of the selected artist's work, the message it communicates, or own point of view	• *Minimally* analyzes the selected artist's work, the message it communicates, or expressing own point of view
Visual Product Recreate artwork	• *Effectively* recreates the selected artist's work of art, using available tools or technology • Visual leaves a lasting impression due to creativity	• *Adequately* recreates the selected artist's work of art, using available tools or technology • Visual product is adequate and creative	• *Somewhat* recreates the selected artist's work of art, using available tools or technology • Visual product may lack creativity	• *Minimally* recreates the selected artist's work of art, using available tools or technology • Visual product demonstrates *minimal* creativity
Presentational Writing 3 Student art work	• *Effectively* develops an organized paragraph on the student art work • *Effectively* describes how the art work was created • *Effectively* evaluates the message • *Effectively* compares similarities and differences between original artwork and student recreation	• *Adequately* develops an organized paragraph on the student art work • *Adequately* describes how the art work was created • *Adequately* evaluates the message • *Adequately* compares similarities and differences between original artwork and student recreation	• Develops a limited paragraph on the student art work • *Limited* description of how the art work was created • *Limited* evaluation of the message • *Limited* comparison of similarities and differences between original artwork and student recreation	• *Minimally* develops an organized paragraph on the student art work • *Minimally* describes how the art work was created • *Minimally* evaluates the message • *Minimally* compares similarities and differences between original artwork and student recreation

continued on next page

HILO 8 Summative Assessment

Communication Mode/Domain	7 Exceeds Expectations	6 Meets Expectations	5 Almost Meets Expectations	4 Does Not Meet Expectations
Interpersonal Q & A	• *Effectively and consistently* asks questions about artwork of other students • *Effectively and consistently* answers questions about own artwork • *Consistently* provides or asks for clarification, such as repeating words, rephrasing questions or providing examples • *Effectively and consistently* uses words, circumlocution, self-correction, phrases and occasional complex sentences to express ideas	• *Adequately* asks questions about artwork of other students • *Adequately* answers questions about own artwork • *Most of the time* provides or asks for clarification, such as repeating words, rephrasing questions or providing examples • *Most of the time* uses words, circumlocution, self-correction, phrases and simple sentences to express ideas	• *Sometimes* asks questions about artwork of other students • *Sometimes* answers questions about own artwork • *Sometimes* provides or asks for clarification, such as repeating words • *Sometimes* uses words, circumlocution, self-correction, phrases and simple sentences to express ideas	• *Rarely* asks questions about artwork of other students • *Rarely* answers questions about own artwork • *Rarely* asks for clarification • May use words and memorized phrases or simple sentences to express ideas
Language Control	*Consistently and effectively* uses the following grammatical structures appropriately: • Past tenses • Present perfect tenses	*Adequately* uses the following grammatical structures appropriately: • Past tenses • Present perfect tenses	*Sometimes* uses the following grammatical structures appropriately: • Past tenses • Present perfect tenses	*Rarely* uses the following grammatical structures appropriately: • Past tenses • Present perfect tenses
Vocabulary	• Uses at least 12 vocabulary words and expressions from the hilo appropriately • *Effectively* uses conjunctions, transition words and idiomatic expressions appropriately	• Uses 10–12 vocabulary words and expressions from the hilo appropriately • *Adequately* uses conjunctions, transition words and idiomatic expressions appropriately	• May use 7–9 vocabulary words and expressions from the hilo appropriately • *Sometimes* uses conjunctions, transition words and idiomatic expressions appropriately	• May use 5–6 vocabulary words and expressions from the hilo appropriately • *Rarely* uses conjunctions, transition words and idiomatic expressions appropriately
Cultural awareness	• Uses mostly culturally appropriate vocabulary and expressions • Indicates awareness of differences in cultural behaviors and perspectives	• Uses some culturally appropriate vocabulary and expressions • May indicate some awareness of differences in cultural behaviors and perspectives	• *Occasionally* uses culturally appropriate vocabulary and/or expressions • May not indicate awareness of differences in cultural behaviors and perspectives	• *Rarely* or may not use culturally appropriate vocabulary or expressions • Does not indicate awareness of differences in cultural behaviors and perspectives

© 2013 Wayside Publishing (This document is editable with permission from publisher)

Hilo 9 Summative Assessment/Evaluación final
¿Con quién cenarías si pudieras?

Mid-High Intermediate

Communication Mode/Domain	7 Exceeds Expectations	6 Meets Expectations	5 Almost Meets Expectations	4 Does Not Meet Expectations
Interpretive Research	• *Effectively* researches a public figure from a minimum of two sources selected from texts and audio/visual materials • *Effectively* interprets and takes notes on the individual's biography and contributions to society, politics, or culture, noting sources	• *Adequately* researches a public figure from a minimum of two sources selected from texts and audio/visual materials • *Adequately* interprets and takes notes on the individual's biography and contributions to society, politics, or culture, noting sources	• *Limited* research on a public figure from two sources selected from texts and audio/visual materials • *Limited* interpretation and note taking on the individual's biography and contributions to society, politics, or culture, noting sources	• *Minimally* researches a public figure from one source • *Minimally* interprets and takes notes on the individual's biography and contributions to society, politics, or culture, noting sources
Presentational Writing Essay	• *Effectively* develops a detailed and organized minimum 3-paragraph essay on the individual's biography • *Effectively* analyzes the individual's contribution to society, politics, or culture • *Effectively* explains why you want to have dinner with the person	• *Adequately* develops an organized 3-paragraph essay on the individual's biography • *Adequately* analyzes the individual's contribution to society, politics, or culture • *Adequately* explains why you want to have dinner with the person	• *Limited* development of a 2-paragraph essay on the individual's biography • *Limited* analysis of the individual's contribution to society, politics, or culture • *Limited* explanation of why you want to have dinner with the person	• *Minimally* develops a 1–2 paragraph essay on the individual's biography • *Minimally* analyzes the individual's contribution to society, politics, or culture • *Minimally* explains why you want to have dinner with the person
Presentational Speaking Monologue/ Dialogue/ Documentary	• *Effectively* delivers a creative presentation based on the individual's life and contributions that made the individual an admired public figure • Communicates the message clearly with good eye contact and poise; minimal hesitation or teacher assistance • Is comprehensible to a native speaker with mostly accurate pronunciation • Occasional errors in targeted structures interfere with communication • Meets all criteria	• *Adequately* delivers a presentation based on the individual's life and contributions that made the individual an admired public figure • Communicates the message adequately with some eye contact and poise; some hesitation, some teacher assistance needed • Is comprehensible to a native speaker with pronunciation • Several errors in targeted structures may interfere with communication • Meets most criteria	• Delivers a limited presentation based on the individual's life and contributions that made the individual an admired public figure • Communicates without clarity and limited eye contact and poise; frequent hesitation, teacher assistance needed • May not be comprehensible to a native speaker; pronunciation is fair • Some errors in targeted structures interfere with communication • Meets some criteria	• *Minimally* delivers a presentation based on the individual's life and contributions that made the individual an admired public figure • Hesitation and pronunciation impede communication; cannot proceed without teacher assistance • Many errors in targeted structures interfere with communication • Meets few criteria
Presentational Delivery	• Visual presentation captures audience attention and leaves a lasting impression due to creativity • *Effectively* presents the information creatively and uniquely using available tools or technology	• Visual presentation is creative and captures audience attention • *Adequately* presents the information using available tools or technology	• Visual presentation may lack creativity • *Limited* presentation using available tools or technology	• Visual presentation demonstrates minimal creativity • *Minimally* presents the information using available tools or technology

continued on next page

HILO 9 Summative Assessment

Communication Mode/Domain	7 Exceeds Expectations	6 Meets Expectations	5 Almost Meets Expectations	4 Does Not Meet Expectations
Interpersonal **Individual** speaking Spanish during Q & A session	• *Effectively* prepares a minimum of 10 questions that you want to know about the individual who changed the world • *Effectively* selects and responds to 5 questions based on the information from research • *Effectively* asks questions of other guests to learn about other influential figures	• *Adequately* prepares a minimum of 10 questions that you want to know about the individual • *Adequately* selects and responds to 4-5 questions based on the information from research • *Most of the time* asks questions of other guests to learn about other influential figures	• *Sometimes* prepares 6–8 questions that you want to know about the individual • *Sometimes* selects and responds to 3–4 questions based on the information from research • *Sometimes* asks questions of other guests to learn about other influential figures	• *Rarely* prepares 4–5 questions that you want to know about the individual • *Rarely* selects and responds to 2-3 questions based on the information from research • *Rarely* asks questions of other guests to learn about other influential figures
Language Control	*Consistently and effectively* uses the following grammatical structures appropriately: • Past tenses • Present perfect tenses • Si clauses and subjunctive tenses	*Adequately* uses the following grammatical structures appropriately: • Past tenses • Present perfect tenses • Si clauses and subjunctive tenses	*Sometimes* uses the following grammatical structures appropriately: • Past tenses • Present perfect tenses • Si clauses and subjunctive tenses	*Rarely* uses the following grammatical structures appropriately: • Past tenses • Present perfect tenses • Si clauses and subjunctive tenses
Vocabulary	• Uses at least 12 vocabulary words and expressions from the hilo appropriately • *Effectively* uses conjunctions, transition words and idiomatic expressions appropriately	• Uses 10–12 vocabulary words and expressions from the hilo appropriately • *Adequately* uses conjunctions, transition words and idiomatic expressions appropriately	• May use 7–9 vocabulary words and expressions from the hilo appropriately • *Sometimes* uses conjunctions, transition words and idiomatic expressions appropriately	• May use 5–6 vocabulary words and expressions from the hilo appropriately • *Rarely* uses conjunctions, transition words and idiomatic expressions appropriately
Cultural awareness	• Uses mostly culturally appropriate vocabulary and expressions • Indicates awareness of differences in cultural behaviors and perspectives	• Uses some culturally appropriate vocabulary and expressions • May indicate some awareness of differences in cultural behaviors and perspectives	• *Occasionally* uses culturally appropriate vocabulary and/or expressions • May not indicate awareness of differences in cultural behaviors and perspectives	• *Rarely* or may not use culturally appropriate vocabulary or expressions • Does not indicate awareness of differences in cultural behaviors and perspectives

© 2013 Wayside Publishing (This document is editable with permission from publisher)

Hilo 10 Summative Assessment/Evaluación final
Los idiomas sí que cuentan/Languages Count

Mid-High Intermediate

Communication Mode/Domain	7 Exceeds Expectations	6 Meets Expectations	5 Almost Meets Expectations	4 Does Not Meet Expectations
Interpersonal Individual collaborative contributions during process	• *Consistently* initiates and maintains discussion by asking questions to get team members to respond • *Consistently* asks for clarification, such as repeating words, rephrasing questions or providing examples • Uses words, circumlocution, self-correction, phrases and occasional complex sentences to express ideas • *Effectively* collaborates with team to complete all requirements	• *Adequately* initiates and maintains discussion by asking questions to get team members to respond • *Sometimes* asks for clarification, such as repeating words, rephrasing questions or providing examples • Uses words, circumlocution, self-correction, phrases and simple sentences to express ideas • *Mostly* collaborates with team to complete most requirements	• *Sometimes* participates in the discussion by asking or answering questions • *Sometimes* asks for clarification, such as repeating words • Uses words, circumlocution, self-correction, phrases and simple sentences to express ideas • *Sometimes* collaborates with team to complete some requirements	• *Minimally* participates in the discussion • *Minimally* asks for clarification • May use words and memorized phrases or simple sentences to express ideas • *Minimally* collaborates with team to complete requirements
Interpretive Individual Research	• *Effectively* interprets a minimum of three sources per group, selected from a variety of texts, visual and audio sources • *Effectively* summarizes each source in one paragraph indicating why they chose that ethnic group to research	• *Adequately* interprets three sources per group, selected from a variety of texts, visual and audio sources • *Adequately* summarizes each source in one paragraph indicating why they chose that ethnic group to research	• *Sometimes* interprets two or more sources selected from a variety of texts, visual and audio sources • *Sometimes* summarizes each source in one paragraph indicating why they chose that ethnic group to research	• *Minimally* interprets sources selected from a variety of texts, visual and audio sources • *Minimally* summarizes a source in one paragraph indicating why they chose that ethnic group to research
Individual Presentational Writing I Research essay	• *Effectively* develops a three-paragraph essay to include history, origin of the language, current statistics and maps addressing all criteria on checklist	• *Adequately* develops a two to three-paragraph essay to include history, origin of the language, current statistics and maps addressing most criteria on checklist	• *Sometimes* develops a one to two paragraph essay to include history, origin of the language, current statistics and maps addressing some criteria on checklist	• *Minimally* develops a one to two paragraph essay to include history, origin of the language, current statistics and maps addressing few criteria on checklist
Team Activity Products	• *Effectively* develops two activities, similar to *Día E*, that promote and protect the mother tongue language of the ethnic group, using technology or other tools • Activities leave a lasting impression due to creativity and organization • Meets all criteria	• *Adequately* develops two activities, similar to *Día E*, that promote and protect the mother tongue language of the ethnic group, using technology or other tools • Activities are mostly creative and organized • Meets most requirements	• *Somewhat* develops one or two activities, similar to *Día E*, that promote and protect the mother tongue language of the ethnic group, using technology or other tools • Activities are somewhat organized but lack creativity • Meets some requirements	• *Minimally* develops one activity, similar to *Día E*, that promotes and protects the mother tongue language of the ethnic group, using technology or other tools • Activity demonstrates minimal organization with minimal creativity • Meets few requirements

continued on next page

© 2013 Wayside Publishing (This document is editable with permission from publisher)

HILO 10 Summative Assessment

Communication Mode/Domain	7 Exceeds Expectations	6 Meets Expectations	5 Almost Meets Expectations	4 Does Not Meet Expectations
Presentational Speaking Persuasive message Individual	• *Effectively* persuades others to protect ethnic languages, using a form of technology • *Effectively* connects language to identity • Communicates the message clearly with good eye contact and poise; minimal hesitation or teacher assistance • Is comprehensible to a native speaker with mostly accurate pronunciation • Occasional errors in targeted structures may interfere with communication	• *Adequately* persuades others to protect ethnic languages, using a form of technology • *Adequately* connects language to identity • Communicates the message *adequately* with some eye contact and poise; some hesitation and/or teacher assistance • Is comprehensible to a native speaker with *adequate* pronunciation • Several errors in targeted structures may interfere with communication	• *Sometimes* persuades others to protect ethnic languages, using a form of technology • *Sometimes* connects language to identity • Communicates without clarity and *limited* eye contact and poise; *frequent* hesitation, teacher assistance needed • *Sometimes* comprehensible to a native speaker and pronunciation is fair. • Some errors in targeted structures interfere with communication.	• *Minimally* persuades others to protect ethnic languages, using a form of technology • *Minimally* connects language to identity • Hesitation and pronunciation impede communication • Cannot proceed without teacher assistance. • Errors in targeted structures interfere with communication
Presentational Writing II Individual reflection	• *Effectively* reflects, in minimum two paragraphs, on what was learned about relationship between identity and language • *Effectively* indicates language comparisons between ethnic language and national language • *Effectively* makes a connection to literacy and relationship to mother tongue	• *Adequately* reflects, in two paragraphs, on what was learned about relationship between identity and language • *Adequately* indicates language comparisons between ethnic language and national language • *Adequately* makes a connection to literacy and relationship to mother tongue	• *Sometimes* reflects, in one or two paragraphs, on what was learned about relationship between identity and language • *Sometimes* indicates language comparisons between ethnic language and national language • *Sometimes* makes a connection to literacy and relationship to mother tongue	• *Minimally* reflects, in one paragraph, on what was learned about relationship between identity and language • *Minimally* indicates language comparisons between ethnic language and national language • *Minimally* makes a connection to literacy and relationship to mother tongue
Language Control	*Effectively* uses the following grammatical structures appropriately: • If clauses with imperfect subjunctive and conditional tenses • Relative pronouns • Familiar commands	*Adequately* uses the following grammatical structures appropriately: • If clauses with imperfect subjunctive and conditional tenses • Relative pronouns • Familiar commands	*Sometimes* uses the following grammatical structures appropriately: • Imperfect subjunctive and conditional tenses • Relative pronouns • Familiar commands	*Rarely* uses the following grammatical structures appropriately: • Imperfect subjunctive and conditional tenses • Relative pronouns • Familiar commands
Vocabulary	• Uses at least 12 vocabulary words and expressions from the hilo appropriately • *Effectively* uses conjunctions, transition words and idiomatic expressions appropriately	• Uses 10–12 vocabulary words and expressions from the hilo appropriately • *Adequately* uses conjunctions, transition words and idiomatic expressions appropriately	• May use 7–9 vocabulary words and expressions from the hilo appropriately • *Sometimes* uses conjunctions, transition words and idiomatic expressions appropriately	• May use 5–6 vocabulary words and expressions from the hilo appropriately • *Minimally* uses conjunctions, transition words and idiomatic expressions appropriately
Cultural awareness	• Uses mostly culturally appropriate vocabulary and expressions • Indicates awareness of differences in cultural behaviors and perspectives	• Uses some culturally appropriate vocabulary and expressions • May indicate some awareness of differences in cultural behaviors and perspectives	• *Occasionally* uses culturally appropriate vocabulary and/or expressions • *Occasionally* indicates awareness of differences in cultural behaviors and perspectives	• *Rarely* or may not use culturally appropriate vocabulary or expressions • *Rarely* indicates awareness of differences in cultural behaviors and perspectives

© 2013 Wayside Publishing (This document is editable with permission from publisher)

Hilo 11 Summative Assessment/Evaluación final
Juntos cuidemos nuestro planeta ¡Haz tu parte!
Mid-High Intermediate

Communication Mode/Domain	7 Exceeds Expectations	6 Meets Expectations	5 Almost Meets Expectations	4 Does Not Meet Expectations
Interpersonal — Individual speaking Spanish during collaborative process	• *Consistently* initiates and maintains discussion by asking questions to get team members to respond • *Consistently* asks for clarification, such as repeating words, rephrasing questions or providing examples • Uses words, circumlocution, self-correction, phrases, and occasional complex sentences to express ideas • *Effectively* collaborates with team to complete all requirements	• *Adequately* initiates and maintains discussion by asking questions to get team members to respond • *Sometimes* asks for clarification, such as repeating words, rephrasing questions or providing examples • Uses words, circumlocution, self-correction, phrases and simple sentences to express ideas • *Mostly* collaborates with team to complete most requirements	• *Occasionally* participates in the discussion by asking or answering questions • *Occasionally* asks for clarification, such as repeating words • Uses words, circumlocution, self-correction, phrases and simple sentences to express ideas • *Sometimes* collaborates with team to complete some requirements	• *Minimally* participates in the discussion • *Minimally* asks for clarification • May use words and memorized phrases or simple sentences to express ideas • *Minimally* collaborates with team to complete requirements
Interpretive — Individual Research	• *Effectively* interprets a minimum of three sources per group, selected from a variety of texts, visual and audio sources • *Effectively* outlines each source addressing all criteria on checklist	• *Adequately* interprets three sources per group, selected from a variety of texts, visual and audio sources • *Adequately* outlines each source addressing most criteria on checklist	• *Sometimes* interprets two or more sources selected from a variety of texts, visual and audio sources • *Sometimes* outlines each source addressing some criteria on checklist	• *Minimally* interprets sources selected from a variety of texts, visual and audio sources • *Minimally* outlines each source addressing few criteria on checklist
Presentational Writing — Team Promotional Product	• *Effectively* develops and produces a four section promotional product to include the environmental threat, causes and effects on living things, and suggestions to remedy the harmful effects, addressing all criteria on checklist • *Effectively* captures audience attention with a strong opening image and/or statement	• *Adequately* develops and produces a four section promotional product to include the environmental threat, causes and effects on living things, and suggestions to remedy the harmful effects, addressing most criteria on checklist • *Adequately* captures audience attention with a good opening image and/or statement	• *Sometimes* develops and produces a four section promotional product to include the environmental threat, causes and effects on living things, and suggestions to remedy the harmful effects, addressing some criteria on checklist • *Sometimes* captures audience attention with a fair opening image and/or statement	• *Minimally* develops and produces a four section promotional product to include the environmental threat, causes and effects on living things, and suggestions to remedy the harmful effects, addressing few criteria on checklist • *Minimally* captures audience attention with an opening image and/or statement
Presentational Writing — Team PSA script	• *Effectively* collaborates with team members to develop and write a two-minute script for the public service announcement • Meets all criteria	• *Adequately* collaborates with team members to develop and write a 90 second to two-minute script for the public service announcement • Meets most criteria	• *Sometimes* collaborates with team members to develop and write a one-minute script for the public service announcement • Meets some criteria	• *Minimally* collaborates with team members to develop and write a script for the public service announcement • Meets few criteria
Individual Presentational Speaking — Persuasive public service announcement	• *Effectively* persuades others to get involved with protecting the environment • *Effectively* uses a form of technology • Communicates the message clearly with good eye contact and poise; minimal hesitation or teacher assistance • Is comprehensible to a native speaker with mostly accurate pronunciation • Occasional errors in targeted structures may interfere with communication	• *Adequately* persuades others to get involved with protecting the environment • *Adequately* uses a form of technology • Communicates the message adequately with some eye contact and poise; some hesitation and/or teacher assistance • Is comprehensible to a native speaker with adequate pronunciation • Several errors in targeted structures interfere with communication	• *Sometimes* persuades others to get involved with protecting the environment • *Sometimes* connects language to identity • Communicates without clarity and with limited eye contact and poise; frequent hesitation, teacher assistance needed • *Sometimes* comprehensible to a native speaker and pronunciation is fair • Some errors in targeted structures interfere with communication	• *Minimally* persuades others to protect ethnic languages, using a form of technology • *Minimally* connects language to identity • Hesitation and pronunciation impede communication • Cannot proceed without teacher assistance • Errors in targeted structures interfere with communication

continued on next page

© 2013 Wayside Publishing (This document is editable with permission from publisher)

Communication Mode/Domain	7 Exceeds Expectations	6 Meets Expectations	5 Almost Meets Expectations	4 Does Not Meet Expectations
Language Control	*Effectively* uses the following grammatical structures appropriately: • Familiar commands with pronouns • Conjunctions with/without subjunctive tenses • Uses of por/para	*Adequately* uses the following grammatical structures appropriately: • Familiar commands with pronouns • Conjunctions with/without subjunctive tenses • Uses of por/para	*Sometimes* uses the following grammatical structures appropriately: • Familiar commands with pronouns • Conjunctions with/without subjunctive tenses • Uses of por/para	*Rarely* uses the following grammatical structures appropriately: • Familiar commands with pronouns • Conjunctions with/without subjunctive tenses • Uses of por/para
Vocabulary	• Uses at least 12 vocabulary words and expressions from the hilo appropriately • *Effectively* uses conjunctions, transition words and idiomatic expressions appropriately	• Uses 10–12 vocabulary words and expressions from the hilo appropriately • *Adequately* uses conjunctions, transition words and idiomatic expressions appropriately	• May use 7–9 vocabulary words and expressions from the hilo appropriately • *Sometimes* uses conjunctions, transition words and idiomatic expressions appropriately	• May use 5–6 vocabulary words and expressions from the hilo appropriately • *Minimally* uses conjunctions, transition words and idiomatic expressions appropriately
Cultural awareness	• Uses *mostly* culturally *appropriate* vocabulary and expressions • Indicates awareness of differences in cultural behaviors and perspectives	• Uses *some* culturally *appropriate* vocabulary and expressions • May indicate some awareness of differences in cultural behaviors and perspectives	• *Occasionally* uses culturally appropriate vocabulary and/or expressions • *Occasionally* indicates awareness of differences in cultural behaviors and perspectives	• *Rarely* or may not use culturally appropriate vocabulary or expressions • *Minimally* indicates awareness of differences in cultural behaviors and perspectives

© 2013 Wayside Publishing (This document is editable with permission from publisher)

Hilo Digital Summative Assessment/Evaluación final
Caras de la emigracón/Faces of emigration
Mid-High Intermediate

Communication Mode/Domain	7 Exceeds Expectations	6 Meets Expectations	5 Almost Meets Expectations	4 Does Not Meet Expectations
Interpretive Individual Research	• *Effectively* interprets a minimum of two appropriate sources about emigration experiences: reasons, challenges, opportunities and acculturation process • *Effectively* outlines each source addressing all criteria	• *Adequately* interprets two appropriate sources about emigration experiences: reasons, challenges, opportunities and acculturation process • *Adequately* outlines each source addressing most criteria	• *Sometimes* interprets two appropriate sources about emigration experiences: reasons, challenges, opportunities and acculturation process • *Sometimes* outlines each source addressing some criteria	• *Minimally* interprets appropriate sources about emigration experiences: reasons, challenges, opportunities and acculturation process • *Minimally* outlines sources, may address a few criteria
Presentational Writing Narrative	• *Effectively* develops a detailed 3–4 paragraph narrative responding to 3 essential questions, comparing and analyzing information about emigration experiences, addressing all criteria • *Effectively* uses cohesive devices and transitions to guide reader	• *Adequately* develops a 3–4 paragraph narrative responding to 3 essential questions, comparing and analyzing information about emigration experiences, addressing most criteria • *Adequately* uses cohesive devices and transitions to guide reader	• *Sometimes* develops a 2–3 paragraph narrative responding to 2 essential questions, comparing and analyzing information about emigration experiences, addressing some criteria • *Sometimes* uses cohesive devices and transitions to guide reader	• *Minimally* develops a 1–2 paragraph narrative responding to 1–2 essential questions, comparing and analyzing information about emigration experiences, addressing few criteria • *Minimally* uses cohesive devices and transitions to guide reader
Presentational Speaking Persuasive conservation	• *Effectively* and *creatively* persuades friends to emigrate, or not, responding to the 3 essential questions, addressing all criteria • Communicates the message with little hesitation and minimal teacher assistance • Is comprehensible to a native speaker with mostly accurate pronunciation • Occasional errors in targeted structures may interfere with communication • Completes all requirements	• *Adequately* and *somewhat creatively* persuades friends to emigrate, or not, responding to the 3 essential questions, addressing most criteria • Communicates the message with some hesitation and some teacher assistance • Is comprehensible to a native speaker with mostly accurate pronunciation • Several errors in targeted structures interfere with communication • Completes most requirements	• *Sometimes* persuades friends to emigrate, or not, responding to the 2 essential questions, addressing some criteria • Has difficulty communicating the message and needs extensive teacher assistance. • May not be comprehensible to a native speaker and pronunciation is poor. • Some errors in targeted structures interfere with communication. • Completes some requirements	• *Minimally* persuades friends to emigrate, or not, responding to 1–2 essential questions, addressing few criteria • Hesitation and pronunciation impede communication • Cannot proceed without teacher assistance. • Many errors in targeted structures interfere with communication • Completes few requirements
Interpersonal Individual speaking Spanish during Q & A session	• *Effectively* asks the presenter a minimum of 2 appropriate questions about the emigration process • Presenter *effectively* responds appropriately to all questions about the emigration process	• *Adequately* asks the presenter 2 appropriate questions about the emigration process • Presenter *adequately* responds appropriately to most questions about the emigration process	• *Sometimes* asks the presenter 1–2 appropriate questions about the emigration process • Presenter *sometimes* responds appropriately to questions about the emigration process	• *Rarely* asks the presenter an appropriate question about the emigration process • Presenter *rarely* responds appropriately to questions about the emigration process
Visual product	• Visual product captures audience attention and leaves a lasting impression due to creativity • *Effectively* presents the information creatively and uniquely using available tools or technology	• Visual presentation is creative and captures audience attention • *Adequately* presents the information using available tools or technology	• Visual presentation may lack creativity • *Limited* presentation using available tools or technology	• Visual presentation demonstrates *minimal* creativity • *Minimally* presents the information using available tools or technology

continued on next page

© 2013 Wayside Publishing (This document is editable with permission from publisher)

Communication Mode/Domain	7 Exceeds Expectations	6 Meets Expectations	5 Almost Meets Expectations	4 Does Not Meet Expectations
Language Control	*Consistently and effectively* uses the following grammatical structures appropriately: • Passive voice • Progressive tenses/uses of gerunds • Uses of *por/para* • Uses of past participles	*Adequately* uses the following grammatical structures appropriately: • Passive voice • Progressive tenses/uses of gerunds • Uses of *por/para* • Uses of past participles	*Sometimes* uses the following grammatical structures appropriately: • Passive voice • Progressive tenses/uses of gerunds • Uses of *por/para* • Uses of past participles	*Rarely* uses the following grammatical structures appropriately: • Passive voice • Progressive tenses/uses of gerunds • Uses of *por/para* • Uses of past participles
Vocabulary	• Uses at least 12 vocabulary words and expressions from the hilo appropriately • *Effectively* uses conjunctions, transition words and idiomatic expressions appropriately	• Uses 10–12 vocabulary words and expressions from the hilo appropriately • *Adequately* uses conjunctions, transition words and idiomatic expressions appropriately	• May use 7–9 vocabulary words and expressions from the hilo • *Sometimes* uses conjunctions, transition words and idiomatic expressions appropriately	• May use 5–6 vocabulary words and expressions from the hilo appropriately • *Rarely* uses conjunctions, transition words and idiomatic expressions appropriately
Cultural awareness	• Indicates awareness of differences in cultural behaviors and perspectives	• May indicate some awareness of differences in cultural behaviors and perspectives	• May not indicate awareness of differences in cultural behaviors and perspectives	• Does not indicate awareness of differences in cultural behaviors and perspectives

© 2013 Wayside Publishing (This document is editable with permission from publisher)

Hilo 12 Summative Assessment/Evaluación final
Feria de la salud/Community Health Fair

Mid-High Intermediate

Communication Mode/Domain	7 Exceeds Expectations	6 Meets Expectations	5 Almost Meets Expectations	4 Does Not Meet Expectations
Interpretive Research	• *Effectively* researches a health issue, causes and effects, from a minimum of two sources selected from texts and audio/visual materials • *Effectively* interprets and takes notes on the health issue, noting sources	• *Adequately* researches a health issue, causes and effects, from a minimum of two sources selected from texts and audio/visual materials • *Adequately* interprets and takes notes on the health issue noting sources	• *Limited* research on a health issue, causes and effects, from one or two sources selected from texts and audio/visual materials • *Limited* interpretation and note taking on the health issue, *sometimes* noting sources	• *Minimally* researches a health issue from one source • *Minimally* interprets and takes notes on the health issue
Presentational Writing Content	• *Effectively* develops a detailed and organized minimum 3-paragraph essay on the health issue, causes and effects, reasons, and suggestions for a healthy lifestyle • Meets all criteria	• *Adequately* develops an organized 3-paragraph essay on the health issue, causes and effects, reasons, and suggestions for a healthy lifestyle • Meets most criteria	• *Limited* development of a 2-paragraph essay on the health issue, causes and effects, reasons, and suggestions for a healthy lifestyle • Meets some criteria	• *Minimally* develops a 1–2 paragraph essay on the health issue, causes and effects, reasons, and suggestions for a healthy lifestyle • Meets few criteria
Presentational Speaking Presents to audience of two or more	• *Effectively* delivers a creative presentation based on the health issue, causes and effects, reasons, and suggestions for a healthy lifestyle • Communicates the message clearly with good eye contact and poise; minimal hesitation, minimal teacher assistance • Is comprehensible to a native speaker with mostly accurate pronunciation • Few errors in targeted structures interfere with communication • Meets all criteria	• *Adequately* delivers a presentation based on the health issue, causes and effects, reasons, and suggestions for a healthy lifestyle • Communicates the message adequately with some eye contact and poise; some hesitation, some teacher assistance needed • Is comprehensible to a native speaker with adequate pronunciation • Several errors in targeted structures may interfere with communication • Meets most criteria	• Delivers a limited presentation based on the health issue, causes and effects, reasons, and suggestions for a healthy lifestyle • Communicates without clarity and limited eye contact and poise; frequent hesitation, teacher assistance needed • May not be comprehensible to a native speaker, pronunciation is fair • Some errors in targeted structures interfere with communication • Meets some criteria	• *Minimally* delivers a presentation based on the health issue, causes and effects, reasons, and suggestions for a healthy lifestyle • Hesitation and pronunciation impede communication; cannot proceed without teacher assistance • Many errors in targeted structures interfere with communication • Meets few criteria
Visual product	• Visual product captures audience attention and leaves a lasting impression due to creativity • *Effectively* presents the information creatively and uniquely using available tools or technology	• Visual presentation is creative and captures audience attention • *Adequately* presents the information using available tools or technology	• Visual presentation may lack creativity • *Limited* presentation using available tools or technology	• Visual presentation demonstrates *minimal* creativity • *Minimally* presents the information using available tools or technology
Interpersonal Speaking Spanish during Q & A session	• *Effectively* asks and responds to questions from other presenters about health issues, causes and effects, reasons, and suggestions for a healthy lifestyle	• *Adequately* asks and responds to questions from other presenters about health issues, causes and effects, reasons, and suggestions for a healthy lifestyle	• *Occasionally* asks and responds to questions from other presenters about health issues, causes and effects, reasons, and suggestions for a healthy lifestyle	• *Rarely* asks and responds to questions from other presenters about health issues, causes and effects, reasons, and suggestions for a healthy lifestyle

continued on next page

Communication Mode/Domain	7 Exceeds Expectations	6 Meets Expectations	5 Almost Meets Expectations	4 Does Not Meet Expectations
Language Control	*Consistently and effectively* uses the following grammatical structures appropriately: • Past tenses • Future and conditional tenses • Si clauses a • Subjunctive tenses for advice • Negation/pero/sino	*Adequately* uses the following grammatical structures appropriately: • Past tenses • Future and conditional tenses • Si clauses a • Subjunctive tenses for advice • Negation/pero/sino	*Sometimes* uses the following grammatical structures appropriately: • Past tenses • Future and conditional tenses • Si clauses a • Subjunctive tenses for advice • Negation/pero/sino	*Rarely* uses the following grammatical structures appropriately. • Past tenses • Future and conditional tenses • Si clauses a • Subjunctive tenses for advice • Negation/pero/sino
Vocabulary	• Uses at least 12 vocabulary words and expressions from the hilo appropriately • *Effectively* uses most conjunctions, transition words and idiomatic expressions appropriately	• Uses 10–12 vocabulary words and expressions from the hilo appropriately • *Adequately* uses some conjunctions, transition words and idiomatic expressions appropriately	• May use 7–9 vocabulary words and expressions from the hilo appropriately • *Sometimes* uses a few conjunctions, transition words and idiomatic expressions appropriately	• May use 5–6 vocabulary words and expressions from the hilo appropriately • *Rarely* uses conjunctions, transition words and idiomatic expressions appropriately
Cultural awareness	• Uses mostly culturally appropriate vocabulary and expressions • Indicates awareness of differences in cultural behaviors and perspectives	• Uses some culturally appropriate vocabulary and expressions • May indicate some awareness of differences in cultural behaviors and perspectives	• *Occasionally* uses culturally appropriate vocabulary and/or expressions • May not indicate awareness of differences in cultural behaviors and perspectives	• *Rarely* uses culturally appropriate vocabulary or expressions • Does not indicate awareness of differences in cultural behaviors and perspectives

© 2013 Wayside Publishing (This document is editable with permission from publisher)

El índice para las referencias del uso del lenguaje en contexto

TIEMPOS VERBALES	HILO	ACTIVIDAD	PÁGINA
El presente del indicativo			
• Cambios ortográficos del presente (o-ue, e-ie, e-i) (soler, mostrar, concordar con, comenzar, seguir)	Hilo 6	Act 1	158
• Uso de deber	Hilo 6	Act 1	159
El pretérito indefinido			
• Cambios ortográficos (verbos -ir: dormir, mentir, seguir, servir…)	Hilo 4	Act 4	102
• Verbos irregulares en el pretérito (decir, hacer, estar…)	Hilo 4	Act 4	102
• Verbos irregulares en el pretérito (huir, traducir, obtener, convertir)	Hilo 9	Act 3	264
Usos del imperfecto y del pretérito	Hilo 5	Act 5	139
El presente perfecto – : he, has, ha + -ado, -ido y participios irregulares (muerto, dicho, hecho…)	Hilo 6	Act 2	166
El pluscuamperfecto	Hilo 6	Act 2	166
El futuro	Hilo 4	Act 4	99
El condicional	Hilo 4	Act 2	93
El condicional perfecto	Hilo 6	Act 2	166
• Podría haber influido	Hilo 10	Act 1	280
El presente del subjuntivo			
• Con imperativo informal	Hilo 2	Act 5	46
• Consejos y recomendaciones	Hilo 5	Act 3	133
• Consejos y recomendaciones	Hilo 11	Act 6	335
• Con cuanto mas	Hilo 11	Act 1	159
• Con conjunciones de finalidad (para que, a fin de que, de manera, de modo, de forma)	Hilo 6	Act 6	79
• Antecedente indefinido- (busco a un amigo vs. busco el amigo)	Hilo 3	Act 6	168
• Gustar	Hilo 6	Act 3	168
El presente perfecto del subjuntivo	Hilo 6	Act 2	166
El imperfecto del subjuntivo			
• Como si	Hilo 6	Act 7	180
• Como si	Hilo 11	Act 5	180
• Como si	Hilo 10	Act 1	280
• Cambios ortográficos (pidiera, siguiera, repitiera, muriera, durmiera)	Hilo 3	Act 2	68
El pluscuamperfecto del subjuntivo	Hilo 6	Act 2	166
Cláusulas con si			
• El futuro / presente	Hilo 3	Act 2	71
• El condicional / imperfecto del subjuntivo	Hilo 3	Act 6	70
El imperativo			
• Familiar	Hilo 1	Act 4	17
• Formal y plural	Hilo 2	Act 5	46
• Nosotros	Hilo 7	Act 5	210
• Pronombres	Hilo 11	Act 5	331

USOS DE VERBOS	HILO	ACTIVIDAD	PÁGINA
Se impersonal	Hilo 8	Act 3	236
Voz pasiva	Hilo 5	Act 1	124
El gerundio con pronombres	Hilo 8	Act 2	233
Usos del participio (-ado, -ido)	Hilo 6	Act 2	168
Estar + participio para describir	Hilo digital	Act 5	Guía digital
Gustar	Hilo 6	Act 7	179

ADJETIVOS			
Comparativos	Hilo 1	Act 1	9
Superlativos	Hilo 1	Act 1	9
Comparativos: tan …como	Hilo 1	Act 1	9

ADVERBIOS			
Modo, tiempo, lugar, cantidad	Hilo 9	Act 2	260

LA NEGACION / PERO / SINO			
	Hilo 12	Antes de empezar	348

PRONOMBRES			
• Indirectos y directos	Hilo 5	Act 4	137
• Posesivos	Hilo 10	Act 4	293

ORACIONES RELATIVAS			
Que, el cual, cuyo, quien, el que, lo que	Hilo 7	Act 2	199

POR Y PARA			
	Hilo 11	Act 4	328

LOS ARTICULOS DEFINIDOS			
Uso de "el" vs. "la"	Hilo 5	Act 3	132

LOS NÚMEROS			
Ordinales y cardinales	Hilo 7	Act 1	197